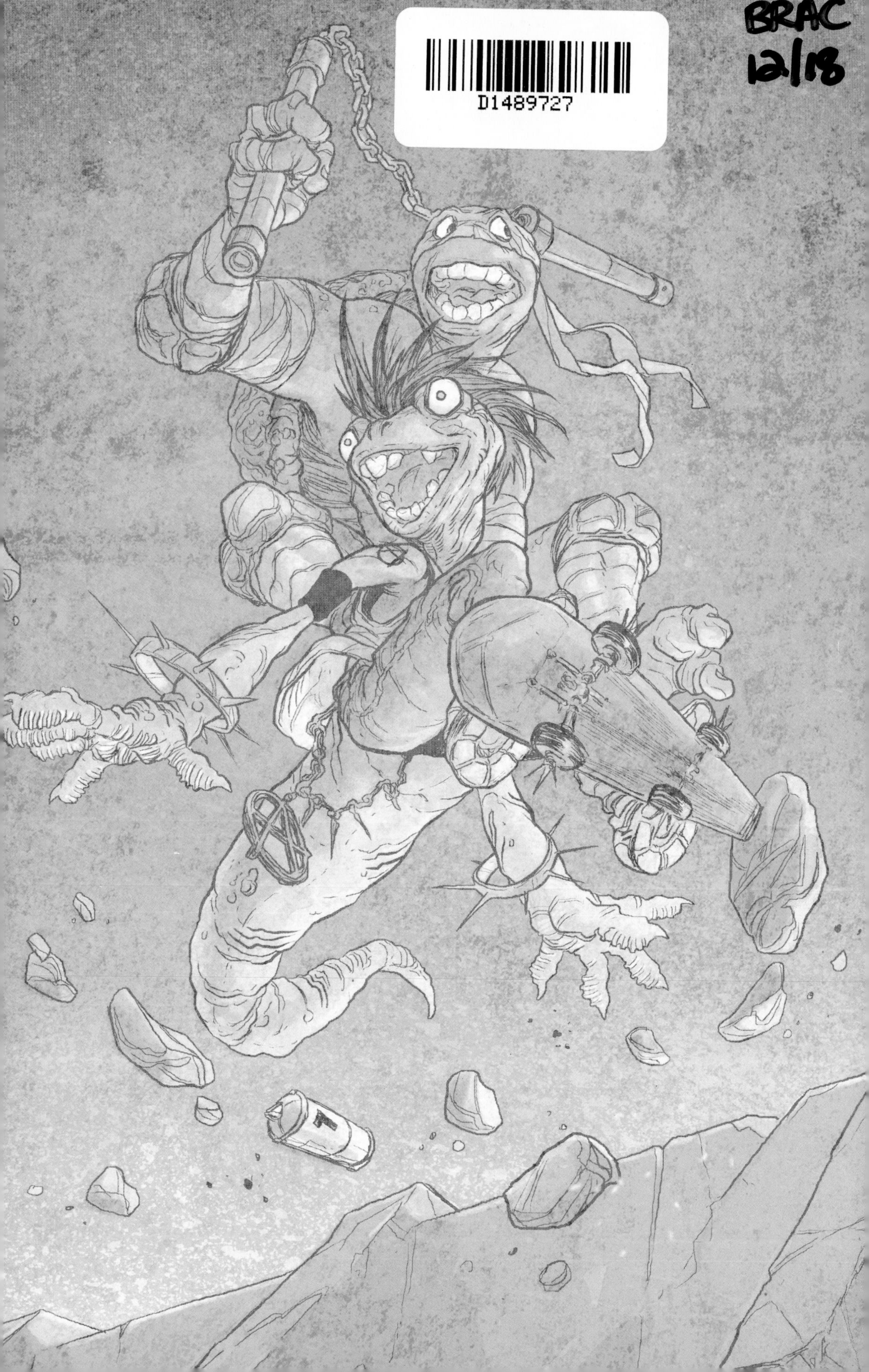

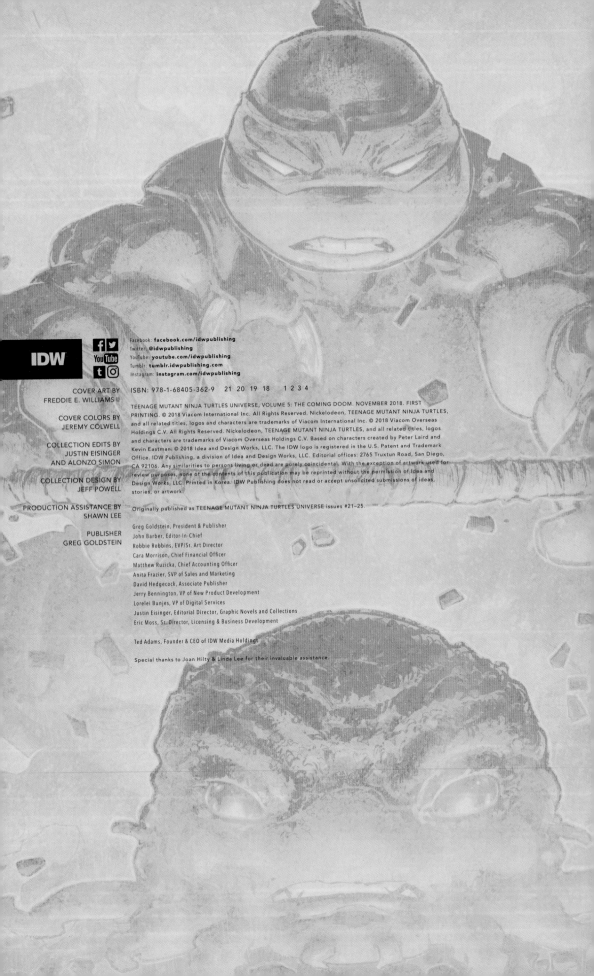

IDW

Facebook: **facebook.com/idwpublishing**
Twitter: **@idwpublishing**
YouTube: **youtube.com/idwpublishing**
Tumblr: **tumblr.idwpublishing.com**
Instagram: **instagram.com/idwpublishing**

ISBN: 978-1-68405-362-9   21 20 19 18   1 2 3 4

COVER ART BY
FREDDIE E. WILLIAMS II

COVER COLORS BY
JEREMY COLWELL

COLLECTION EDITS BY
JUSTIN EISINGER
AND ALONZO SIMON

COLLECTION DESIGN BY
JEFF POWELL

PRODUCTION ASSISTANCE BY
SHAWN LEE

PUBLISHER
GREG GOLDSTEIN

Originally published as TEENAGE MUTANT NINJA TURTLES UNIVERSE issues #21–25.

Greg Goldstein, President & Publisher
John Barber, Editor-In-Chief
Robbie Robbins, EVP/Sr. Art Director
Cara Morrison, Chief Financial Officer
Matthew Ruzicka, Chief Accounting Officer
Anita Frazier, SVP of Sales and Marketing
David Hedgecock, Associate Publisher
Jerry Bennington, VP of New Product Development
Lorelei Bunjes, VP of Digital Services
Justin Eisinger, Editorial Director, Graphic Novels and Collections
Eric Moss, Sr. Director, Licensing & Business Development

Ted Adams, Founder & CEO of IDW Media Holdings

Special thanks to Joan Hilty & Linda Lee for their invaluable assistance.

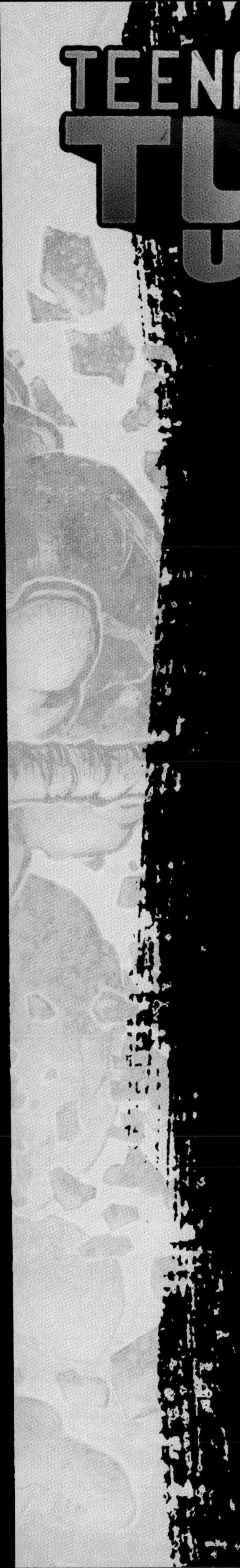

TEENAGE MUTANT NINJA TURTLES UNIVERSE

LOST CAUSES

WRITTEN BY **PAUL ALLOR**
ART BY **MARK TORRES**
COLORS BY **RONDA PATTISON**

HOW WOODY SPENT HIS TRICERATON INVASION

WRITTEN BY **CALEB GOELLNER**
ART BY **PABLO TUNICA**
COLORS BY **PATRICIO DELPECHE**

DANGEROUS WATERS

WRITTEN BY **ROSS MAY**
ART BY **CHRIS JOHNSON**
COLORS BY **MARK ENGLERT**

...AND OUT CAME THE REPTILES

WRITTEN BY **RYAN FERRIER**
ART BY **PABLO TUNICA**
COLORS BY **PATRICIO DELPECHE**

NOBODY CARES

WRITTEN BY **RICH DOUEK**
ART BY **BRAHM REVEL**

LIFE AT SEA

WRITTEN BY **RICH DOUEK**
ART BY **BUSTER MOODY**

SPIRIT WALK

WRITTEN BY **IAN FLYNN**
ART BY **NELSON DANIEL**

LETTERS BY **SHAWN LEE**
SERIES EDITS BY **BOBBY CURNOW**

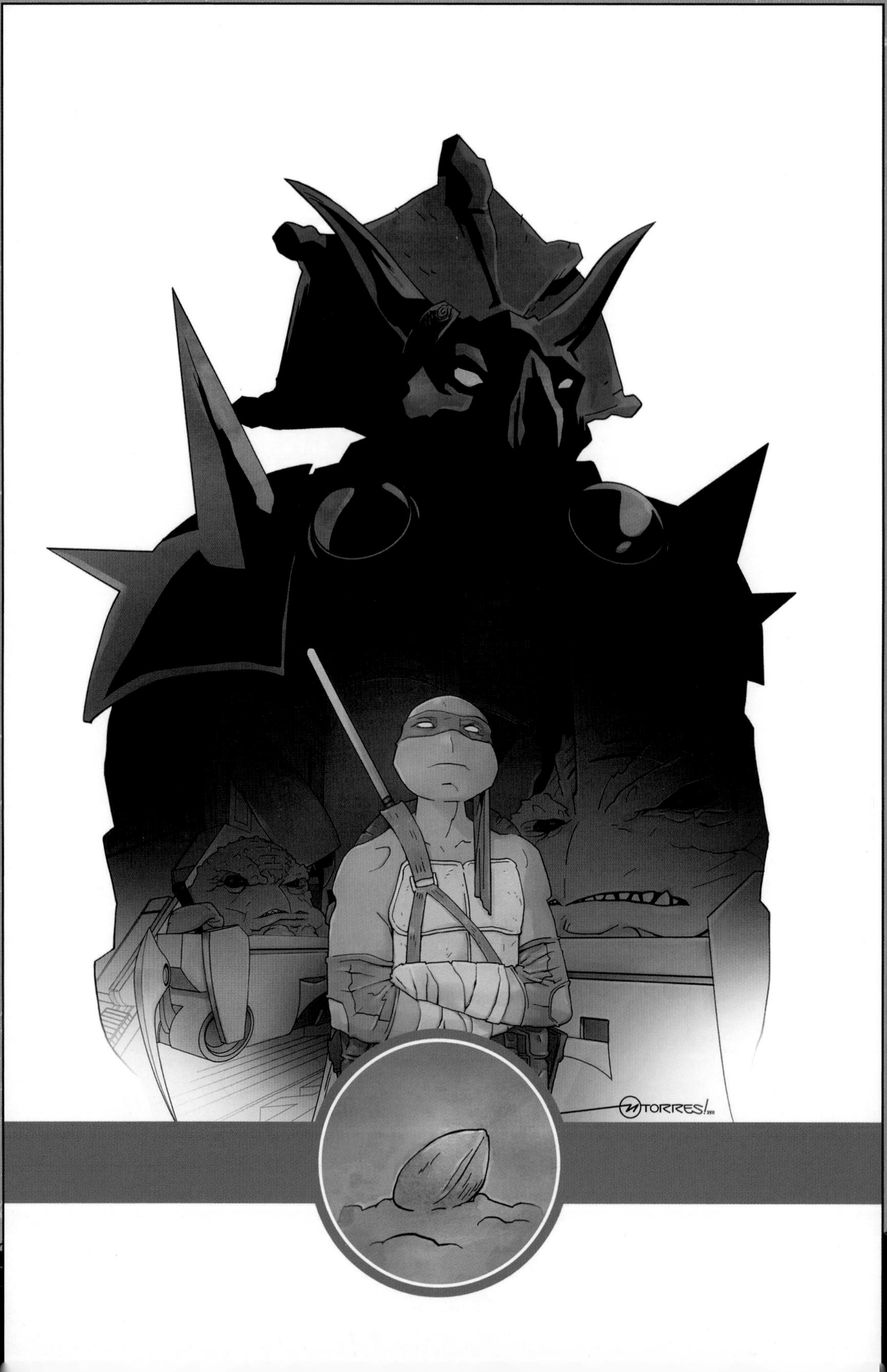
TORRES!

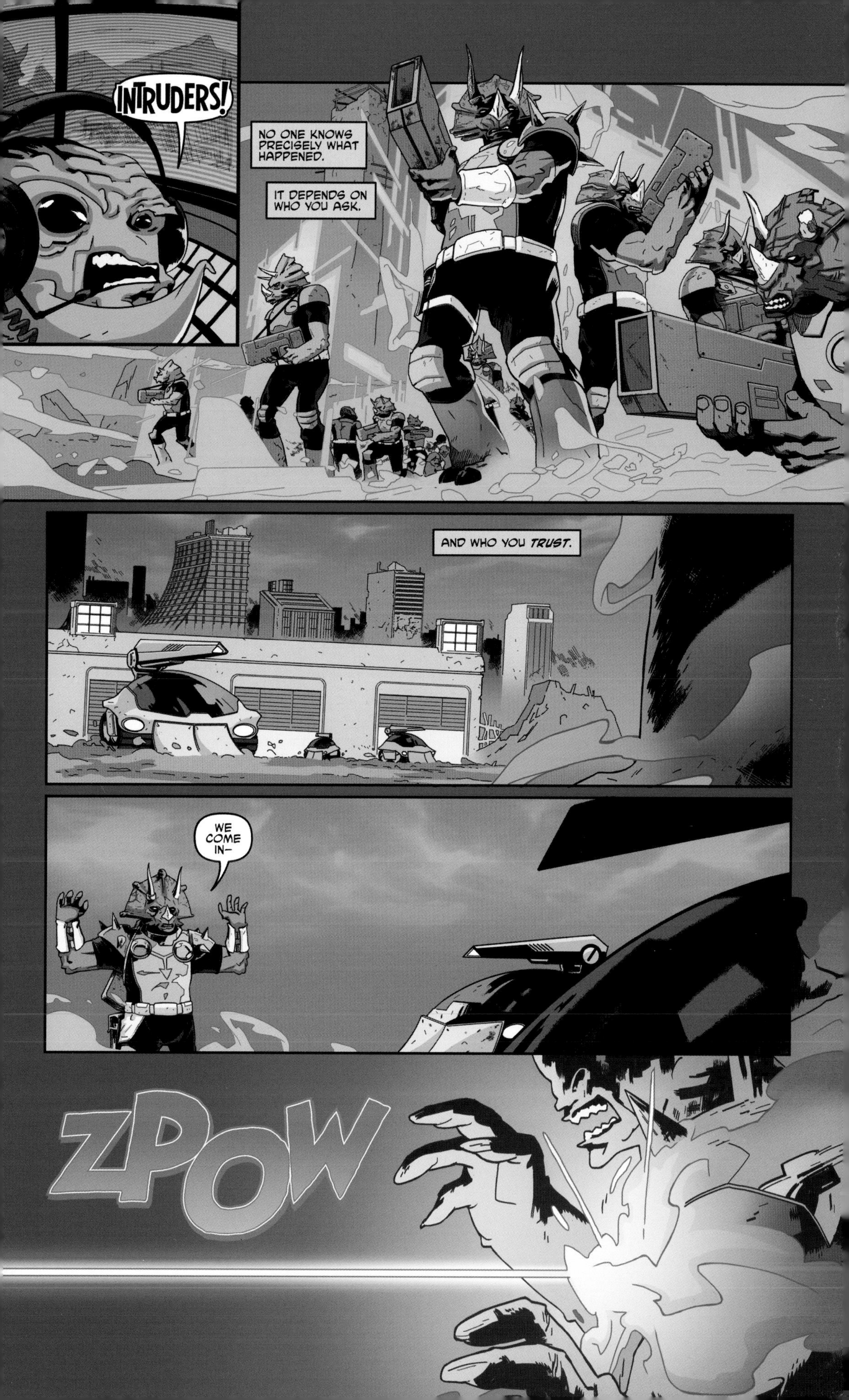
INTRUDERS!
NO ONE KNOWS PRECISELY WHAT HAPPENED.
IT DEPENDS ON WHO YOU ASK.
AND WHO YOU TRUST.
WE COME IN—
ZPOW

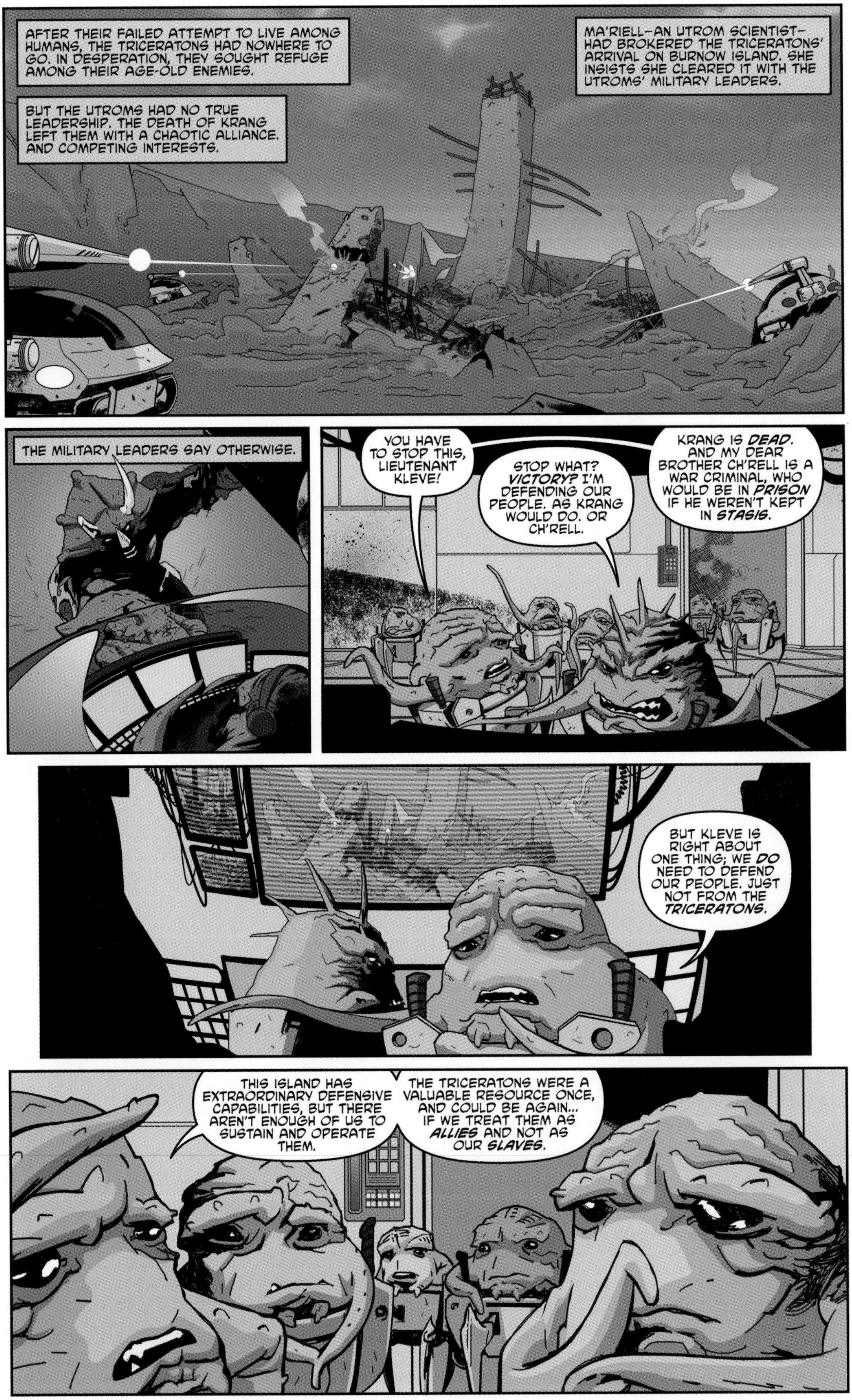
AFTER THEIR FAILED ATTEMPT TO LIVE AMONG HUMANS, THE TRICERATONS HAD NOWHERE TO GO. IN DESPERATION, THEY SOUGHT REFUGE AMONG THEIR AGE-OLD ENEMIES.
BUT THE UTROMS HAD NO TRUE LEADERSHIP. THE DEATH OF KRANG LEFT THEM WITH A CHAOTIC ALLIANCE. AND COMPETING INTERESTS.
MA'RIELL—AN UTROM SCIENTIST—HAD BROKERED THE TRICERATONS' ARRIVAL ON BURNOW ISLAND. SHE INSISTS SHE CLEARED IT WITH THE UTROMS' MILITARY LEADERS.
THE MILITARY LEADERS SAY OTHERWISE.
YOU HAVE TO STOP THIS, LIEUTENANT KLEVE!
STOP WHAT? VICTORY? I'M DEFENDING OUR PEOPLE. AS KRANG WOULD DO. OR CH'RELL.
KRANG IS DEAD. AND MY DEAR BROTHER CH'RELL IS A WAR CRIMINAL, WHO WOULD BE IN PRISON IF HE WEREN'T KEPT IN STASIS.
BUT KLEVE IS RIGHT ABOUT ONE THING; WE DO NEED TO DEFEND OUR PEOPLE. JUST NOT FROM THE TRICERATONS.
THIS ISLAND HAS EXTRAORDINARY DEFENSIVE CAPABILITIES, BUT THERE AREN'T ENOUGH OF US TO SUSTAIN AND OPERATE THEM.
THE TRICERATONS WERE A VALUABLE RESOURCE ONCE, AND COULD BE AGAIN... IF WE TREAT THEM AS ALLIES AND NOT AS OUR SLAVES.

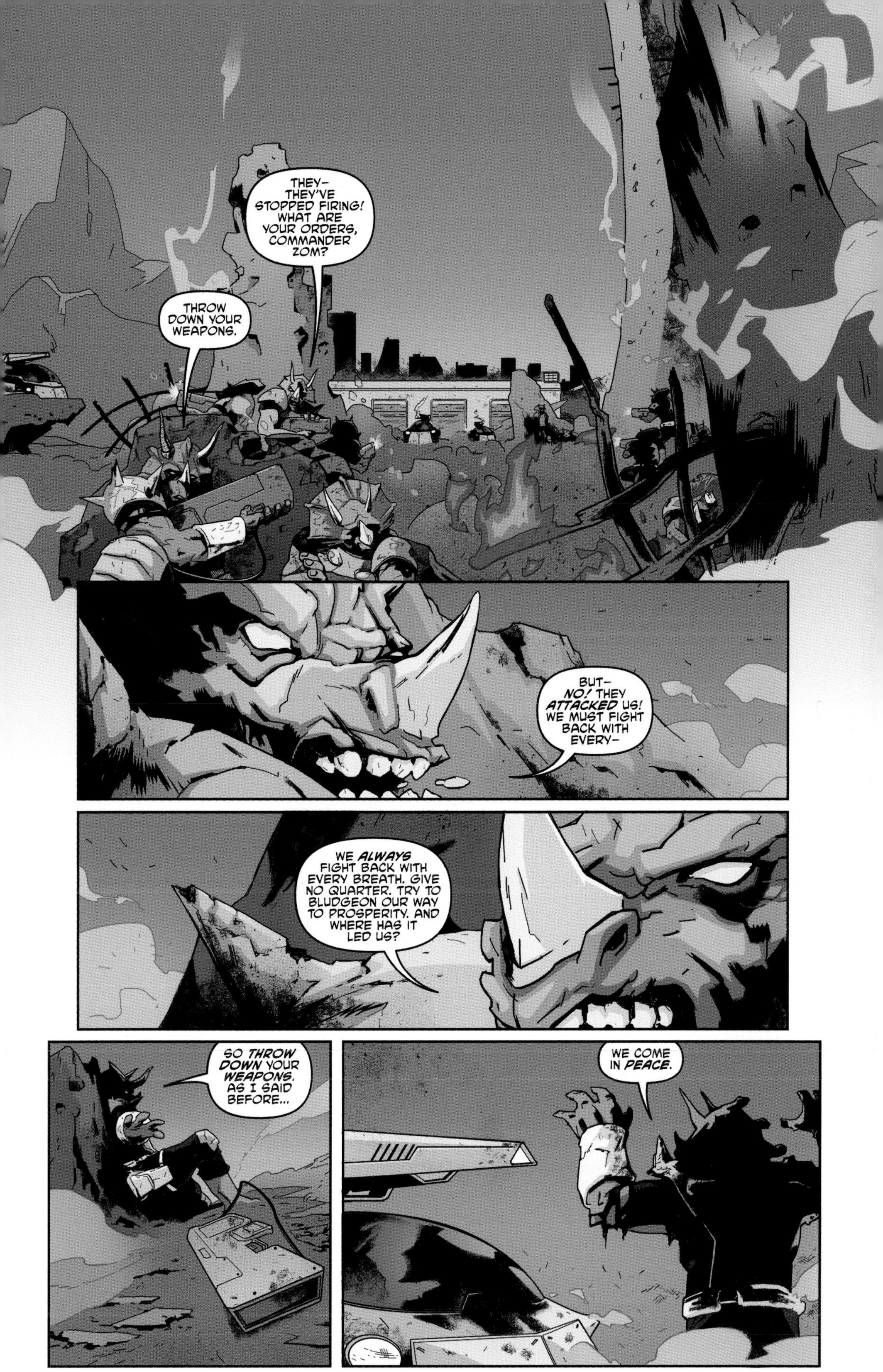
THEY— THEY'VE STOPPED FIRING! WHAT ARE YOUR ORDERS, COMMANDER ZOM?
THROW DOWN YOUR WEAPONS.
BUT— NO! THEY ATTACKED US! WE MUST FIGHT BACK WITH EVERY—
WE ALWAYS FIGHT BACK WITH EVERY BREATH. GIVE NO QUARTER. TRY TO BLUDGEON OUR WAY TO PROSPERITY. AND WHERE HAS IT LED US?
SO THROW DOWN YOUR WEAPONS, AS I SAID BEFORE...
WE COME IN PEACE.

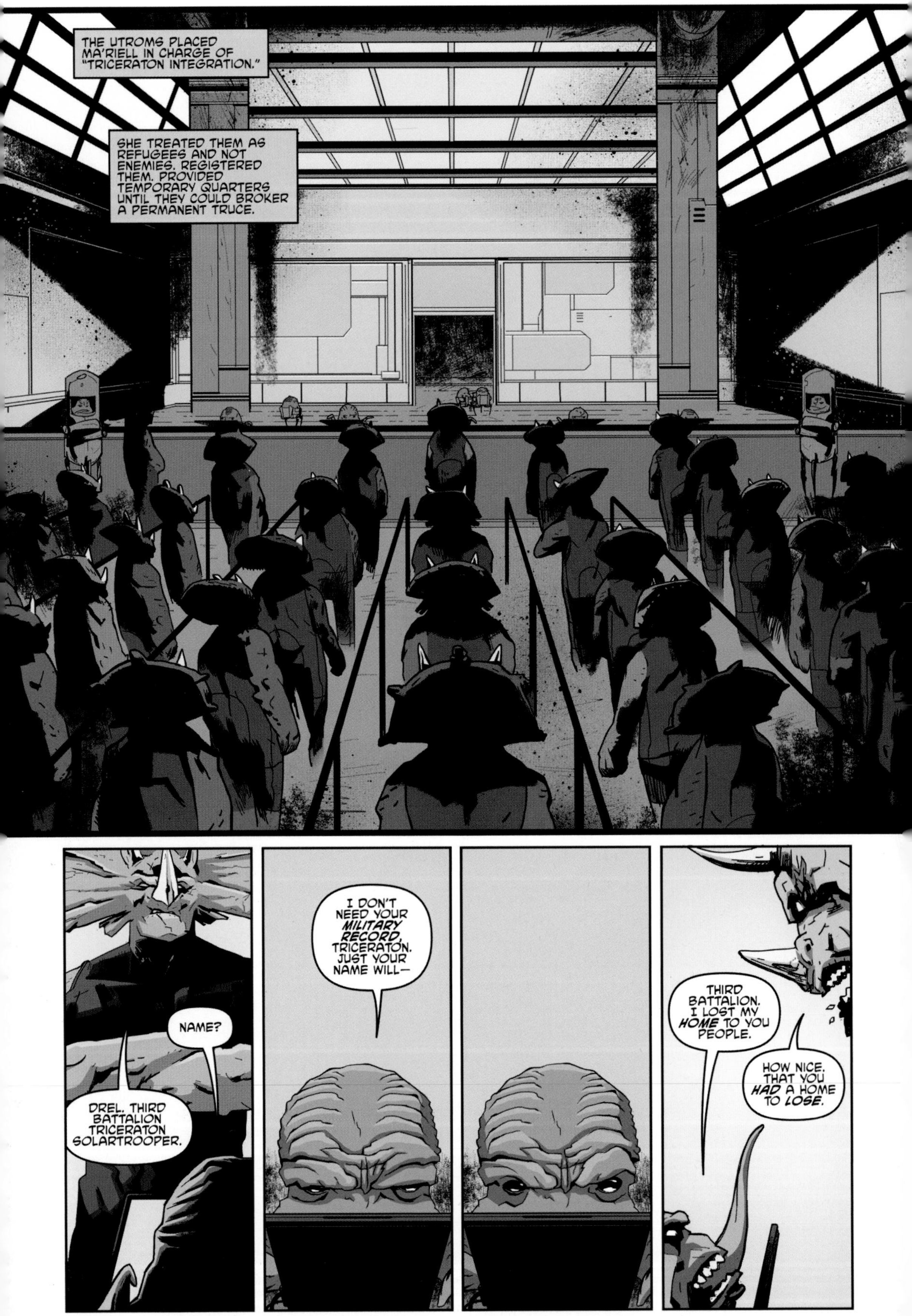
THE UTROMS PLACED MA'RIELL IN CHARGE OF "TRICERATON INTEGRATION."
SHE TREATED THEM AS REFUGEES AND NOT ENEMIES. REGISTERED THEM. PROVIDED TEMPORARY QUARTERS UNTIL THEY COULD BROKER A PERMANENT TRUCE.
NAME?
DREL. THIRD BATTALION TRICERATON SOLARTROOPER.
I DON'T NEED YOUR MILITARY RECORD, TRICERATON. JUST YOUR NAME WILL—
THIRD BATTALION. I LOST MY HOME TO YOU PEOPLE.
HOW NICE. THAT YOU HAD A HOME TO LOSE.

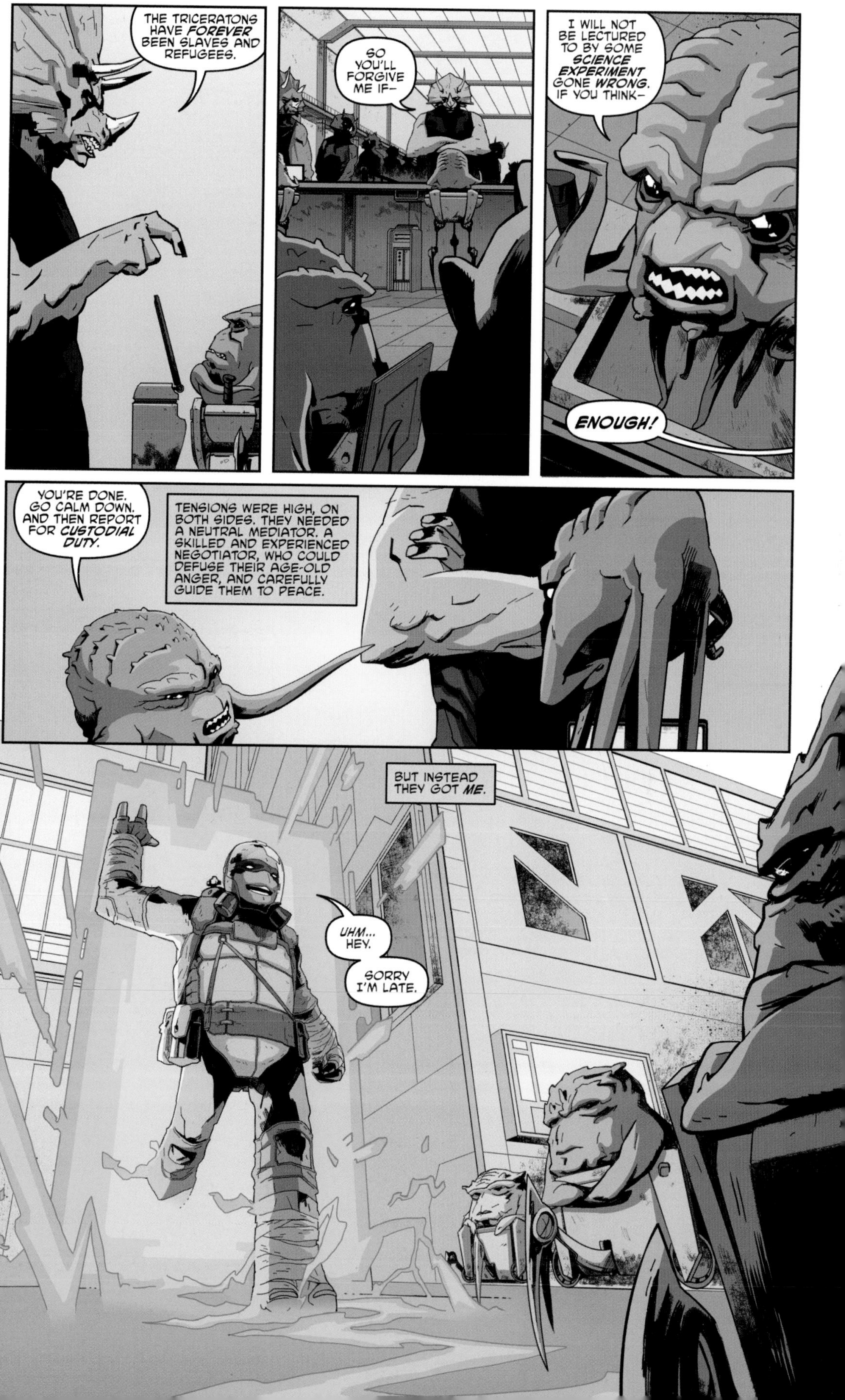
THE TRICERATONS HAVE *FOREVER* BEEN SLAVES AND REFUGEES.
SO YOU'LL FORGIVE ME IF–
I WILL NOT BE LECTURED TO BY SOME *SCIENCE EXPERIMENT* GONE *WRONG*. IF YOU THINK–
ENOUGH!
YOU'RE DONE. GO CALM DOWN. AND THEN REPORT FOR *CUSTODIAL DUTY*.
TENSIONS WERE HIGH, ON BOTH SIDES. THEY NEEDED A NEUTRAL MEDIATOR. A SKILLED AND EXPERIENCED NEGOTIATOR, WHO COULD DEFUSE THEIR AGE-OLD ANGER, AND CAREFULLY GUIDE THEM TO PEACE.
BUT INSTEAD THEY GOT *ME*.
UHM... HEY.
SORRY I'M LATE.

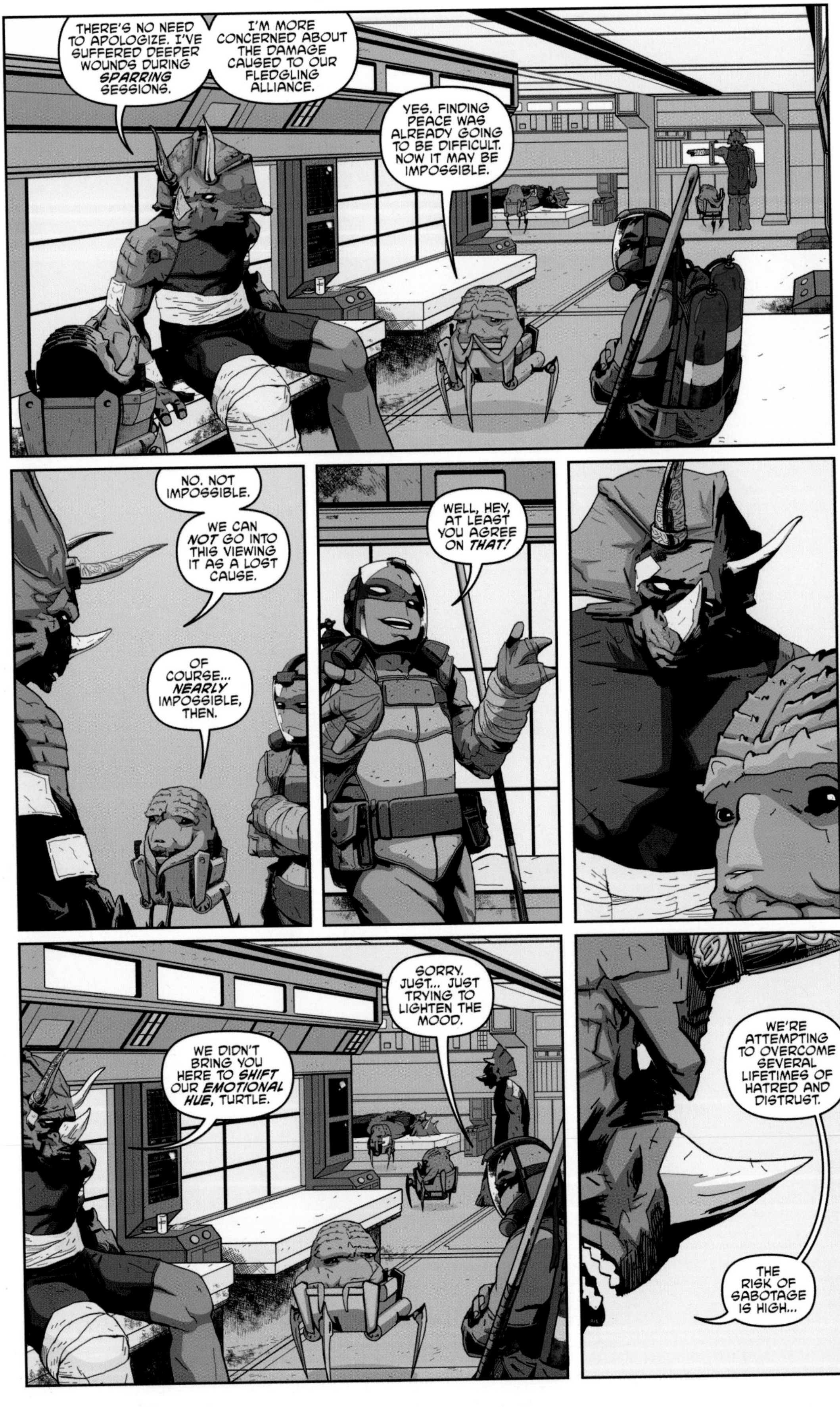
THERE'S NO NEED TO APOLOGIZE. I'VE SUFFERED DEEPER WOUNDS DURING SPARRING SESSIONS.
I'M MORE CONCERNED ABOUT THE DAMAGE CAUSED TO OUR FLEDGLING ALLIANCE.
YES. FINDING PEACE WAS ALREADY GOING TO BE DIFFICULT. NOW IT MAY BE IMPOSSIBLE.
NO. NOT IMPOSSIBLE.
WE CAN NOT GO INTO THIS VIEWING IT AS A LOST CAUSE.
OF COURSE... NEARLY IMPOSSIBLE, THEN.
WELL, HEY, AT LEAST YOU AGREE ON THAT!
WE DIDN'T BRING YOU HERE TO SHIFT OUR EMOTIONAL HUE, TURTLE.
SORRY. JUST... JUST TRYING TO LIGHTEN THE MOOD.
WE'RE ATTEMPTING TO OVERCOME SEVERAL LIFETIMES OF HATRED AND DISTRUST.
THE RISK OF SABOTAGE IS HIGH...

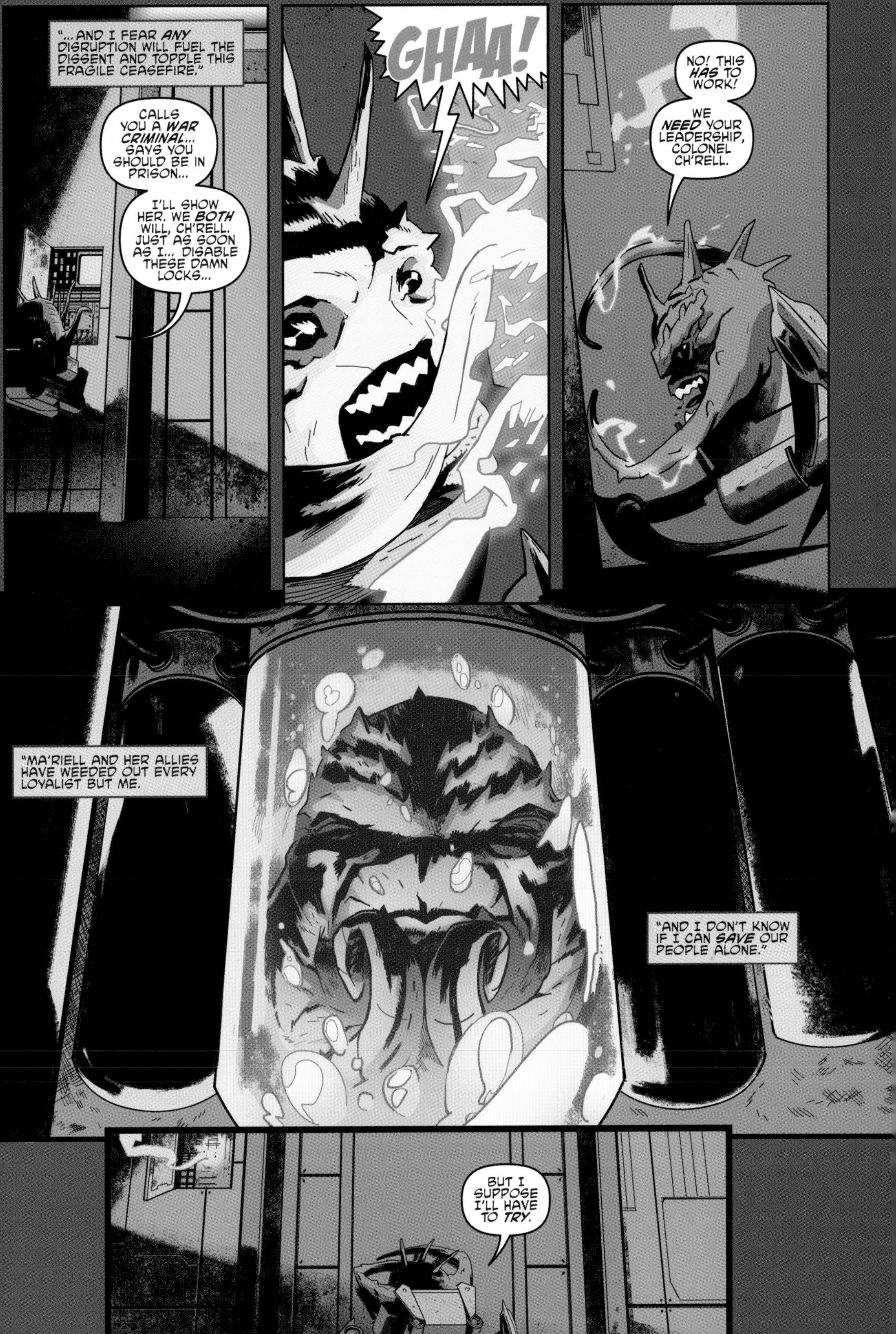

"...AND I FEAR *ANY* DISRUPTION WILL FUEL THE DISSENT AND TOPPLE THIS FRAGILE CEASEFIRE."
CALLS YOU A *WAR CRIMINAL*... SAYS YOU SHOULD BE IN PRISON...
I'LL SHOW HER. WE *BOTH* WILL, CH'RELL. JUST AS SOON AS I... DISABLE THESE DAMN LOCKS...
GHAA!
NO! THIS *HAS* TO WORK!
WE *NEED* YOUR LEADERSHIP, COLONEL CH'RELL.
"MA'RIELL AND HER ALLIES HAVE WEEDED OUT EVERY LOYALIST BUT ME.
"AND I DON'T KNOW IF I CAN *SAVE* OUR PEOPLE ALONE."
BUT I SUPPOSE I'LL HAVE TO *TRY*.

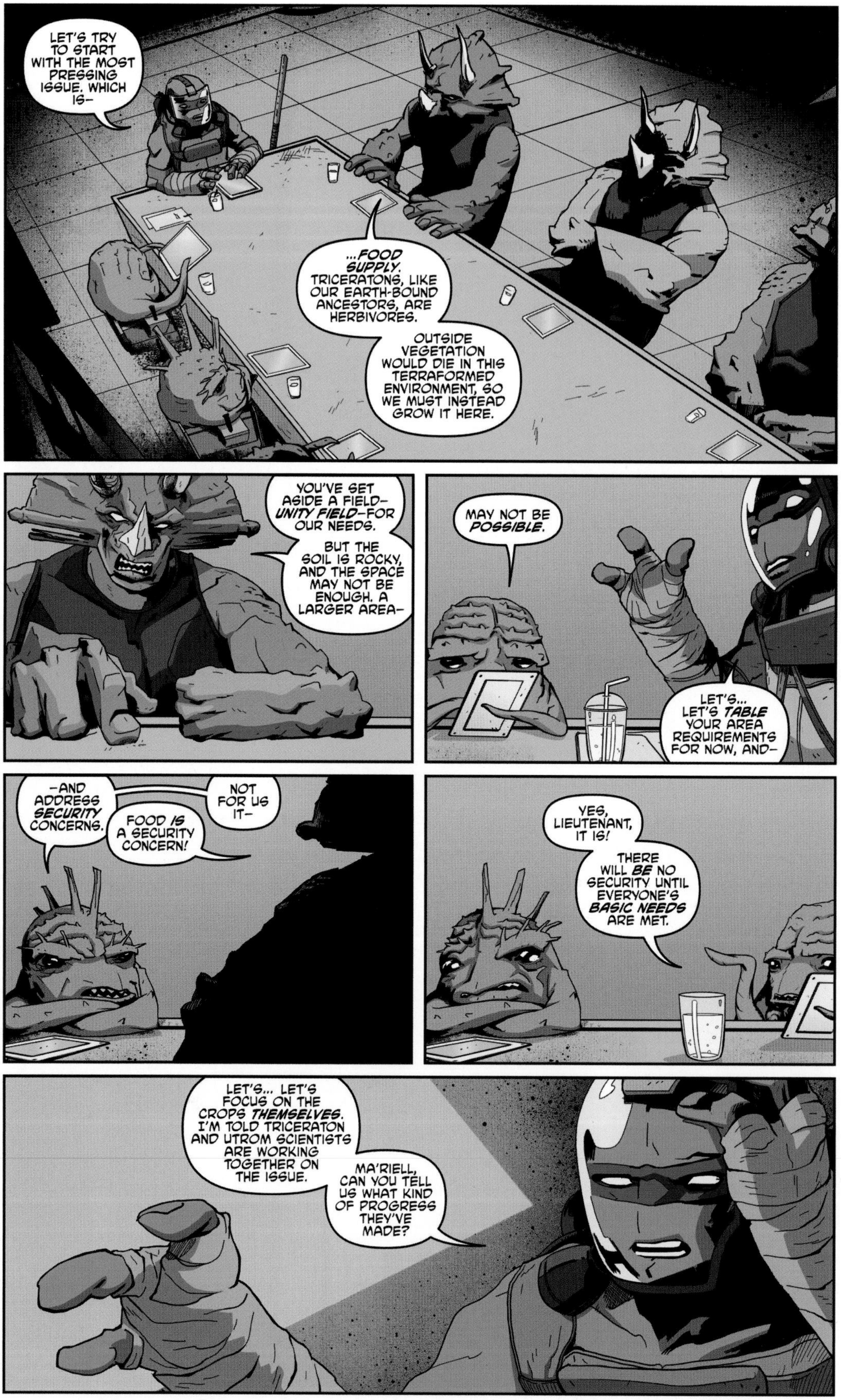

LET'S TRY TO START WITH THE MOST PRESSING ISSUE. WHICH IS–
...FOOD SUPPLY. TRICERATONS, LIKE OUR EARTH-BOUND ANCESTORS, ARE HERBIVORES.
OUTSIDE VEGETATION WOULD DIE IN THIS TERRAFORMED ENVIRONMENT, SO WE MUST INSTEAD GROW IT HERE.
YOU'VE SET ASIDE A FIELD– UNITY FIELD–FOR OUR NEEDS.
BUT THE SOIL IS ROCKY, AND THE SPACE MAY NOT BE ENOUGH. A LARGER AREA–
MAY NOT BE POSSIBLE.
LET'S... LET'S TABLE YOUR AREA REQUIREMENTS FOR NOW, AND–
–AND ADDRESS SECURITY CONCERNS.
NOT FOR US IT–
FOOD IS A SECURITY CONCERN!
YES, LIEUTENANT, IT IS!
THERE WILL BE NO SECURITY UNTIL EVERYONE'S BASIC NEEDS ARE MET.
LET'S... LET'S FOCUS ON THE CROPS THEMSELVES. I'M TOLD TRICERATON AND UTROM SCIENTISTS ARE WORKING TOGETHER ON THE ISSUE.
MA'RIELL, CAN YOU TELL US WHAT KIND OF PROGRESS THEY'VE MADE?

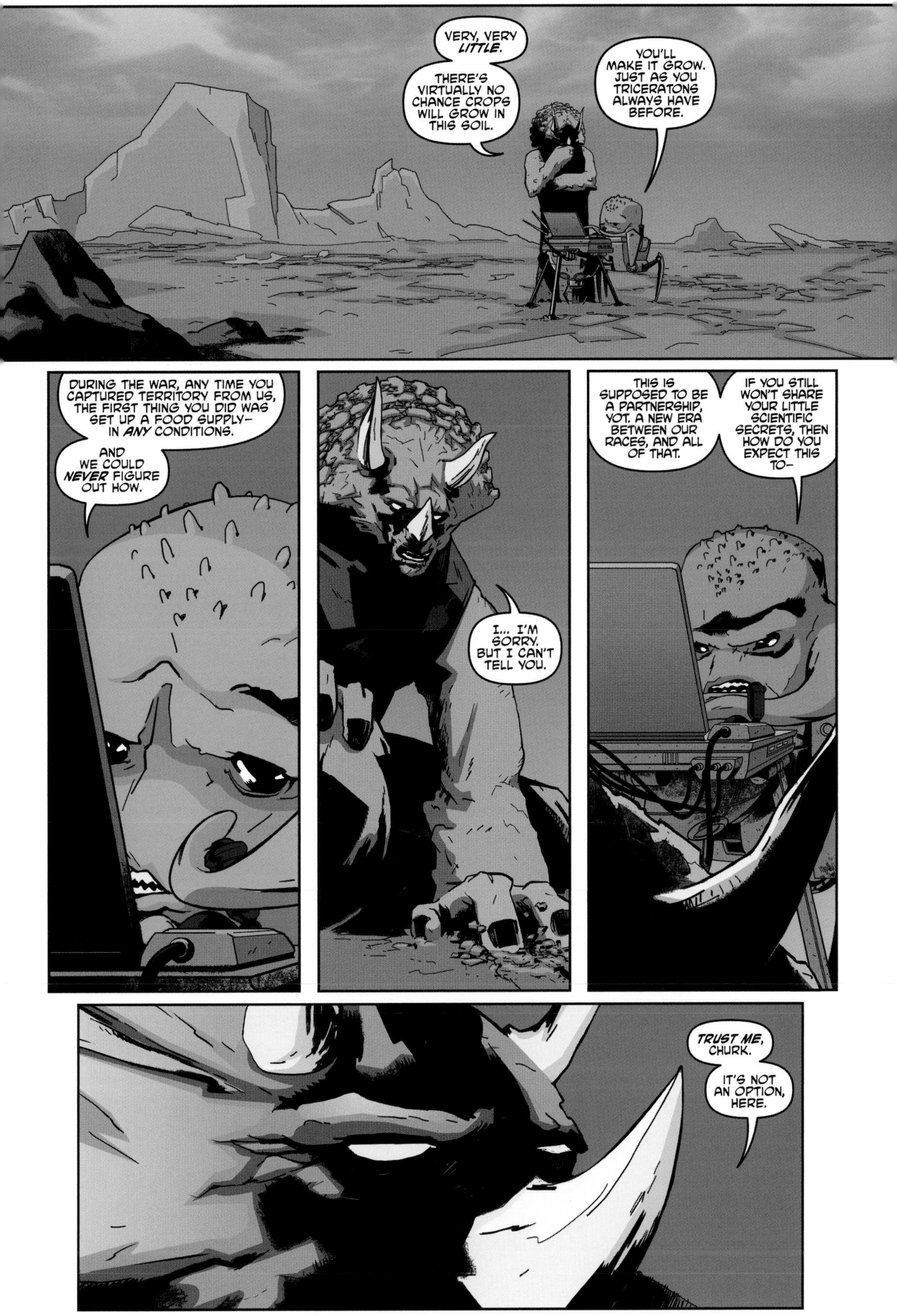
VERY, VERY LITTLE.
THERE'S VIRTUALLY NO CHANCE CROPS WILL GROW IN THIS SOIL.
YOU'LL MAKE IT GROW. JUST AS YOU TRICERATONS ALWAYS HAVE BEFORE.
DURING THE WAR, ANY TIME YOU CAPTURED TERRITORY FROM US, THE FIRST THING YOU DID WAS SET UP A FOOD SUPPLY-- IN ANY CONDITIONS.
AND WE COULD NEVER FIGURE OUT HOW.
I... I'M SORRY. BUT I CAN'T TELL YOU.
THIS IS SUPPOSED TO BE A PARTNERSHIP, YOT. A NEW ERA BETWEEN OUR RACES, AND ALL OF THAT.
IF YOU STILL WON'T SHARE YOUR LITTLE SCIENTIFIC SECRETS, THEN HOW DO YOU EXPECT THIS TO--
TRUST ME, CHURK.
IT'S NOT AN OPTION, HERE.

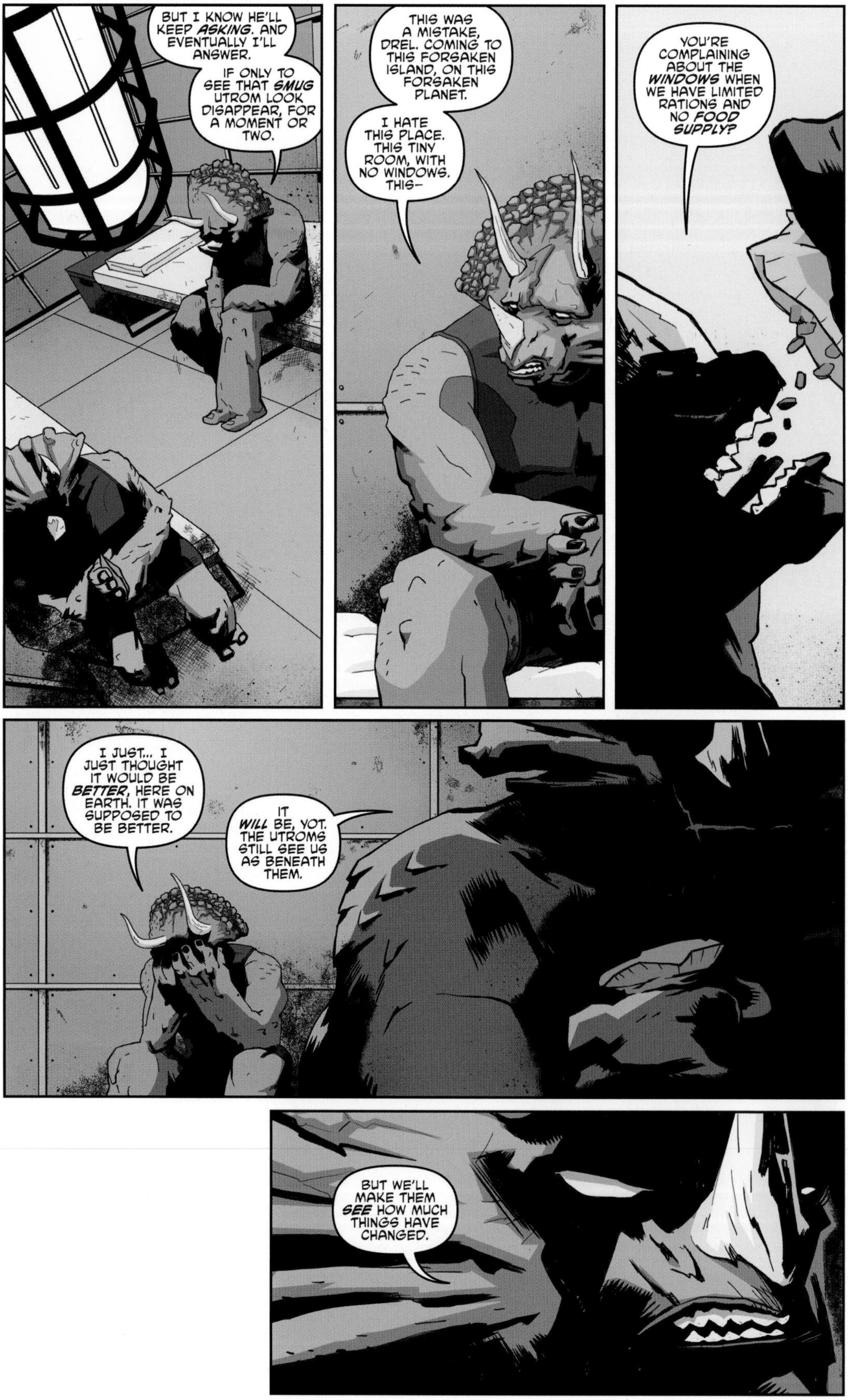
BUT I KNOW HE'LL KEEP ASKING. AND EVENTUALLY I'LL ANSWER.
IF ONLY TO SEE THAT SMUG UTROM LOOK DISAPPEAR, FOR A MOMENT OR TWO.
THIS WAS A MISTAKE, DREL. COMING TO THIS FORSAKEN ISLAND, ON THIS FORSAKEN PLANET.
I HATE THIS PLACE. THIS TINY ROOM, WITH NO WINDOWS. THIS–
YOU'RE COMPLAINING ABOUT THE WINDOWS WHEN WE HAVE LIMITED RATIONS AND NO FOOD SUPPLY?
I JUST... I JUST THOUGHT IT WOULD BE BETTER, HERE ON EARTH. IT WAS SUPPOSED TO BE BETTER.
IT WILL BE, YOT. THE UTROMS STILL SEE US AS BENEATH THEM.
BUT WE'LL MAKE THEM SEE HOW MUCH THINGS HAVE CHANGED.

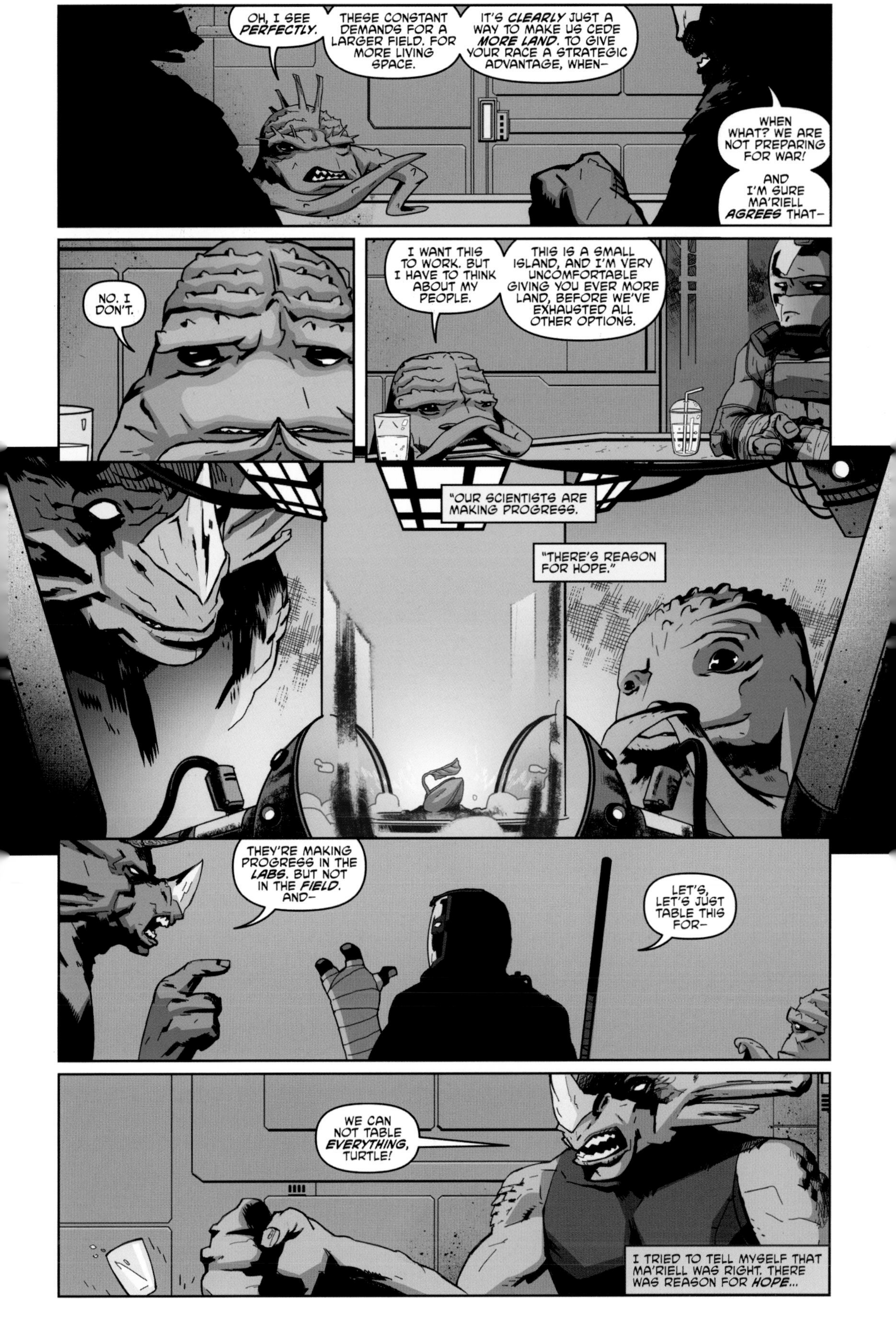
OH, I SEE PERFECTLY.
THESE CONSTANT DEMANDS FOR A LARGER FIELD. FOR MORE LIVING SPACE.
IT'S CLEARLY JUST A WAY TO MAKE US CEDE MORE LAND. TO GIVE YOUR RACE A STRATEGIC ADVANTAGE, WHEN–
WHEN WHAT? WE ARE NOT PREPARING FOR WAR!
AND I'M SURE MA'RIELL AGREES THAT–
NO. I DON'T.
I WANT THIS TO WORK. BUT I HAVE TO THINK ABOUT MY PEOPLE.
THIS IS A SMALL ISLAND, AND I'M VERY UNCOMFORTABLE GIVING YOU EVER MORE LAND, BEFORE WE'VE EXHAUSTED ALL OTHER OPTIONS.
"OUR SCIENTISTS ARE MAKING PROGRESS.
"THERE'S REASON FOR HOPE."
THEY'RE MAKING PROGRESS IN THE LABS. BUT NOT IN THE FIELD. AND–
LET'S, LET'S JUST TABLE THIS FOR–
WE CAN NOT TABLE EVERYTHING, TURTLE!
I TRIED TO TELL MYSELF THAT MA'RIELL WAS RIGHT. THERE WAS REASON FOR HOPE...

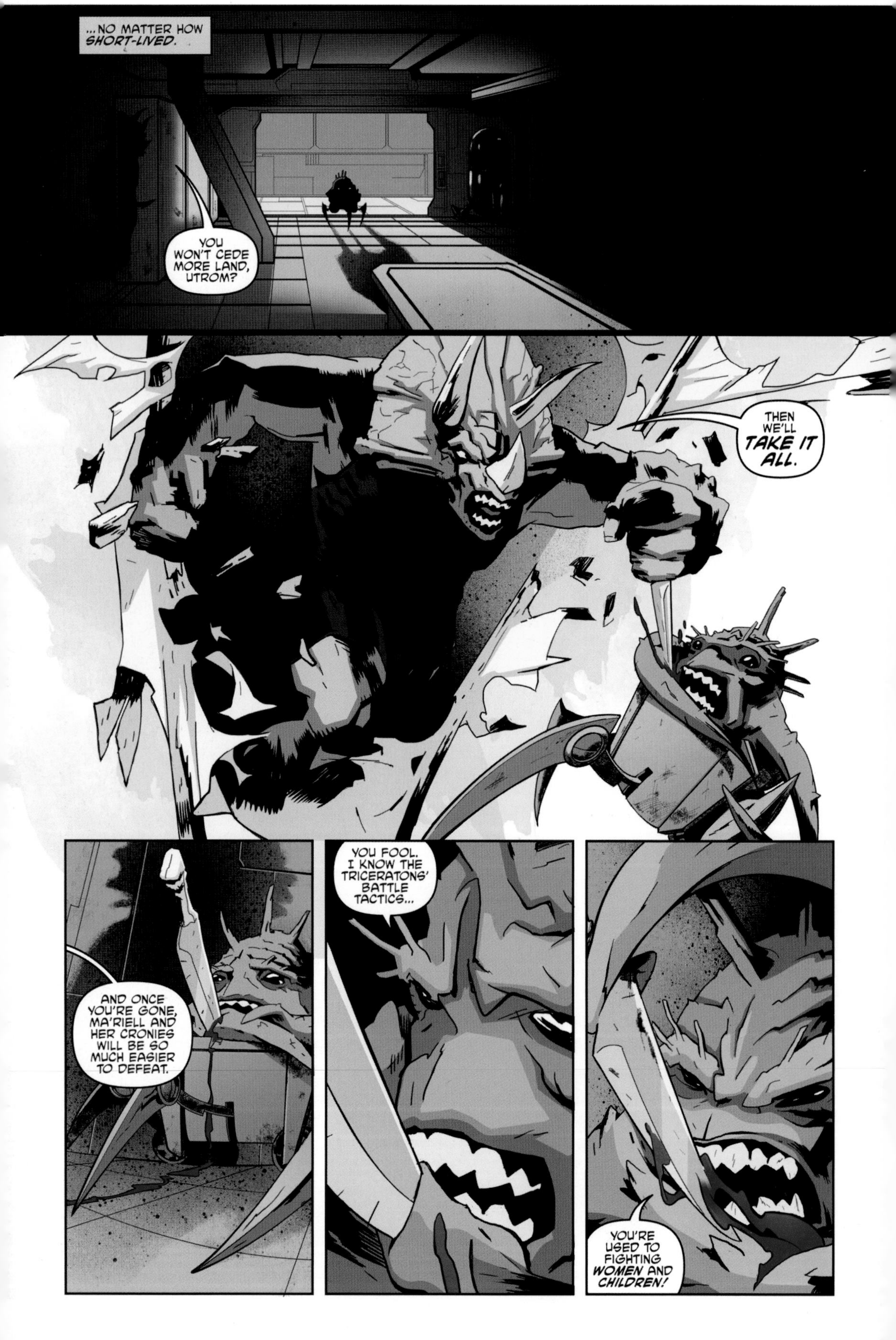
...NO MATTER HOW SHORT-LIVED.
YOU WON'T CEDE MORE LAND, UTROM?
THEN WE'LL TAKE IT ALL.
AND ONCE YOU'RE GONE, MA'RIELL AND HER CRONIES WILL BE SO MUCH EASIER TO DEFEAT.
YOU FOOL. I KNOW THE TRICERATONS' BATTLE TACTICS...
YOU'RE USED TO FIGHTING WOMEN AND CHILDREN!

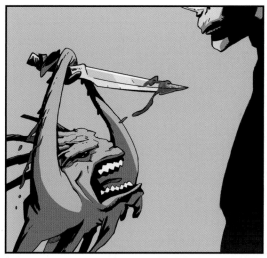

YOU THINK I'D BRING A WEAPON THAT COULD BE SO EASILY TURNED AGAINST ME? I KNOW HOW DECEITFUL THE UTROMS ARE.

CRACK

NO MATTER.

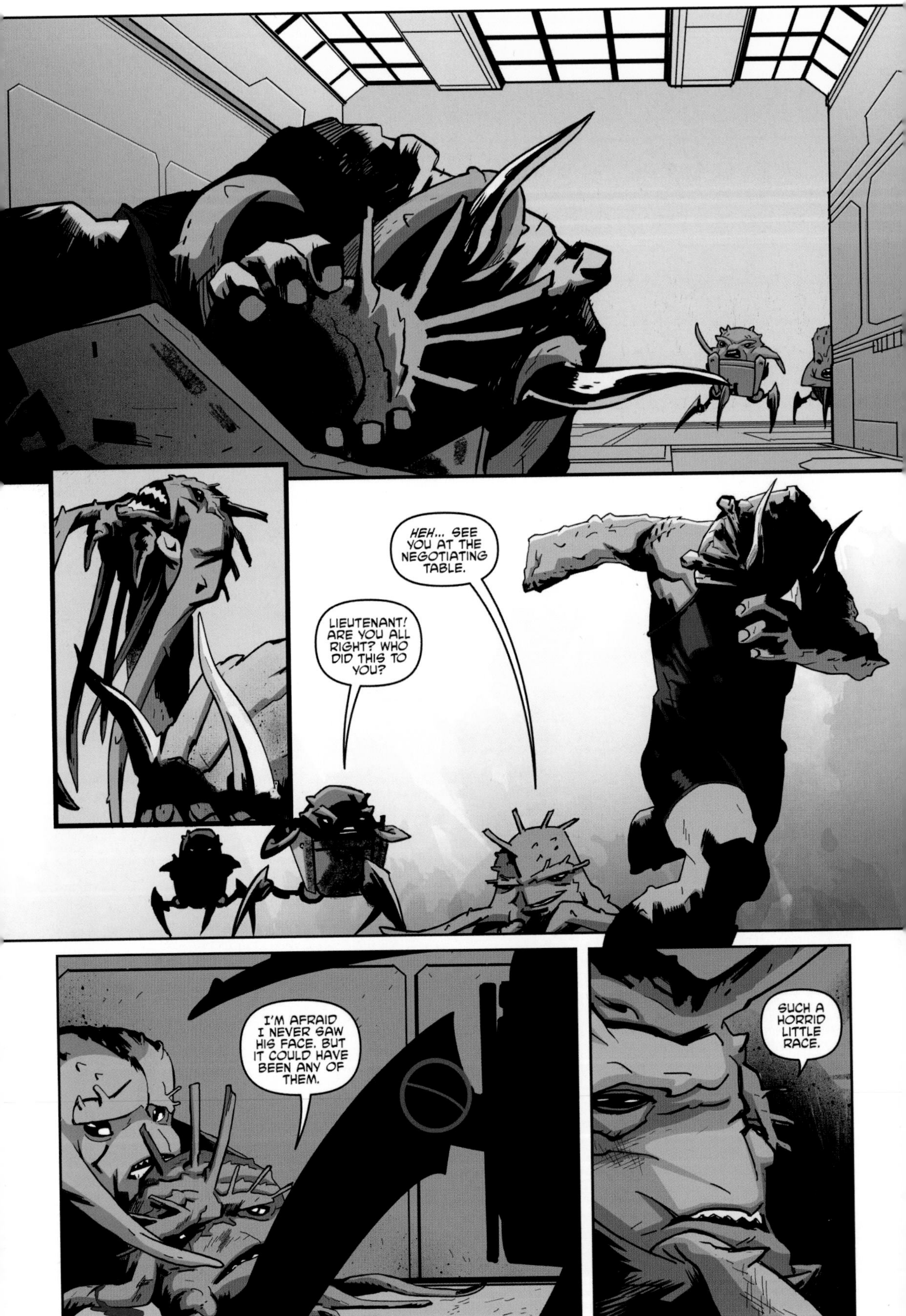
LIEUTENANT! ARE YOU ALL RIGHT? WHO DID THIS TO YOU?
HEH... SEE YOU AT THE NEGOTIATING TABLE.
I'M AFRAID I NEVER SAW HIS FACE. BUT IT COULD HAVE BEEN ANY OF THEM.
SUCH A HORRID LITTLE RACE.

VIOLENT. DUPLICITOUS. *DISTRUSTFUL.*

IF WE *KNEW* WHO MY ASSAILANT WAS, THEN PERHAPS HE COULD BE DETAINED AND THESE NEGOTIATIONS COULD CONTINUE.

BUT WE DON'T. AND SO THEY CANNOT.

MA'RIELL! *CONTROL* YOUR PEOPLE!

WAIT!

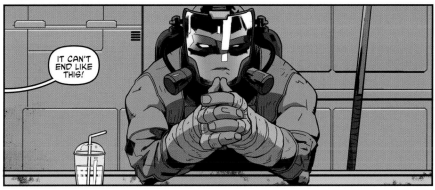

IT CAN'T END LIKE THIS!

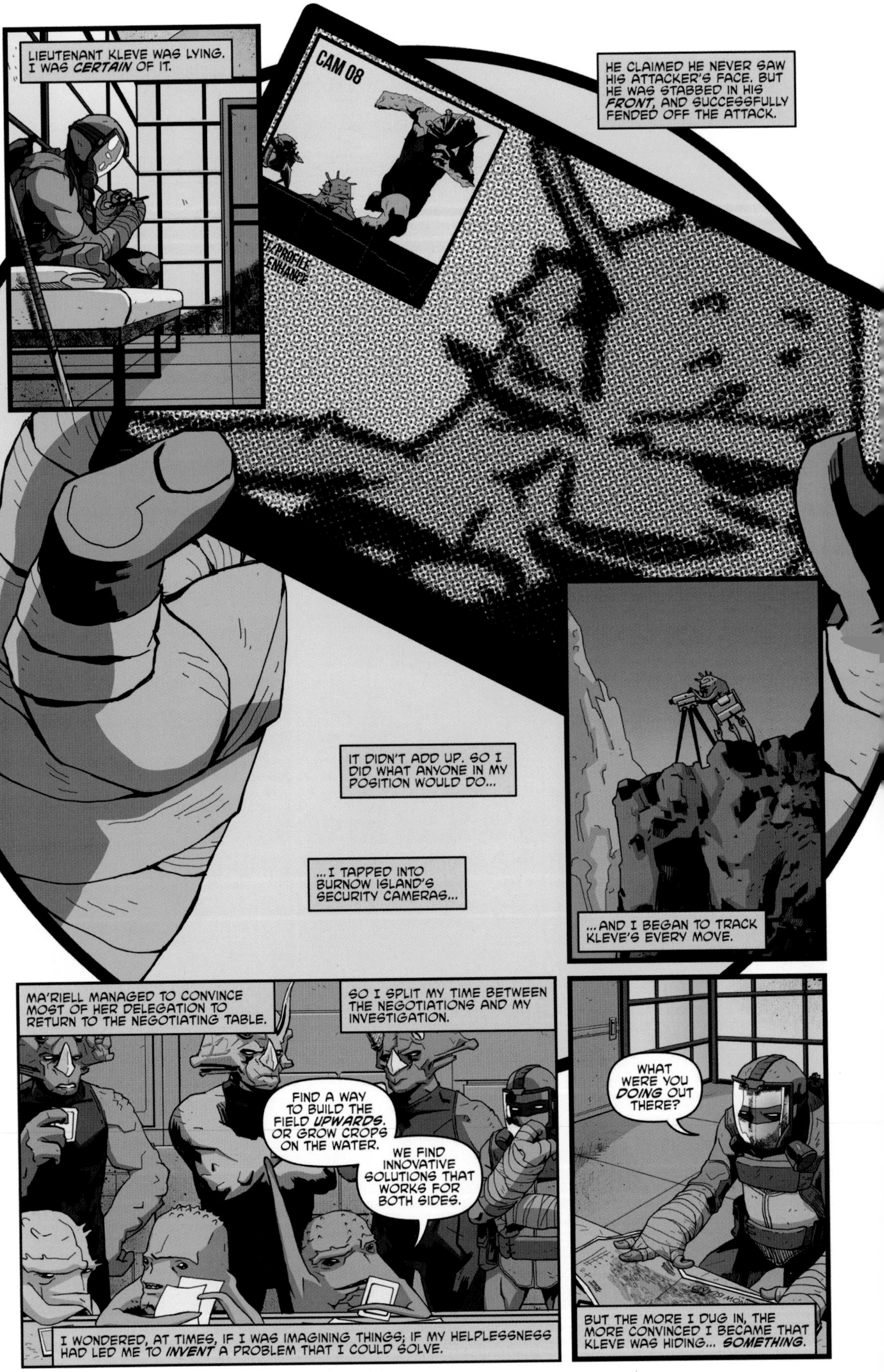
LIEUTENANT KLEVE WAS LYING. I WAS *CERTAIN* OF IT.
CAM 08
HE CLAIMED HE NEVER SAW HIS ATTACKER'S FACE. BUT HE WAS STABBED IN HIS *FRONT*, AND SUCCESSFULLY FENDED OFF THE ATTACK.
IT DIDN'T ADD UP. SO I DID WHAT ANYONE IN MY POSITION WOULD DO...
...I TAPPED INTO BURNOW ISLAND'S SECURITY CAMERAS...
...AND I BEGAN TO TRACK KLEVE'S EVERY MOVE.
MA'RIELL MANAGED TO CONVINCE MOST OF HER DELEGATION TO RETURN TO THE NEGOTIATING TABLE.
SO I SPLIT MY TIME BETWEEN THE NEGOTIATIONS AND MY INVESTIGATION.
FIND A WAY TO BUILD THE FIELD *UPWARDS*. OR GROW CROPS ON THE WATER.
WE FIND INNOVATIVE SOLUTIONS THAT WORKS FOR BOTH SIDES.
I WONDERED, AT TIMES, IF I WAS IMAGINING THINGS; IF MY HELPLESSNESS HAD LED ME TO *INVENT* A PROBLEM THAT I COULD SOLVE.
WHAT WERE YOU *DOING* OUT THERE?
BUT THE MORE I DUG IN, THE MORE CONVINCED I BECAME THAT KLEVE WAS HIDING... ***SOMETHING***.

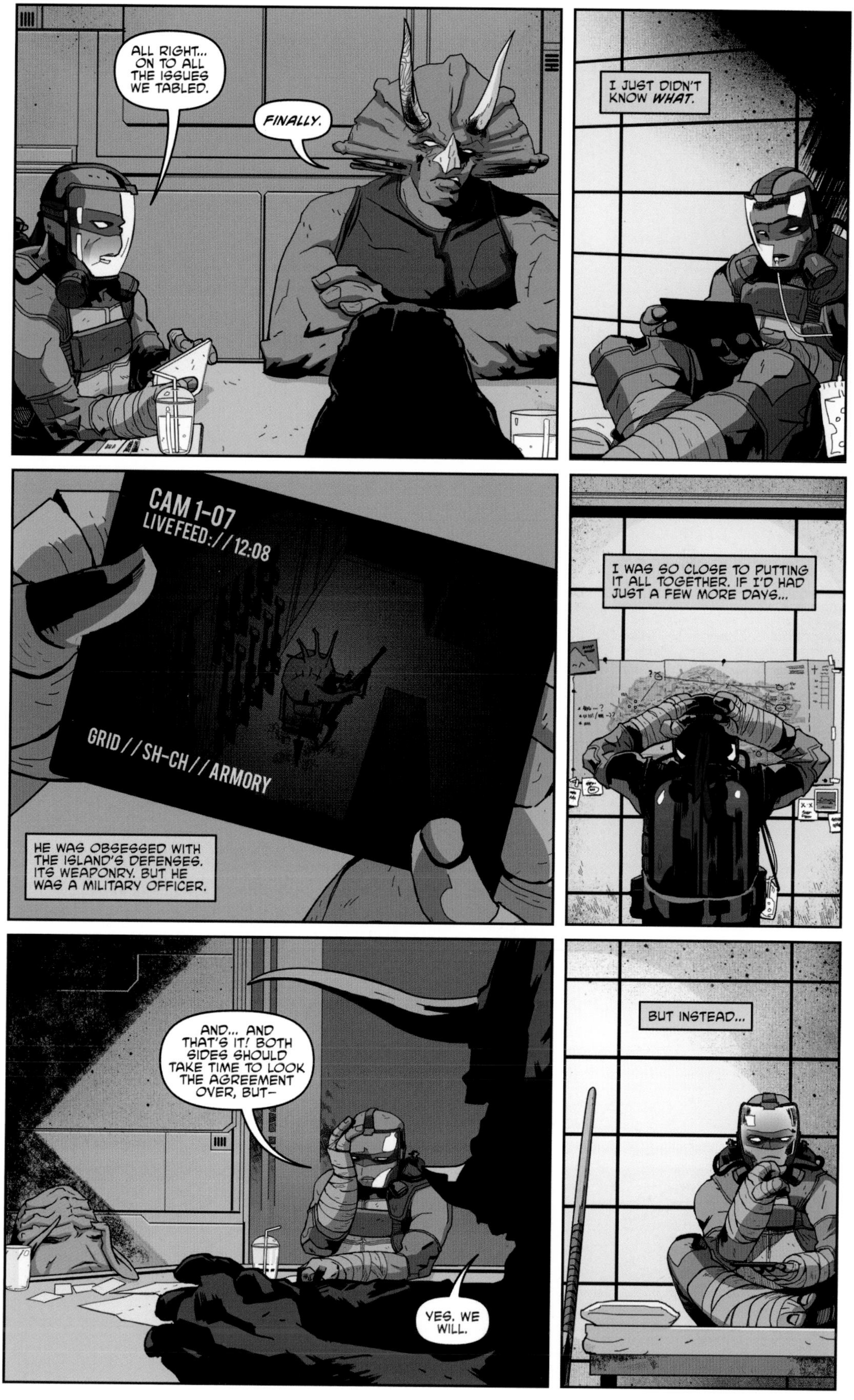
ALL RIGHT... ON TO ALL THE ISSUES WE TABLED.
FINALLY.
I JUST DIDN'T KNOW WHAT.
CAM 1-07
LIVEFEED:// 12:08
GRID//SH-CH//ARMORY
HE WAS OBSESSED WITH THE ISLAND'S DEFENSES. ITS WEAPONRY. BUT HE WAS A MILITARY OFFICER.
I WAS SO CLOSE TO PUTTING IT ALL TOGETHER. IF I'D HAD JUST A FEW MORE DAYS...
AND... AND THAT'S IT! BOTH SIDES SHOULD TAKE TIME TO LOOK THE AGREEMENT OVER, BUT–
YES. WE WILL.
BUT INSTEAD...

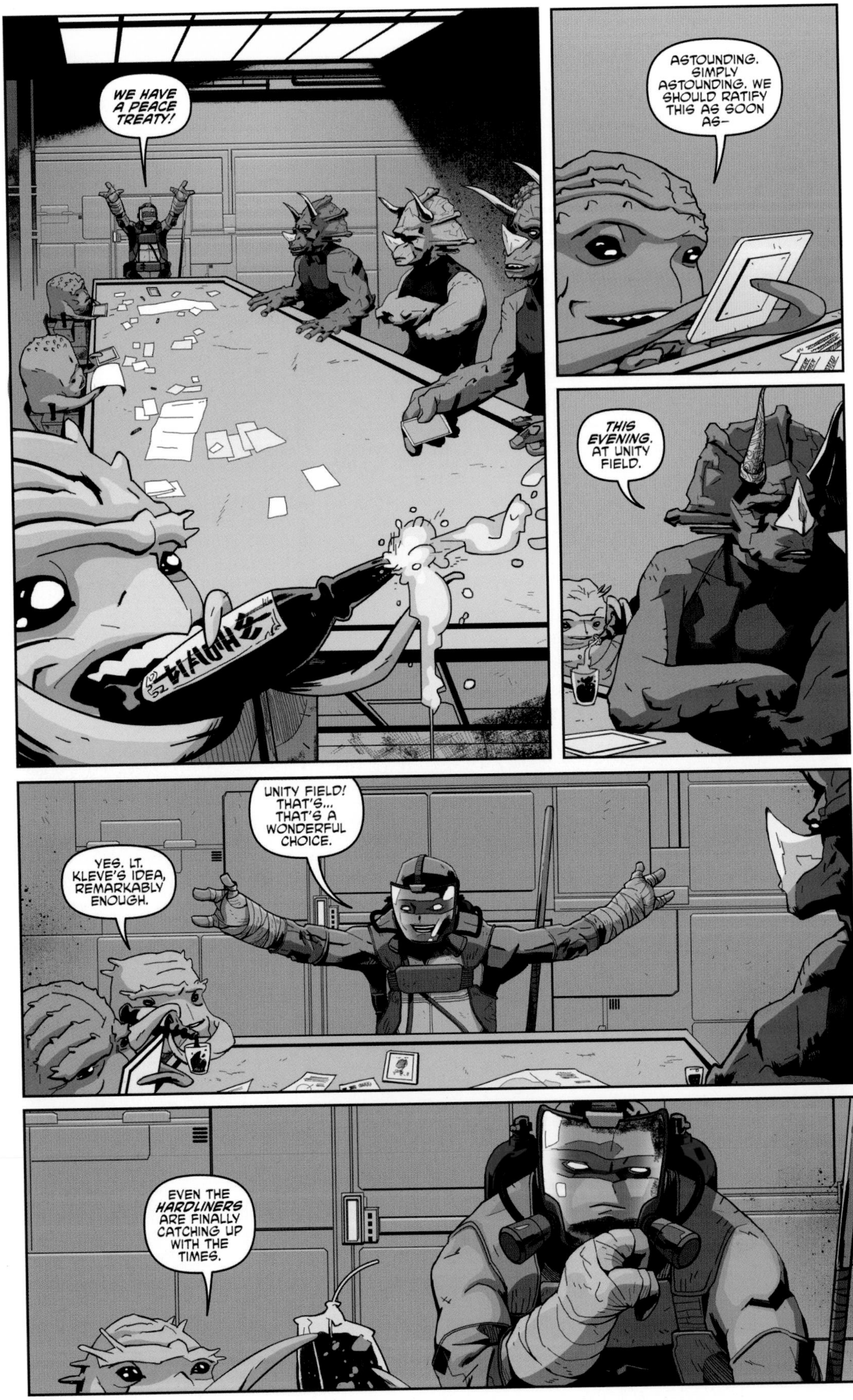
WE HAVE A PEACE TREATY!
ASTOUNDING. SIMPLY ASTOUNDING. WE SHOULD RATIFY THIS AS SOON AS–
THIS EVENING. AT UNITY FIELD.
UNITY FIELD! THAT'S... THAT'S A WONDERFUL CHOICE.
YES. LT. KLEVE'S IDEA, REMARKABLY ENOUGH.
EVEN THE HARDLINERS ARE FINALLY CATCHING UP WITH THE TIMES.

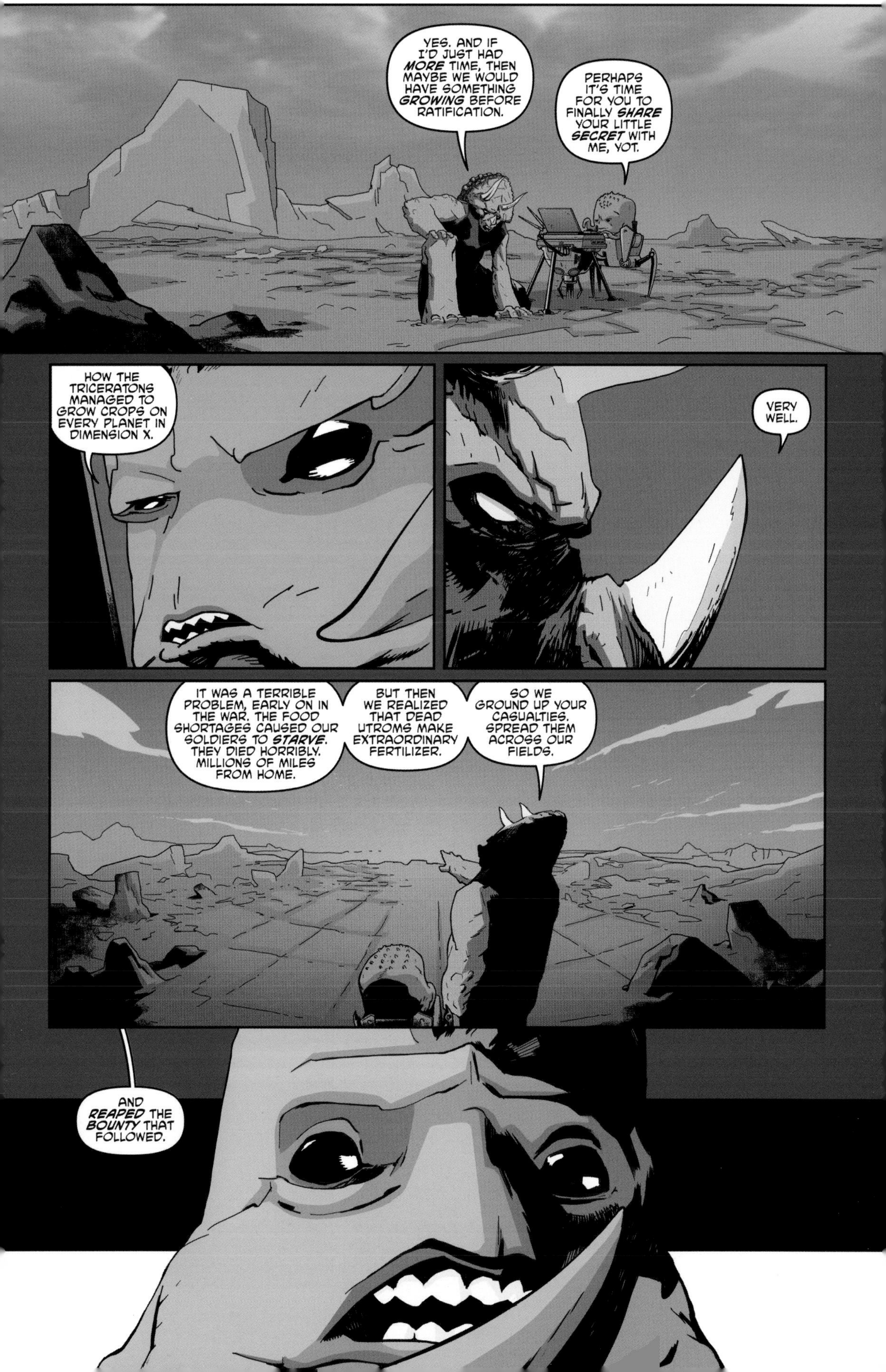
YES. AND IF I'D JUST HAD *MORE* TIME, THEN MAYBE WE WOULD HAVE SOMETHING *GROWING* BEFORE RATIFICATION.
PERHAPS IT'S TIME FOR YOU TO FINALLY *SHARE* YOUR LITTLE *SECRET* WITH ME, YOT.
HOW THE TRICERATONS MANAGED TO GROW CROPS ON EVERY PLANET IN DIMENSION X.
VERY WELL.
IT WAS A TERRIBLE PROBLEM, EARLY ON IN THE WAR. THE FOOD SHORTAGES CAUSED OUR SOLDIERS TO *STARVE*. THEY DIED HORRIBLY. MILLIONS OF MILES FROM HOME.
BUT THEN WE REALIZED THAT DEAD UTROMS MAKE EXTRAORDINARY FERTILIZER.
SO WE GROUND UP YOUR CASUALTIES. SPREAD THEM ACROSS OUR FIELDS.
AND *REAPED* THE *BOUNTY* THAT FOLLOWED.

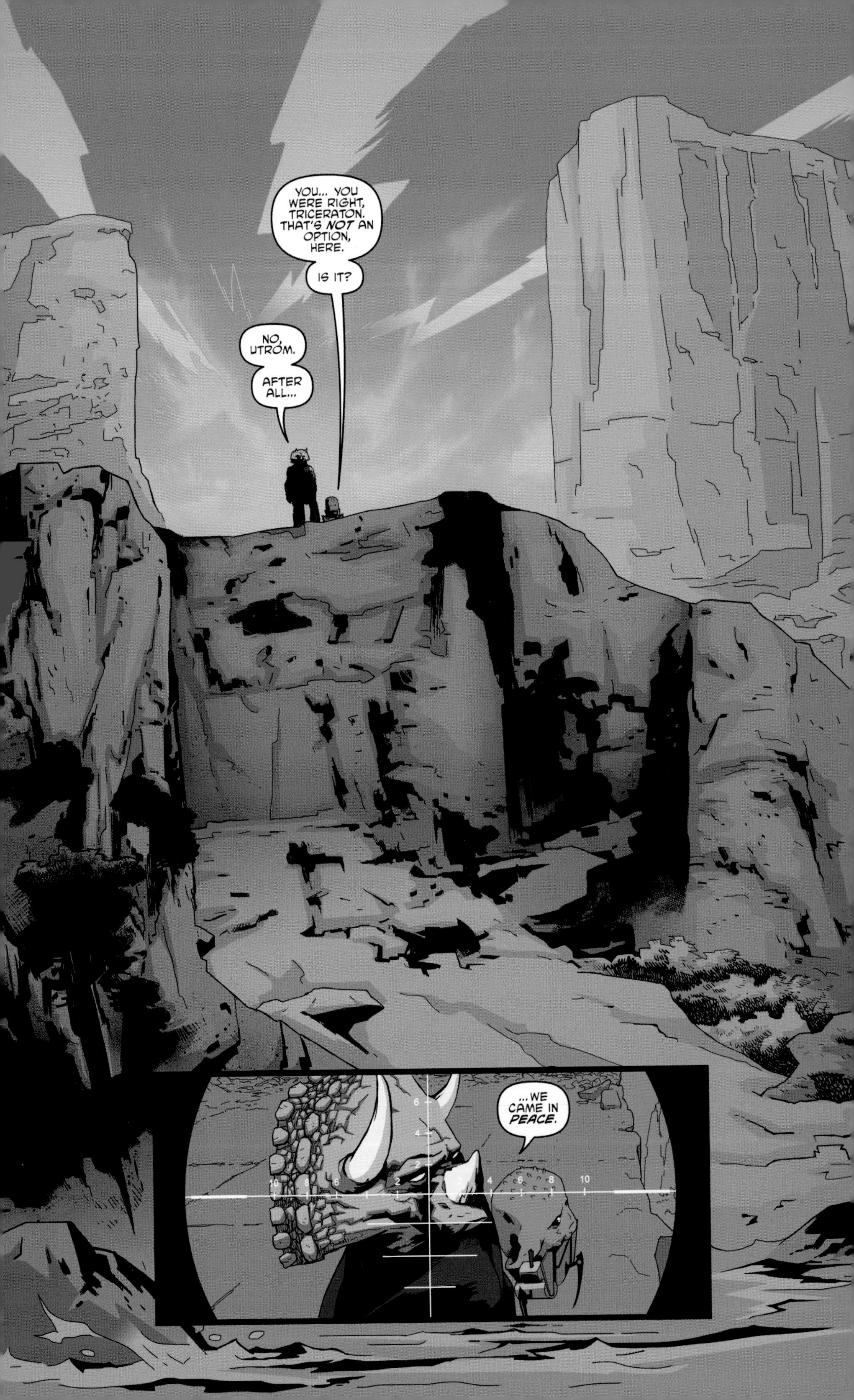
YOU... YOU WERE RIGHT, TRICERATON. THAT'S *NOT* AN OPTION, HERE.
IS IT?
NO, UTROM.
AFTER ALL...
...WE CAME IN *PEACE*.

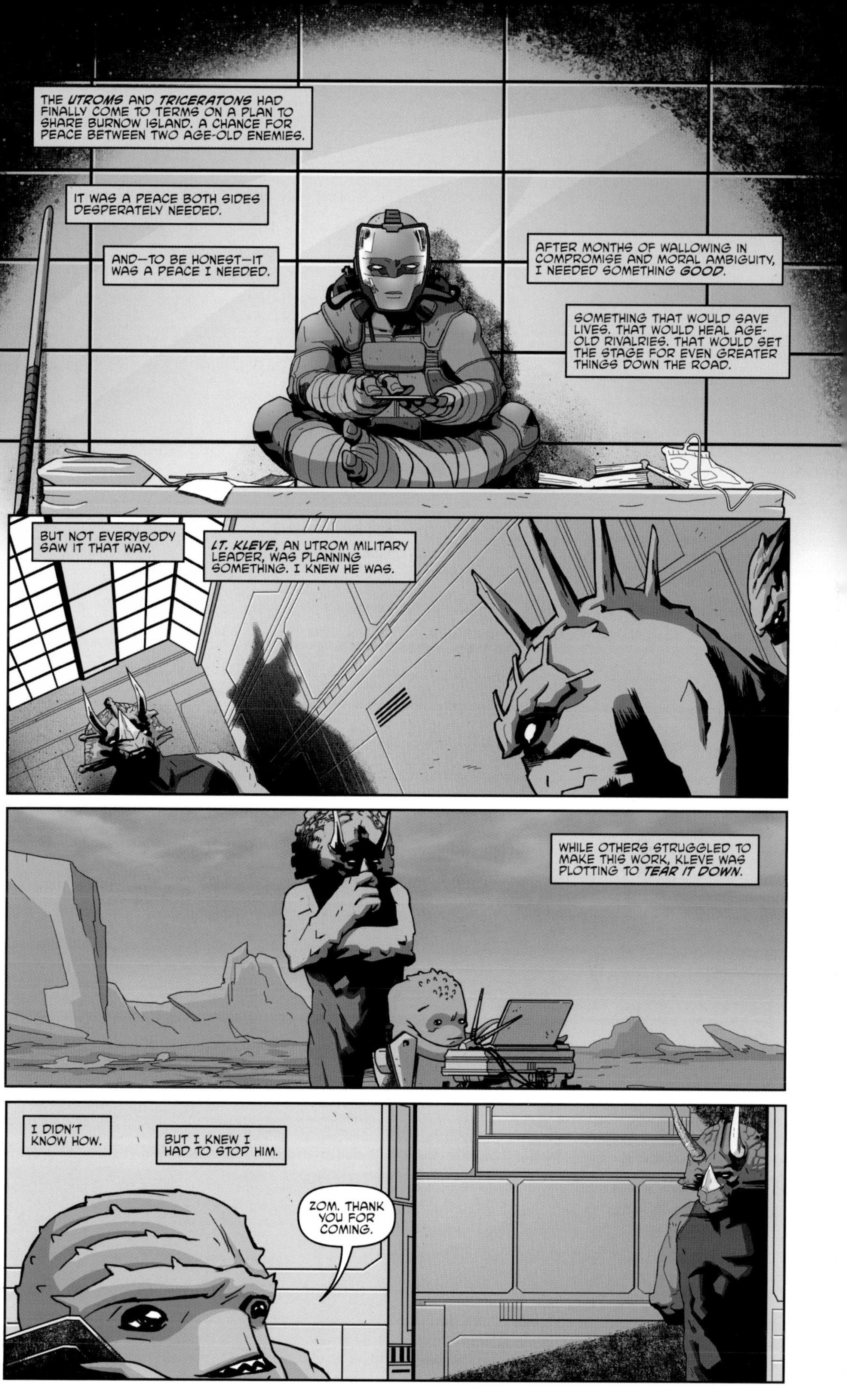
THE UTROMS AND TRICERATONS HAD FINALLY COME TO TERMS ON A PLAN TO SHARE BURNOW ISLAND. A CHANCE FOR PEACE BETWEEN TWO AGE-OLD ENEMIES.
IT WAS A PEACE BOTH SIDES DESPERATELY NEEDED.
AND—TO BE HONEST—IT WAS A PEACE I NEEDED.
AFTER MONTHS OF WALLOWING IN COMPROMISE AND MORAL AMBIGUITY, I NEEDED SOMETHING GOOD.
SOMETHING THAT WOULD SAVE LIVES. THAT WOULD HEAL AGE-OLD RIVALRIES. THAT WOULD SET THE STAGE FOR EVEN GREATER THINGS DOWN THE ROAD.
BUT NOT EVERYBODY SAW IT THAT WAY.
LT. KLEVE, AN UTROM MILITARY LEADER, WAS PLANNING SOMETHING. I KNEW HE WAS.
WHILE OTHERS STRUGGLED TO MAKE THIS WORK, KLEVE WAS PLOTTING TO TEAR IT DOWN.
I DIDN'T KNOW HOW.
BUT I KNEW I HAD TO STOP HIM.
ZOM. THANK YOU FOR COMING.

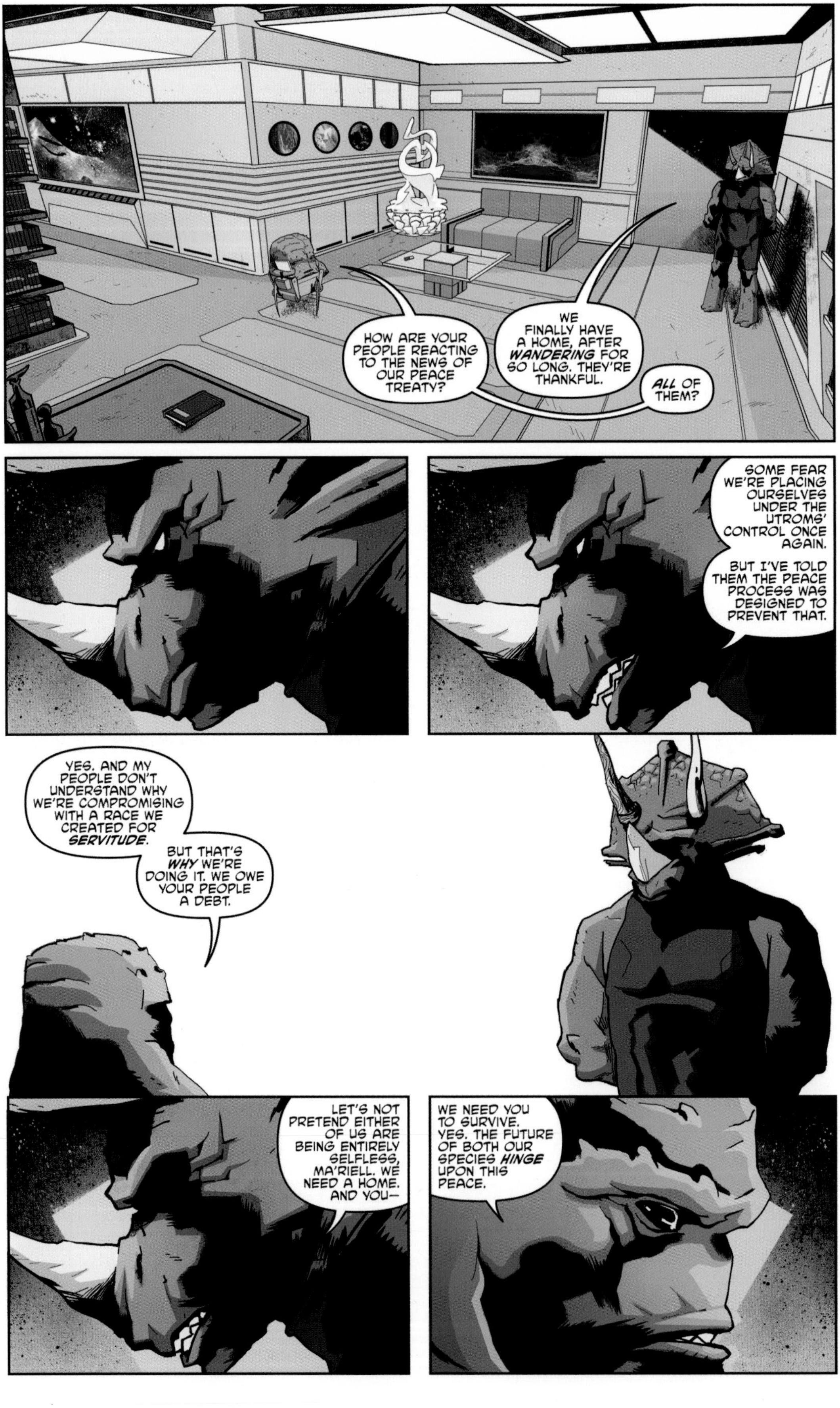
HOW ARE YOUR PEOPLE REACTING TO THE NEWS OF OUR PEACE TREATY?
WE FINALLY HAVE A HOME, AFTER WANDERING FOR SO LONG. THEY'RE THANKFUL.
ALL OF THEM?
SOME FEAR WE'RE PLACING OURSELVES UNDER THE UTROMS' CONTROL ONCE AGAIN.
BUT I'VE TOLD THEM THE PEACE PROCESS WAS DESIGNED TO PREVENT THAT.
YES. AND MY PEOPLE DON'T UNDERSTAND WHY WE'RE COMPROMISING WITH A RACE WE CREATED FOR SERVITUDE.
BUT THAT'S WHY WE'RE DOING IT. WE OWE YOUR PEOPLE A DEBT.
LET'S NOT PRETEND EITHER OF US ARE BEING ENTIRELY SELFLESS, MA'RIELL. WE NEED A HOME. AND YOU–
WE NEED YOU TO SURVIVE. YES. THE FUTURE OF BOTH OUR SPECIES HINGE UPON THIS PEACE.

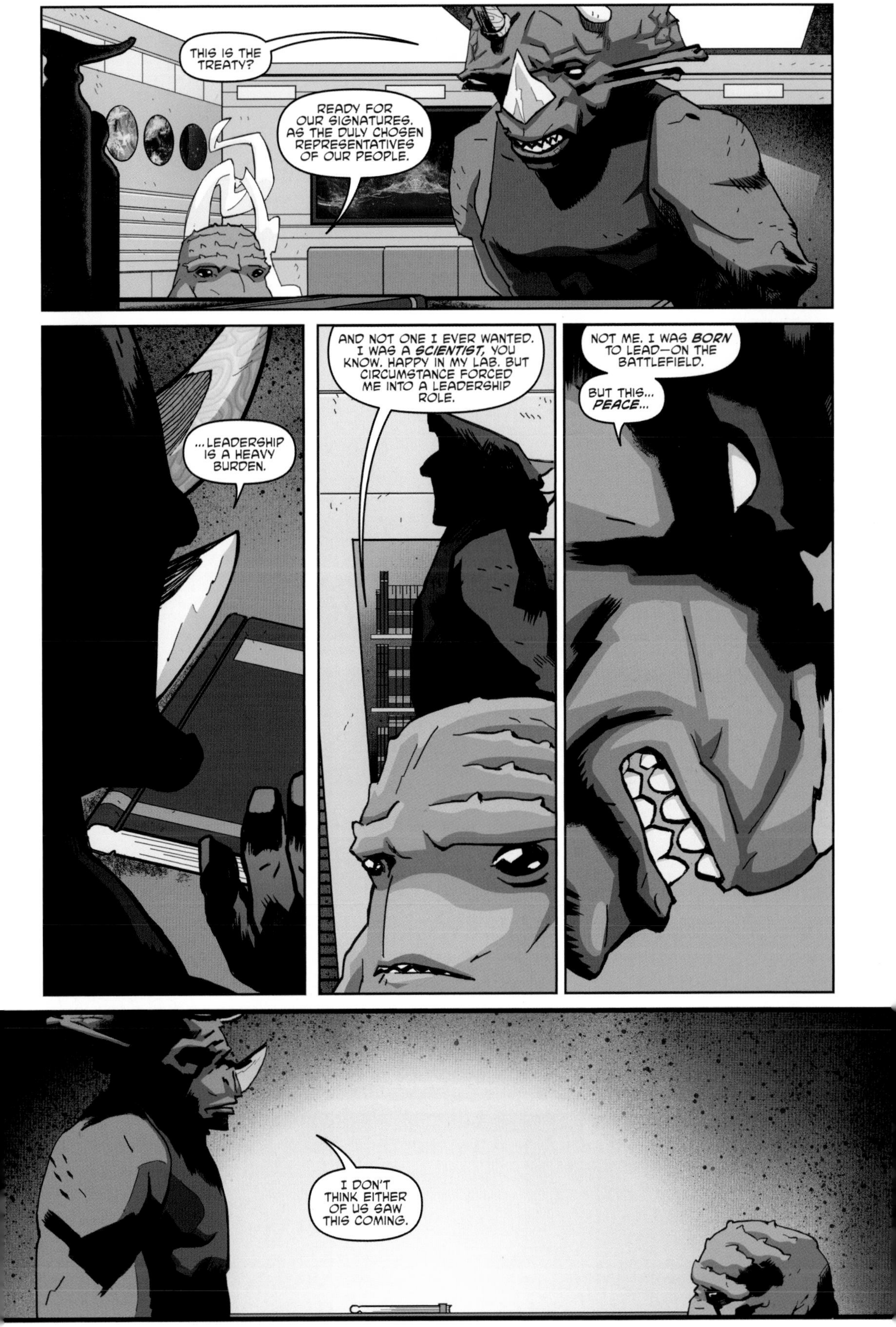
THIS IS THE TREATY?
READY FOR OUR SIGNATURES. AS THE DULY CHOSEN REPRESENTATIVES OF OUR PEOPLE.
...LEADERSHIP IS A HEAVY BURDEN.
AND NOT ONE I EVER WANTED. I WAS A *SCIENTIST,* YOU KNOW. HAPPY IN MY LAB. BUT CIRCUMSTANCE FORCED ME INTO A LEADERSHIP ROLE.
NOT ME. I WAS *BORN* TO LEAD—ON THE BATTLEFIELD.
BUT THIS... *PEACE*...
I DON'T THINK EITHER OF US SAW THIS COMING.

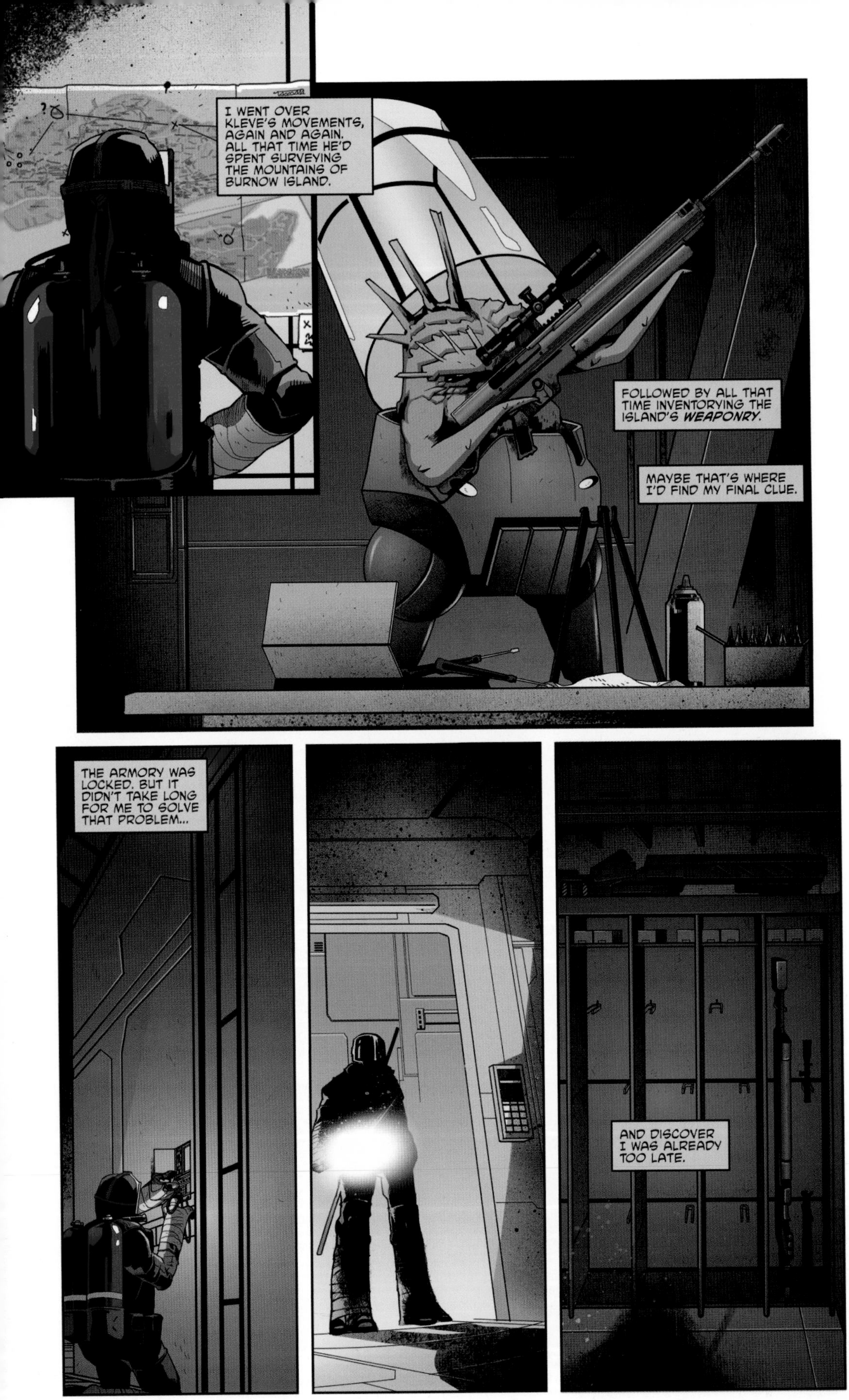
I WENT OVER KLEVE'S MOVEMENTS, AGAIN AND AGAIN. ALL THAT TIME HE'D SPENT SURVEYING THE MOUNTAINS OF BURNOW ISLAND.
FOLLOWED BY ALL THAT TIME INVENTORYING THE ISLAND'S *WEAPONRY*.
MAYBE THAT'S WHERE I'D FIND MY FINAL CLUE.
THE ARMORY WAS LOCKED. BUT IT DIDN'T TAKE LONG FOR ME TO SOLVE THAT PROBLEM...
AND DISCOVER I WAS ALREADY TOO LATE.

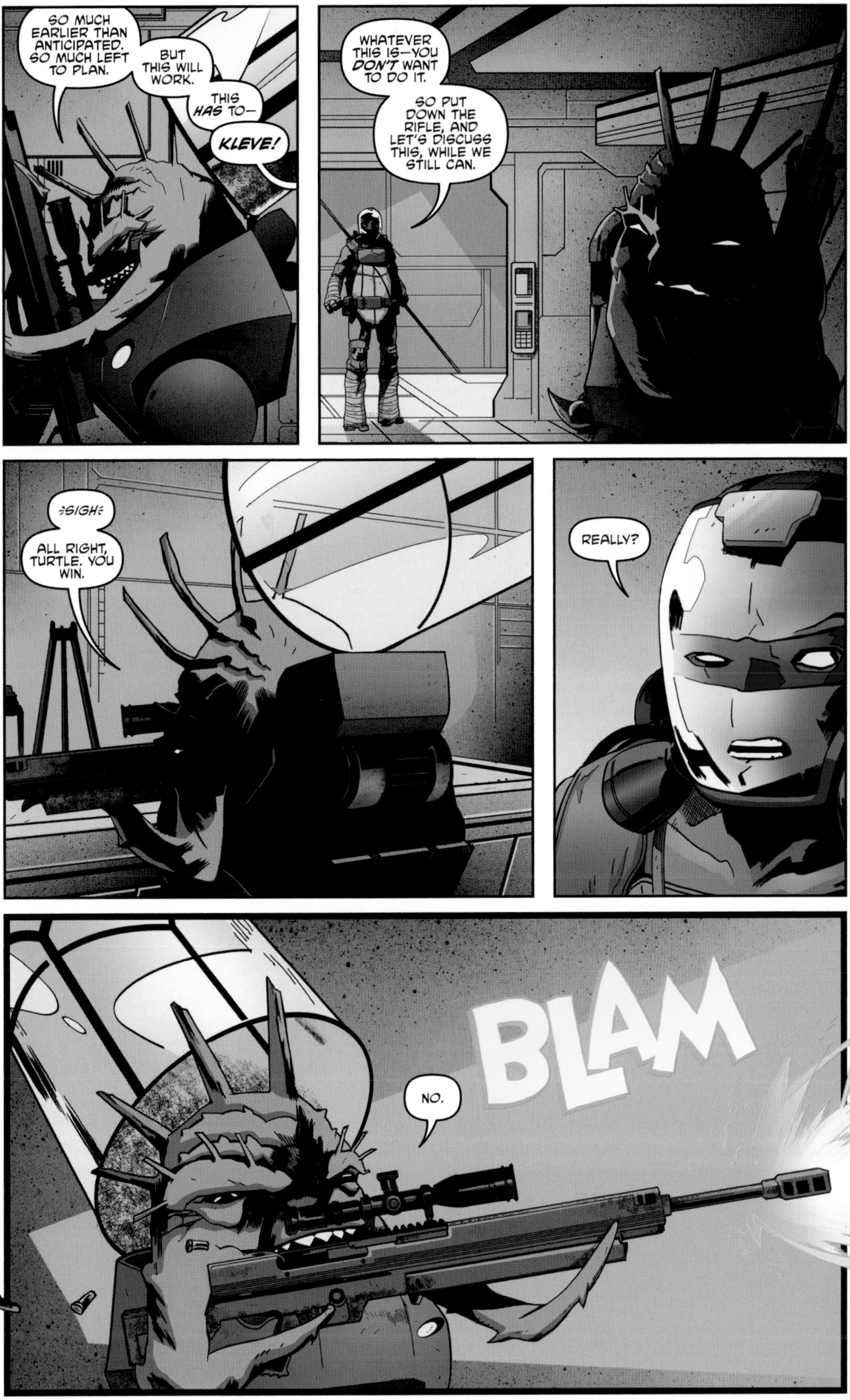
SO MUCH EARLIER THAN ANTICIPATED. SO MUCH LEFT TO PLAN.
BUT THIS WILL WORK.
THIS *HAS* TO—
KLEVE!
WHATEVER THIS IS—YOU *DON'T* WANT TO DO IT.
SO PUT DOWN THE RIFLE, AND LET'S DISCUSS THIS, WHILE WE STILL CAN.
SIGH
ALL RIGHT, TURTLE. YOU WIN.
REALLY?
NO.
BLAM

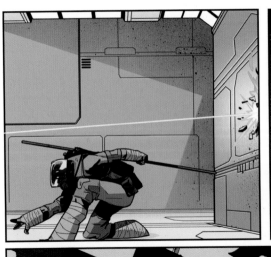

BWAM

WOW. STURDY TECH.

OF *COURSE.* IT CAN CERTAINLY WITHSTAND THE LIKES OF—

HOW DOES IT WORK WHEN YOU'RE NOT *INSIDE* IT?

NO!

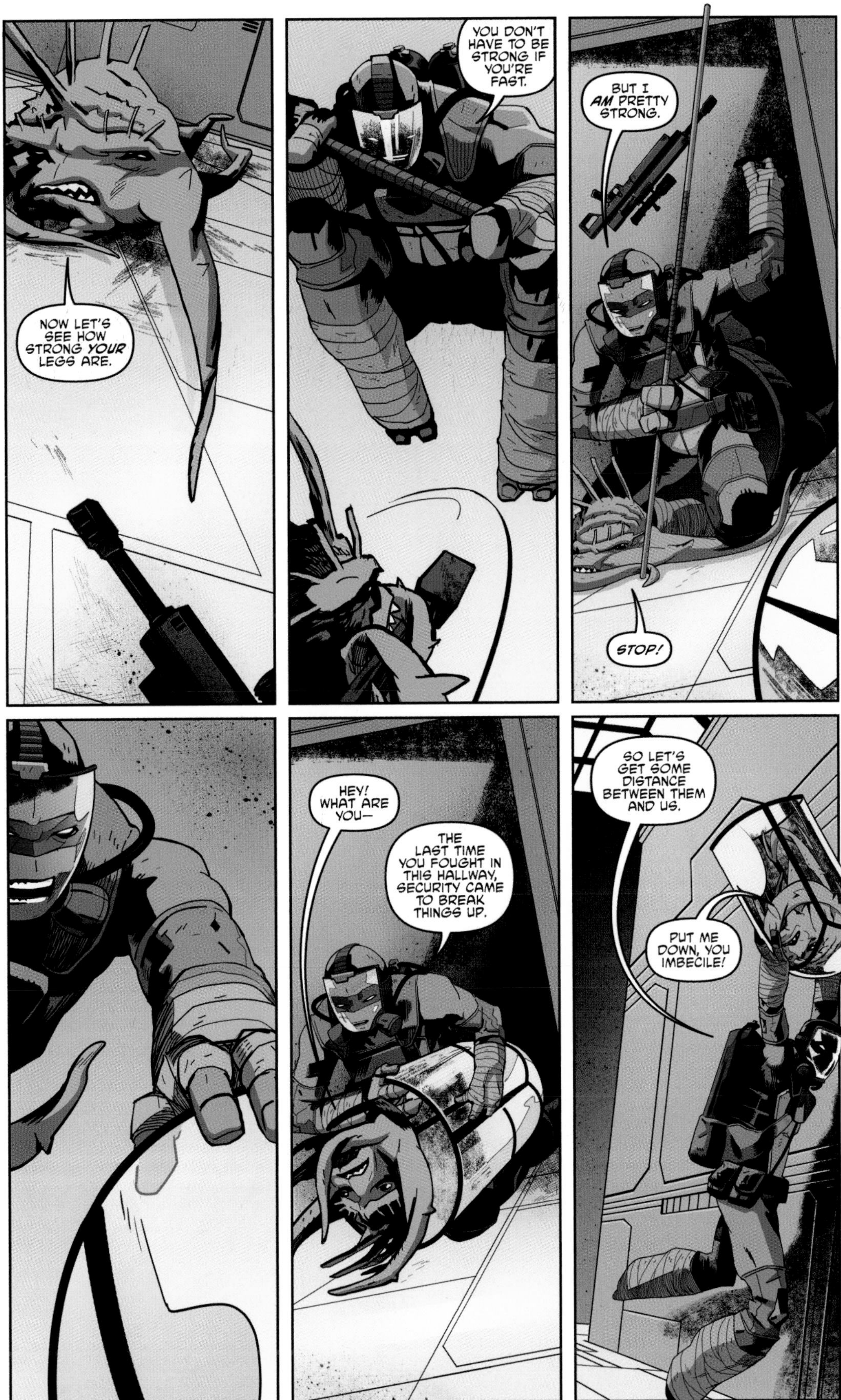
NOW LET'S SEE HOW STRONG YOUR LEGS ARE.
YOU DON'T HAVE TO BE STRONG IF YOU'RE FAST.
BUT I AM PRETTY STRONG.
STOP!
HEY! WHAT ARE YOU—
THE LAST TIME YOU FOUGHT IN THIS HALLWAY, SECURITY CAME TO BREAK THINGS UP.
SO LET'S GET SOME DISTANCE BETWEEN THEM AND US.
PUT ME DOWN, YOU IMBECILE!

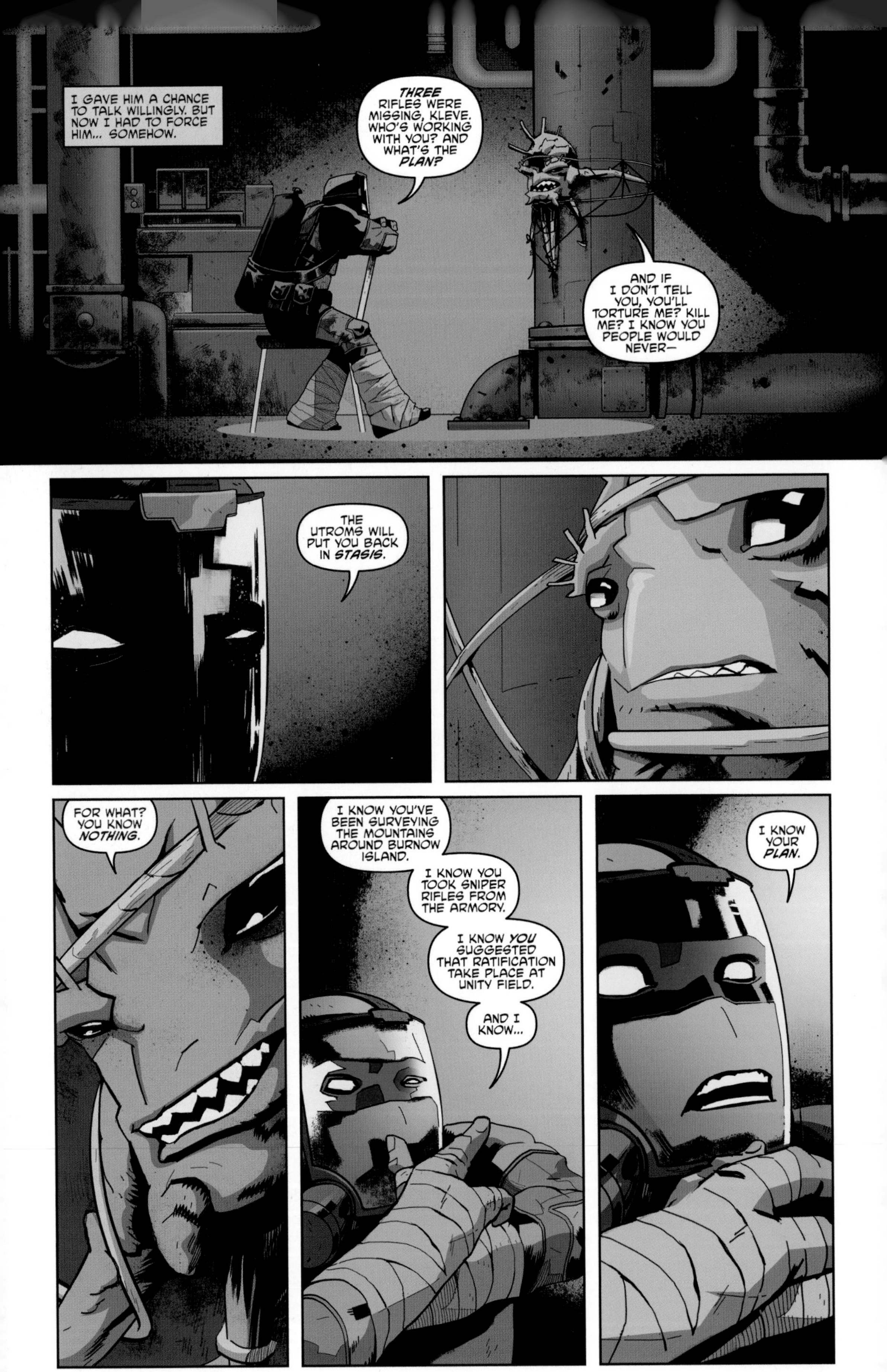
I GAVE HIM A CHANCE TO TALK WILLINGLY. BUT NOW I HAD TO FORCE HIM... SOMEHOW.
THREE RIFLES WERE MISSING, KLEVE. WHO'S WORKING WITH YOU? AND WHAT'S THE PLAN?
AND IF I DON'T TELL YOU, YOU'LL TORTURE ME? KILL ME? I KNOW YOU PEOPLE WOULD NEVER—
THE UTROMS WILL PUT YOU BACK IN STASIS.
FOR WHAT? YOU KNOW NOTHING.
I KNOW YOU'VE BEEN SURVEYING THE MOUNTAINS AROUND BURNOW ISLAND.
I KNOW YOU TOOK SNIPER RIFLES FROM THE ARMORY.
I KNOW YOU SUGGESTED THAT RATIFICATION TAKE PLACE AT UNITY FIELD.
AND I KNOW...
I KNOW YOUR PLAN.

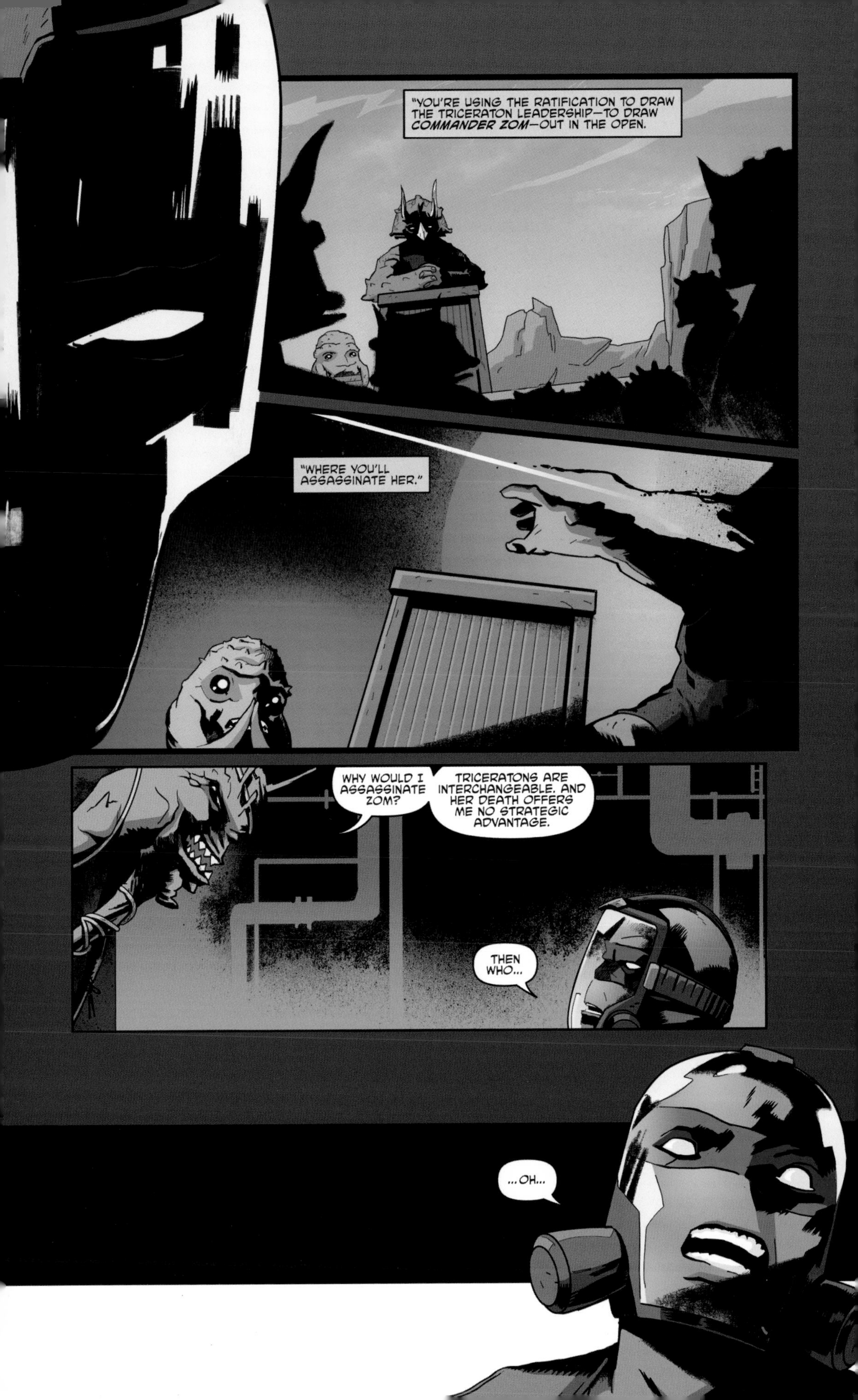
"YOU'RE USING THE RATIFICATION TO DRAW THE TRICERATON LEADERSHIP—TO DRAW *COMMANDER ZOM*—OUT IN THE OPEN.
"WHERE YOU'LL ASSASSINATE HER."
WHY WOULD I ASSASSINATE ZOM?
TRICERATONS ARE INTERCHANGEABLE. AND HER DEATH OFFERS ME NO STRATEGIC ADVANTAGE.
THEN WHO...
...OH...

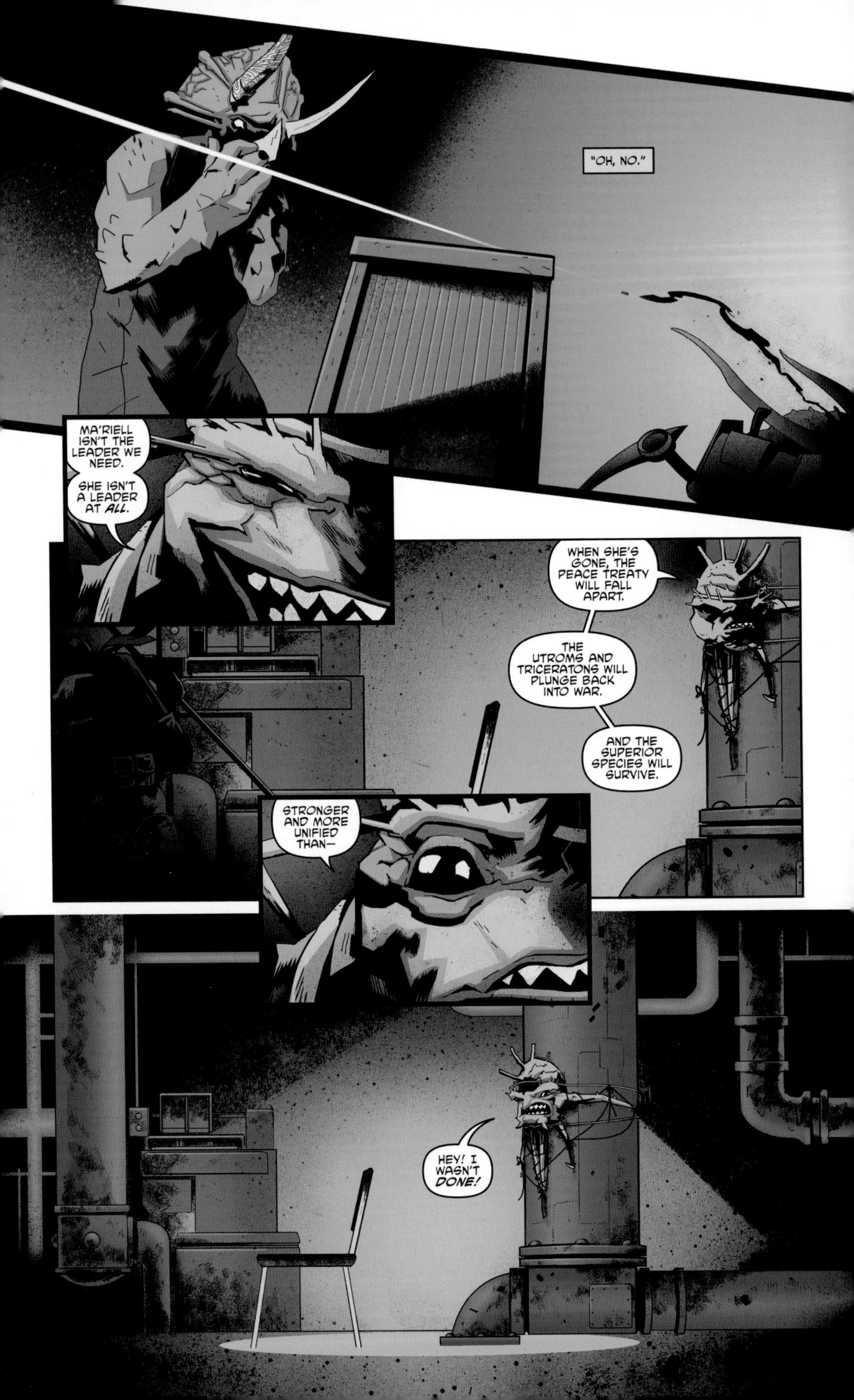
"OH, NO."
MA'RIELL ISN'T THE LEADER WE NEED.
SHE ISN'T A LEADER AT *ALL*.
WHEN SHE'S GONE, THE PEACE TREATY WILL FALL APART.
THE UTROMS AND TRICERATONS WILL PLUNGE BACK INTO WAR.
AND THE SUPERIOR SPECIES WILL SURVIVE.
STRONGER AND MORE UNIFIED THAN—
HEY! I WASN'T *DONE*!

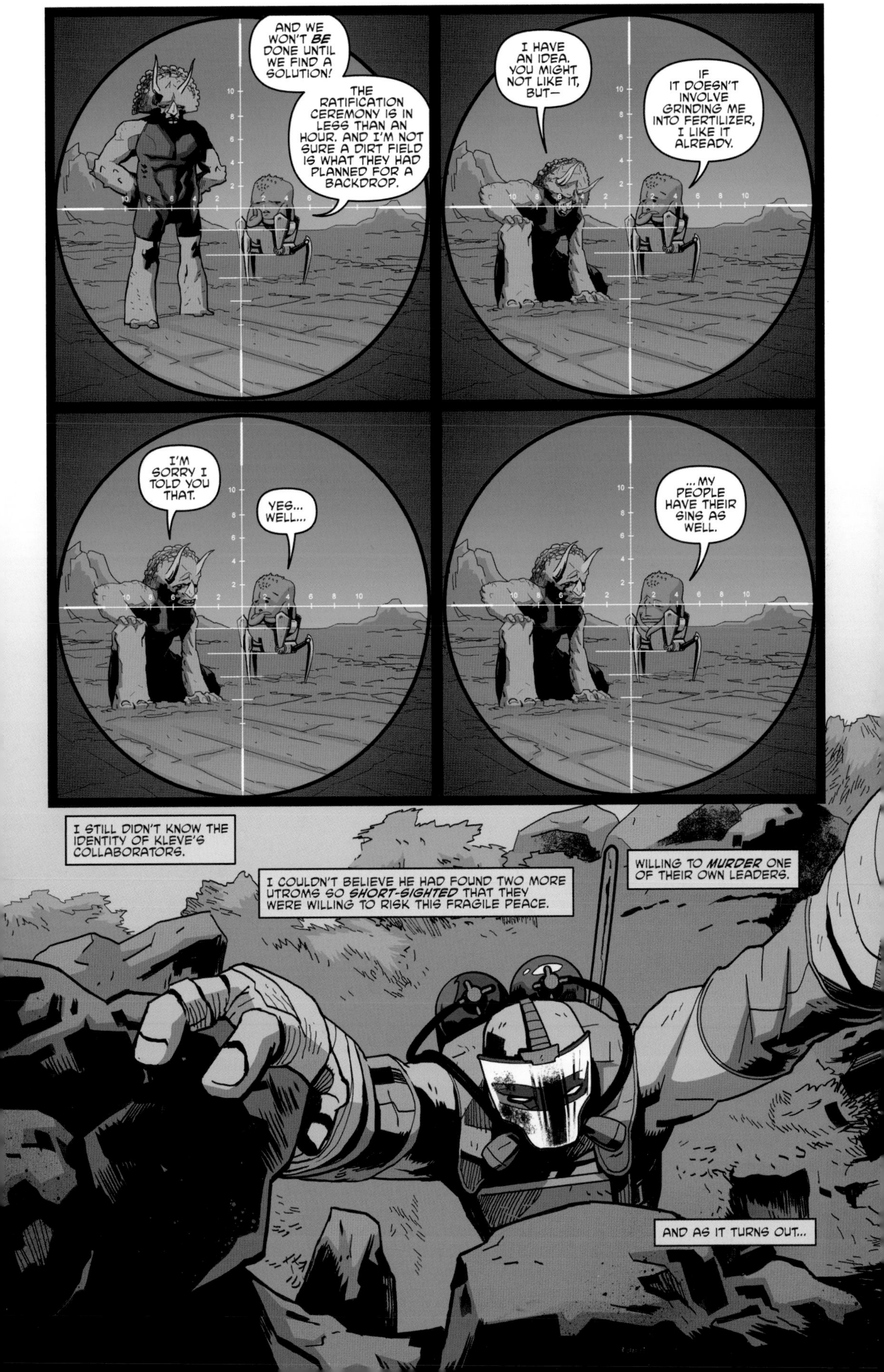

AND WE WON'T *BE* DONE UNTIL WE FIND A SOLUTION!
THE RATIFICATION CEREMONY IS IN LESS THAN AN HOUR. AND I'M NOT SURE A DIRT FIELD IS WHAT THEY HAD PLANNED FOR A BACKDROP.
I HAVE AN IDEA. YOU MIGHT NOT LIKE IT, BUT—
IF IT DOESN'T INVOLVE GRINDING ME INTO FERTILIZER, I LIKE IT ALREADY.
I'M SORRY I TOLD YOU THAT.
YES... WELL...
...MY PEOPLE HAVE THEIR SINS AS WELL.
I STILL DIDN'T KNOW THE IDENTITY OF KLEVE'S COLLABORATORS.
I COULDN'T BELIEVE HE HAD FOUND TWO MORE UTROMS SO *SHORT-SIGHTED* THAT THEY WERE WILLING TO RISK THIS FRAGILE PEACE.
WILLING TO *MURDER* ONE OF THEIR OWN LEADERS.
AND AS IT TURNS OUT...

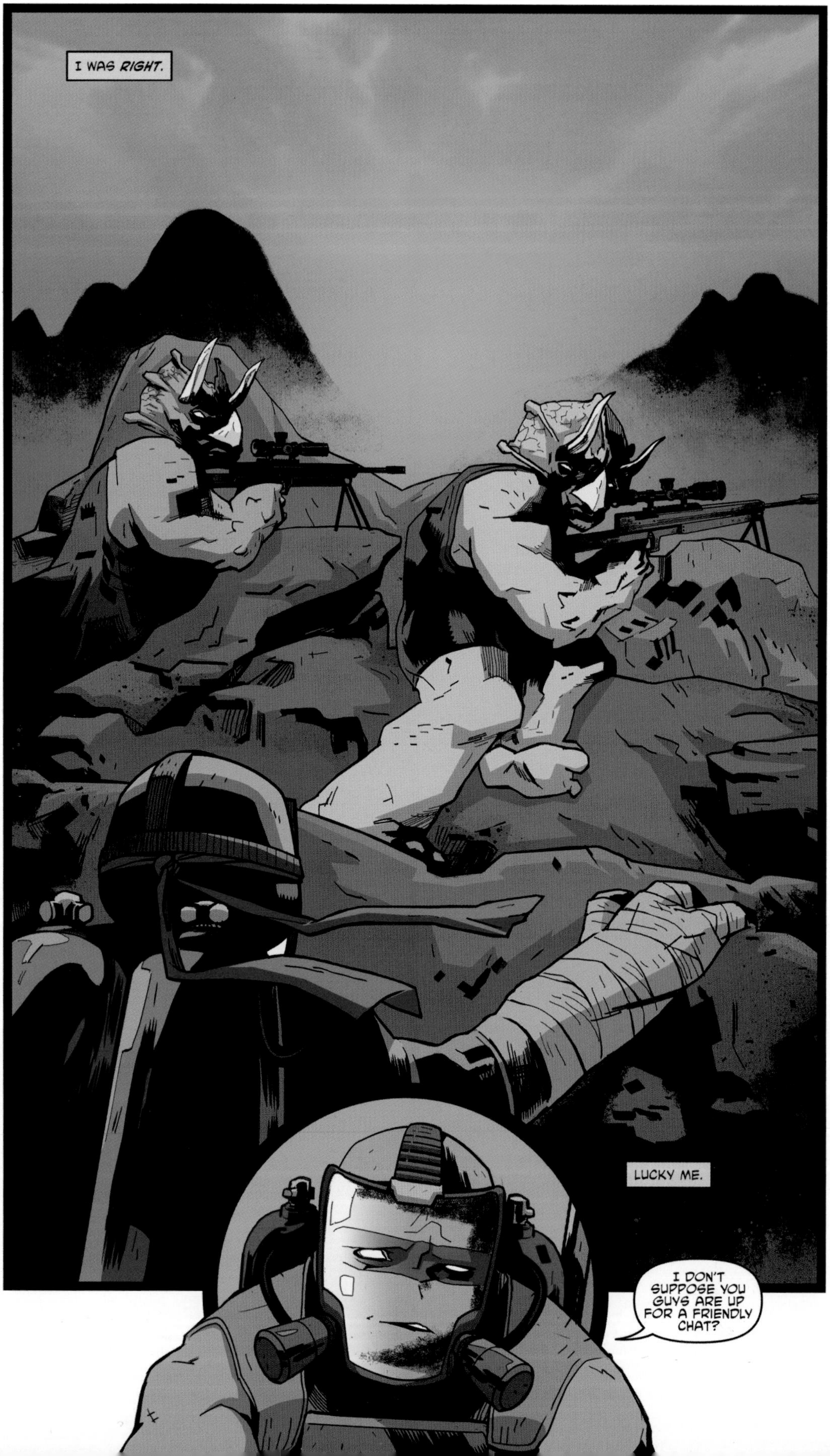
I WAS RIGHT.
LUCKY ME.
I DON'T SUPPOSE YOU GUYS ARE UP FOR A FRIENDLY CHAT?

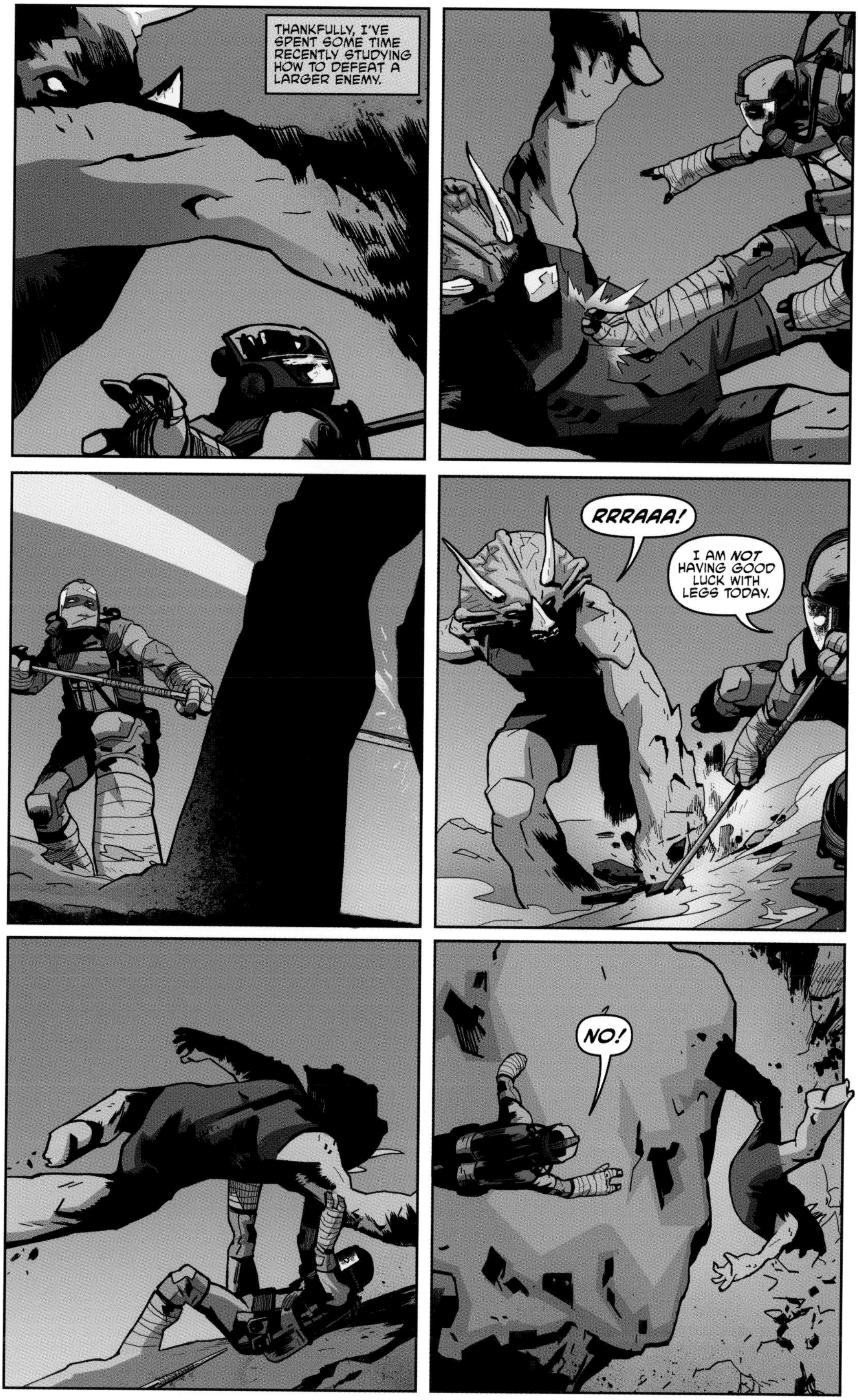
THANKFULLY, I'VE SPENT SOME TIME RECENTLY STUDYING HOW TO DEFEAT A LARGER ENEMY.
RRRAAA!
I AM NOT HAVING GOOD LUCK WITH LEGS TODAY.
NO!

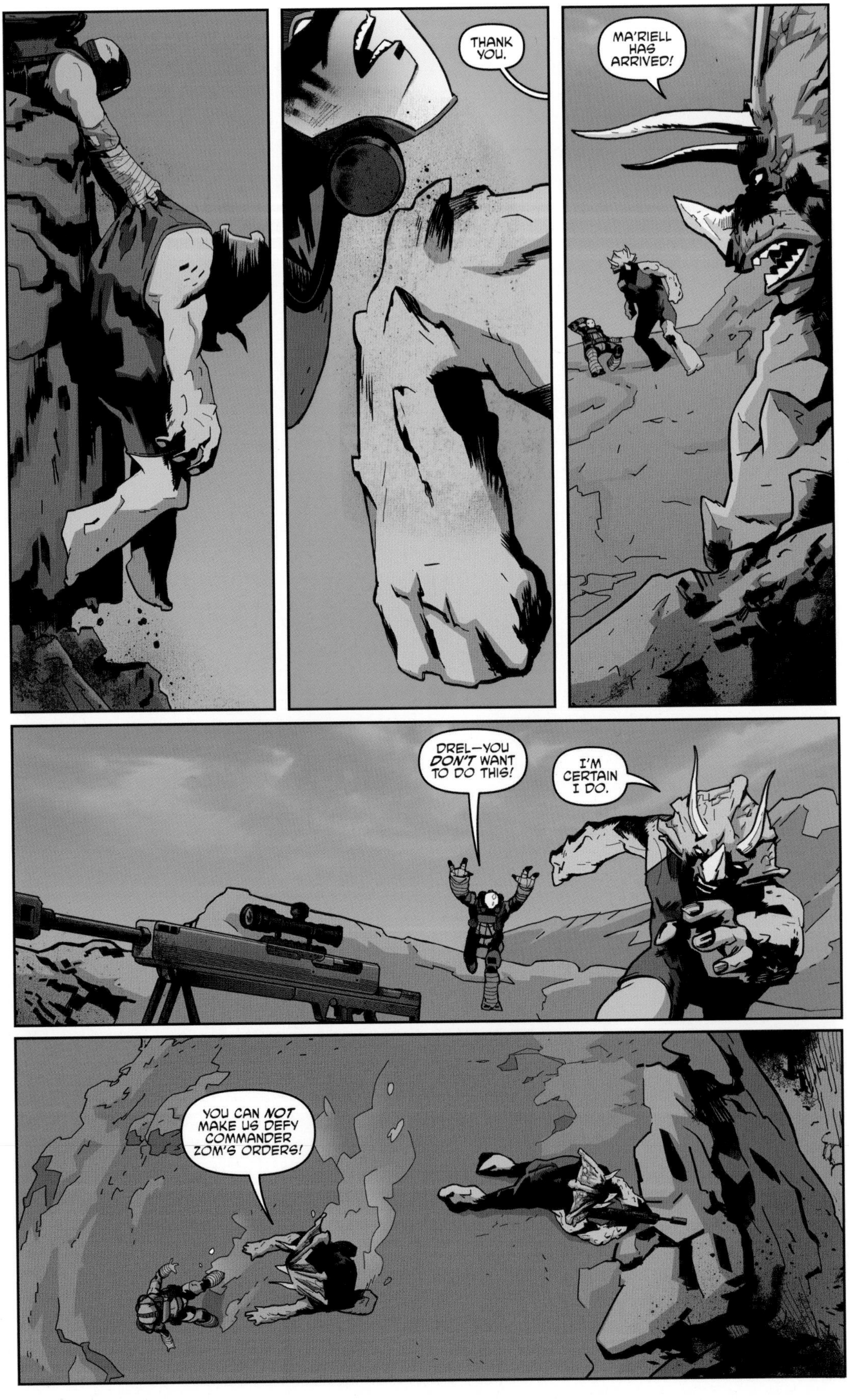
THANK YOU.
MA'RIELL HAS ARRIVED!
DREL—YOU DON'T WANT TO DO THIS!
I'M CERTAIN I DO.
YOU CAN NOT MAKE US DEFY COMMANDER ZOM'S ORDERS!

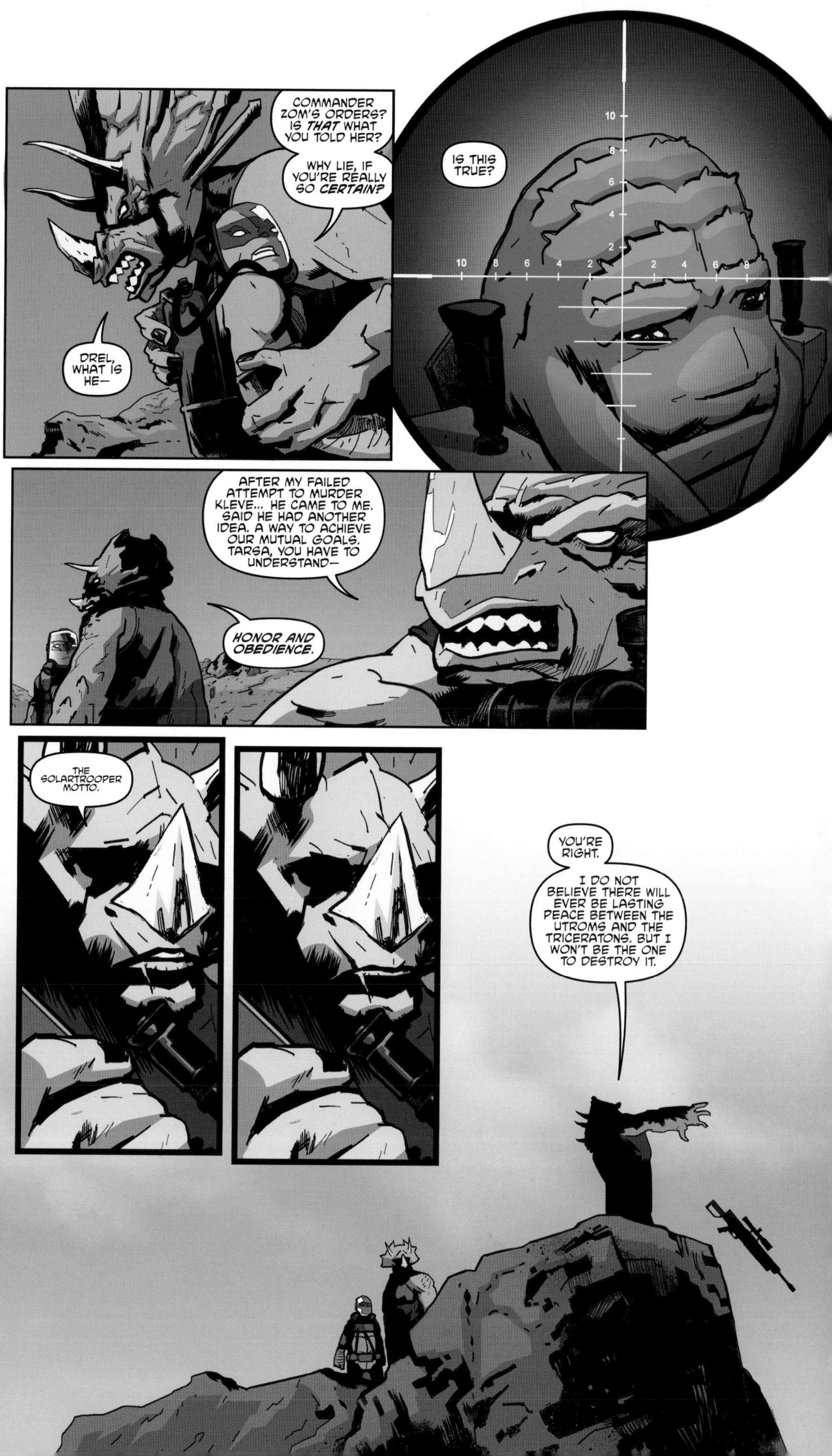
COMMANDER ZOM'S ORDERS? IS *THAT* WHAT YOU TOLD HER?
WHY LIE, IF YOU'RE REALLY SO *CERTAIN?*
DREL, WHAT IS HE—
IS THIS TRUE?
10
8
6
4
2
AFTER MY FAILED ATTEMPT TO MURDER KLEVE... HE CAME TO ME. SAID HE HAD ANOTHER IDEA. A WAY TO ACHIEVE OUR MUTUAL GOALS. TARSA, YOU HAVE TO UNDERSTAND—
HONOR AND OBEDIENCE.
THE SOLARTROOPER MOTTO.
YOU'RE RIGHT.
I DO NOT BELIEVE THERE WILL EVER BE LASTING PEACE BETWEEN THE UTROMS AND THE TRICERATONS. BUT I WON'T BE THE ONE TO DESTROY IT.

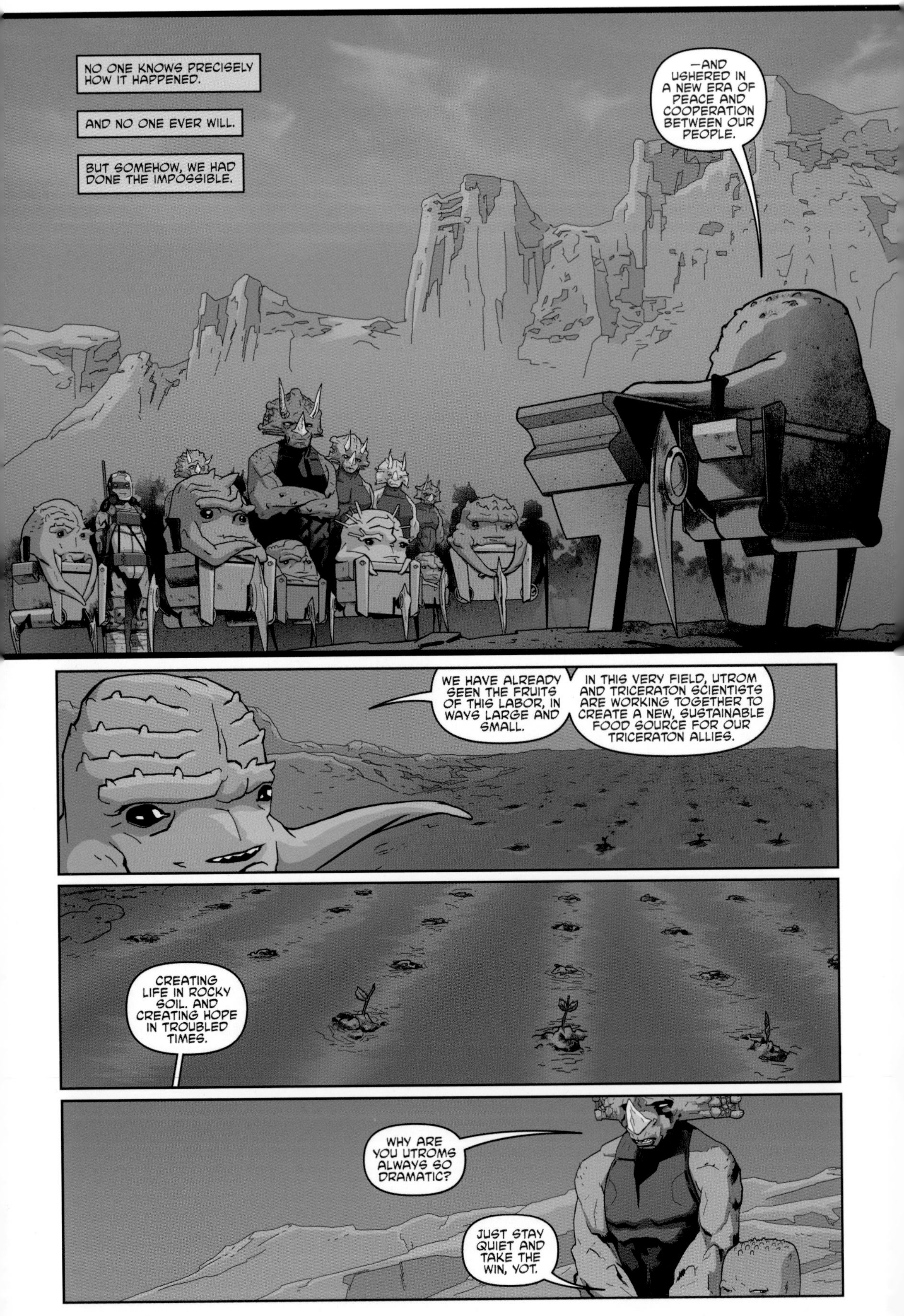
NO ONE KNOWS PRECISELY HOW IT HAPPENED.
AND NO ONE EVER WILL.
BUT SOMEHOW, WE HAD DONE THE IMPOSSIBLE.
—AND USHERED IN A NEW ERA OF PEACE AND COOPERATION BETWEEN OUR PEOPLE.
WE HAVE ALREADY SEEN THE FRUITS OF THIS LABOR, IN WAYS LARGE AND SMALL.
IN THIS VERY FIELD, UTROM AND TRICERATON SCIENTISTS ARE WORKING TOGETHER TO CREATE A NEW, SUSTAINABLE FOOD SOURCE FOR OUR TRICERATON ALLIES.
CREATING LIFE IN ROCKY SOIL. AND CREATING HOPE IN TROUBLED TIMES.
WHY ARE YOU UTROMS ALWAYS SO DRAMATIC?
JUST STAY QUIET AND TAKE THE WIN, YOT.

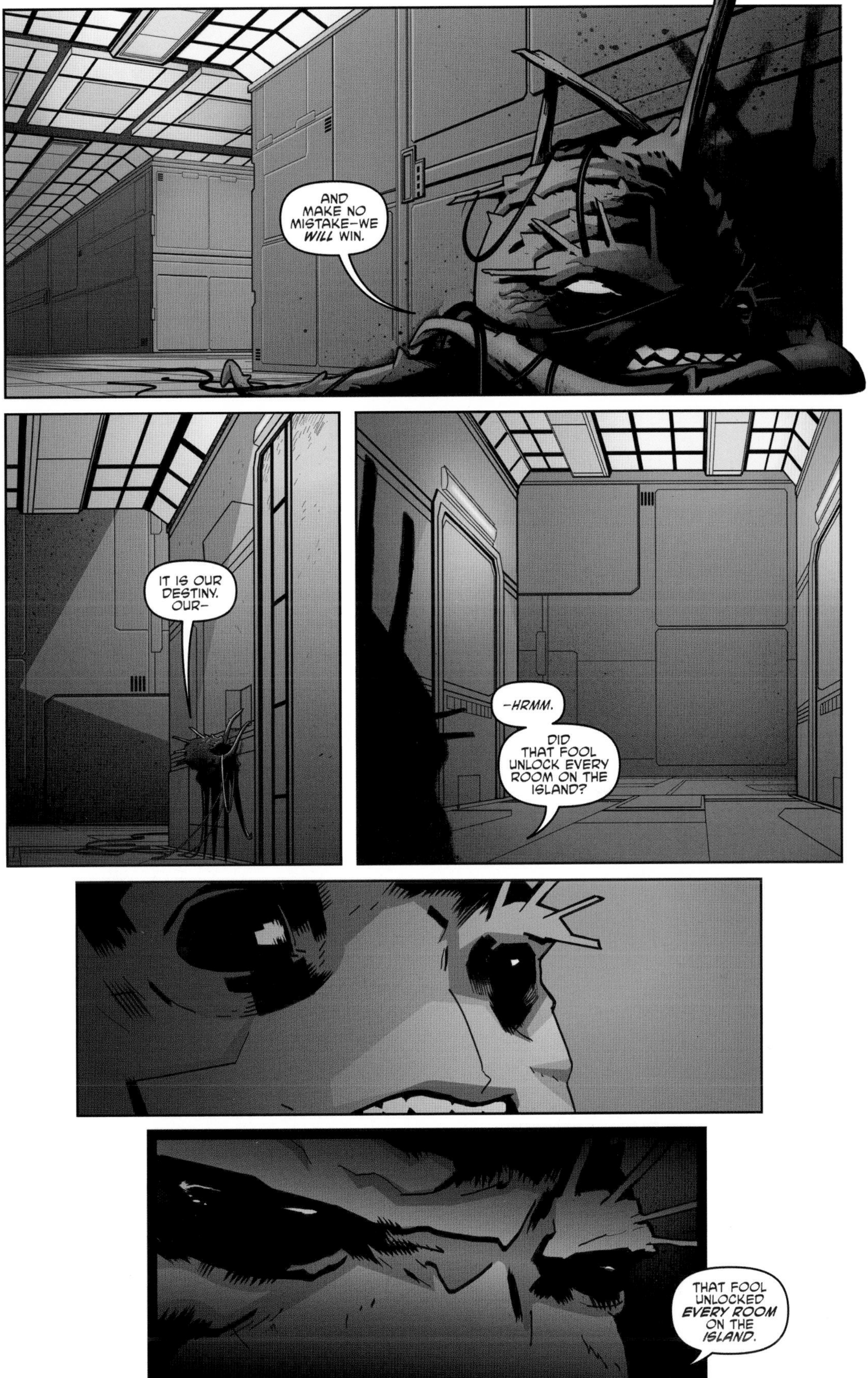
AND MAKE NO MISTAKE—WE *WILL* WIN.
IT IS OUR DESTINY. OUR—
—HRMM.
DID THAT FOOL UNLOCK EVERY ROOM ON THE ISLAND?
THAT FOOL UNLOCKED *EVERY ROOM* ON THE *ISLAND*.

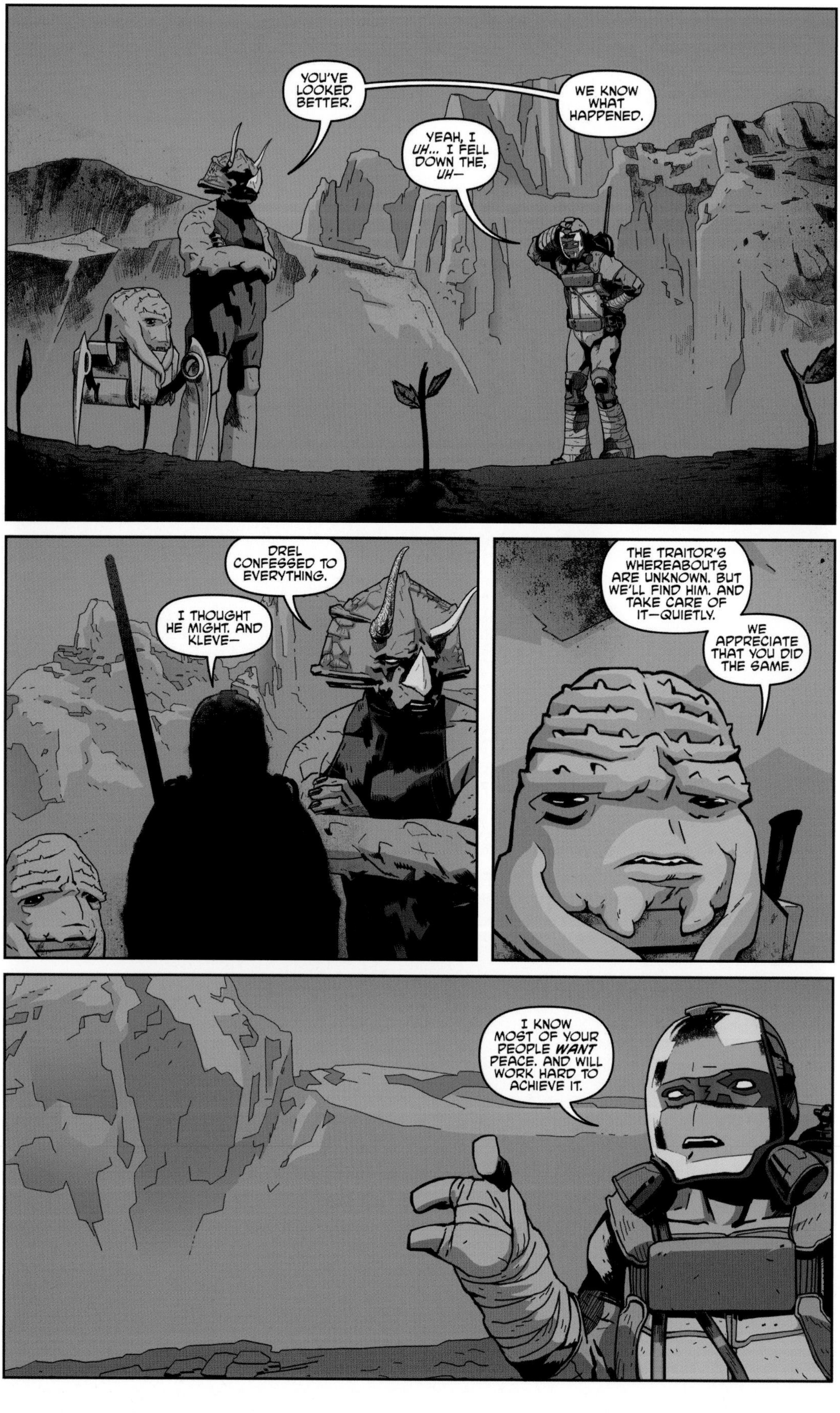
YOU'VE LOOKED BETTER.
WE KNOW WHAT HAPPENED.
YEAH, I UH... I FELL DOWN THE, UH—
DREL CONFESSED TO EVERYTHING.
I THOUGHT HE MIGHT. AND KLEVE—
THE TRAITOR'S WHEREABOUTS ARE UNKNOWN. BUT WE'LL FIND HIM. AND TAKE CARE OF IT—QUIETLY.
WE APPRECIATE THAT YOU DID THE SAME.
I KNOW MOST OF YOUR PEOPLE *WANT* PEACE. AND WILL WORK HARD TO ACHIEVE IT.

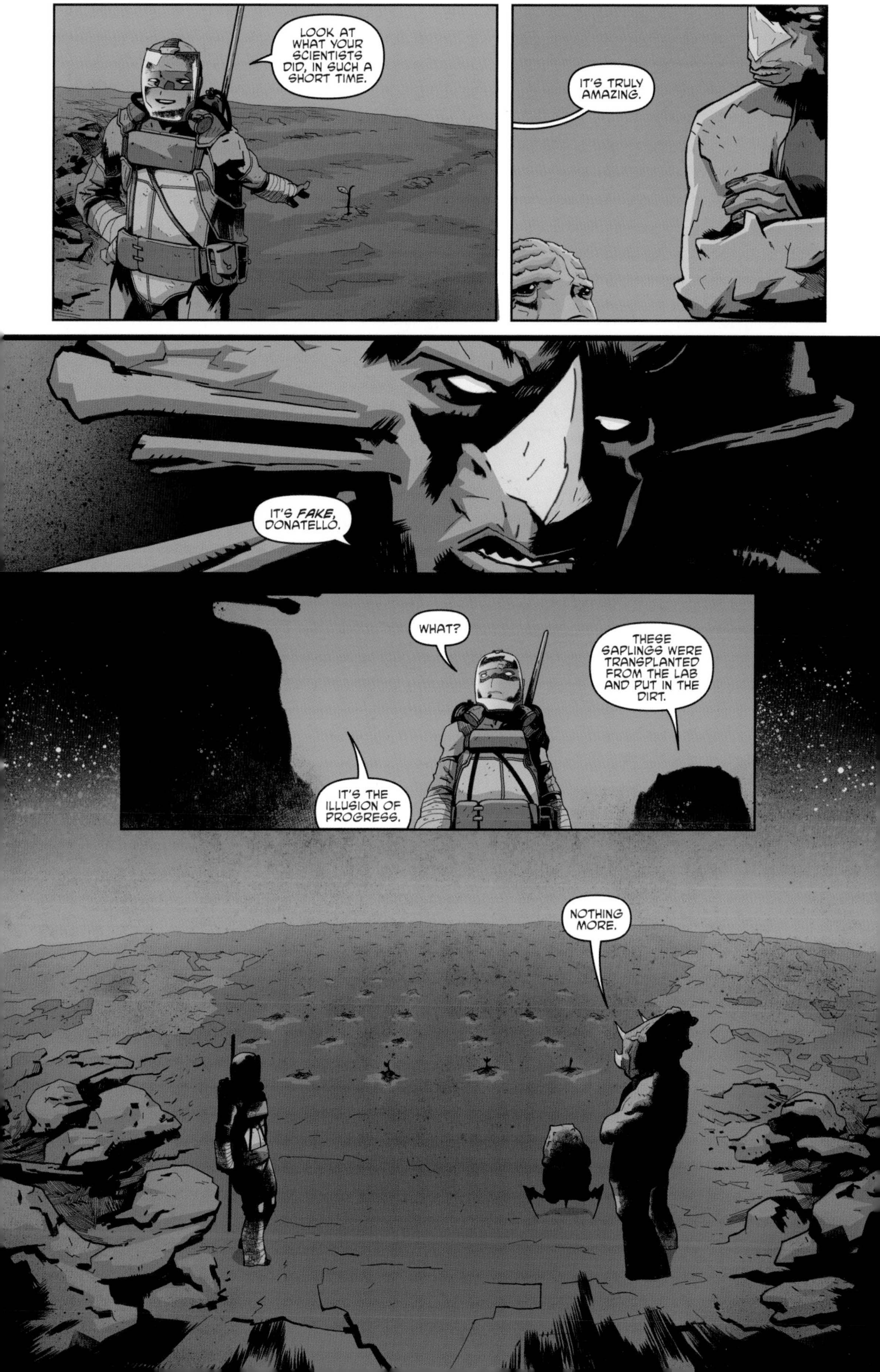
LOOK AT WHAT YOUR SCIENTISTS DID, IN SUCH A SHORT TIME.
IT'S TRULY AMAZING.
IT'S *FAKE,* DONATELLO.
WHAT?
THESE SAPLINGS WERE TRANSPLANTED FROM THE LAB AND PUT IN THE DIRT.
IT'S THE ILLUSION OF PROGRESS.
NOTHING MORE.

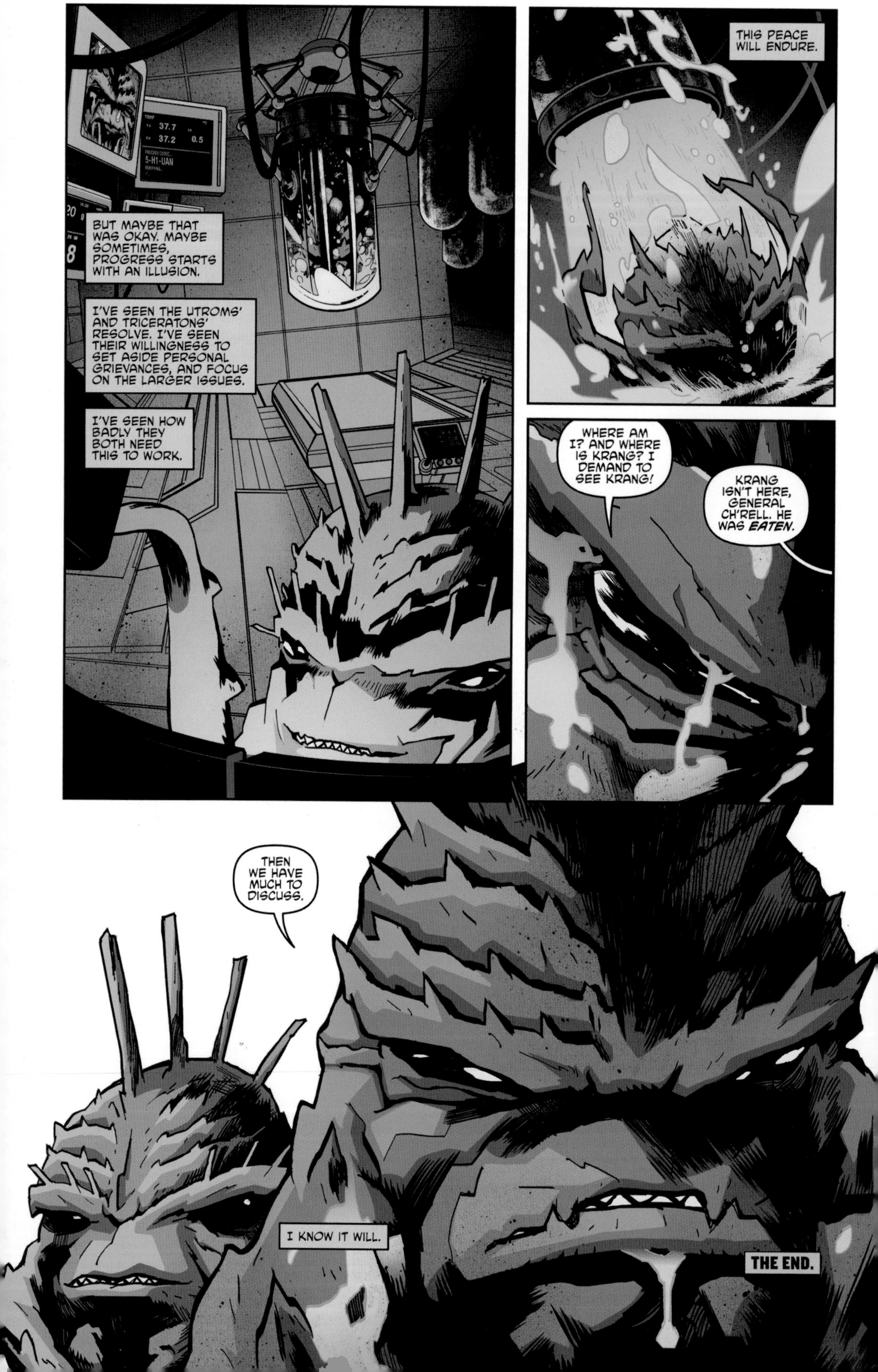
BUT MAYBE THAT WAS OKAY. MAYBE SOMETIMES, PROGRESS STARTS WITH AN ILLUSION.
I'VE SEEN THE UTROMS' AND TRICERATONS' RESOLVE. I'VE SEEN THEIR WILLINGNESS TO SET ASIDE PERSONAL GRIEVANCES, AND FOCUS ON THE LARGER ISSUES.
I'VE SEEN HOW BADLY THEY BOTH NEED THIS TO WORK.
THIS PEACE WILL ENDURE.
WHERE AM I? AND WHERE IS KRANG? I DEMAND TO SEE KRANG!
KRANG ISN'T HERE, GENERAL CH'RELL. HE WAS *EATEN*.
THEN WE HAVE MUCH TO DISCUSS.
I KNOW IT WILL.
THE END.

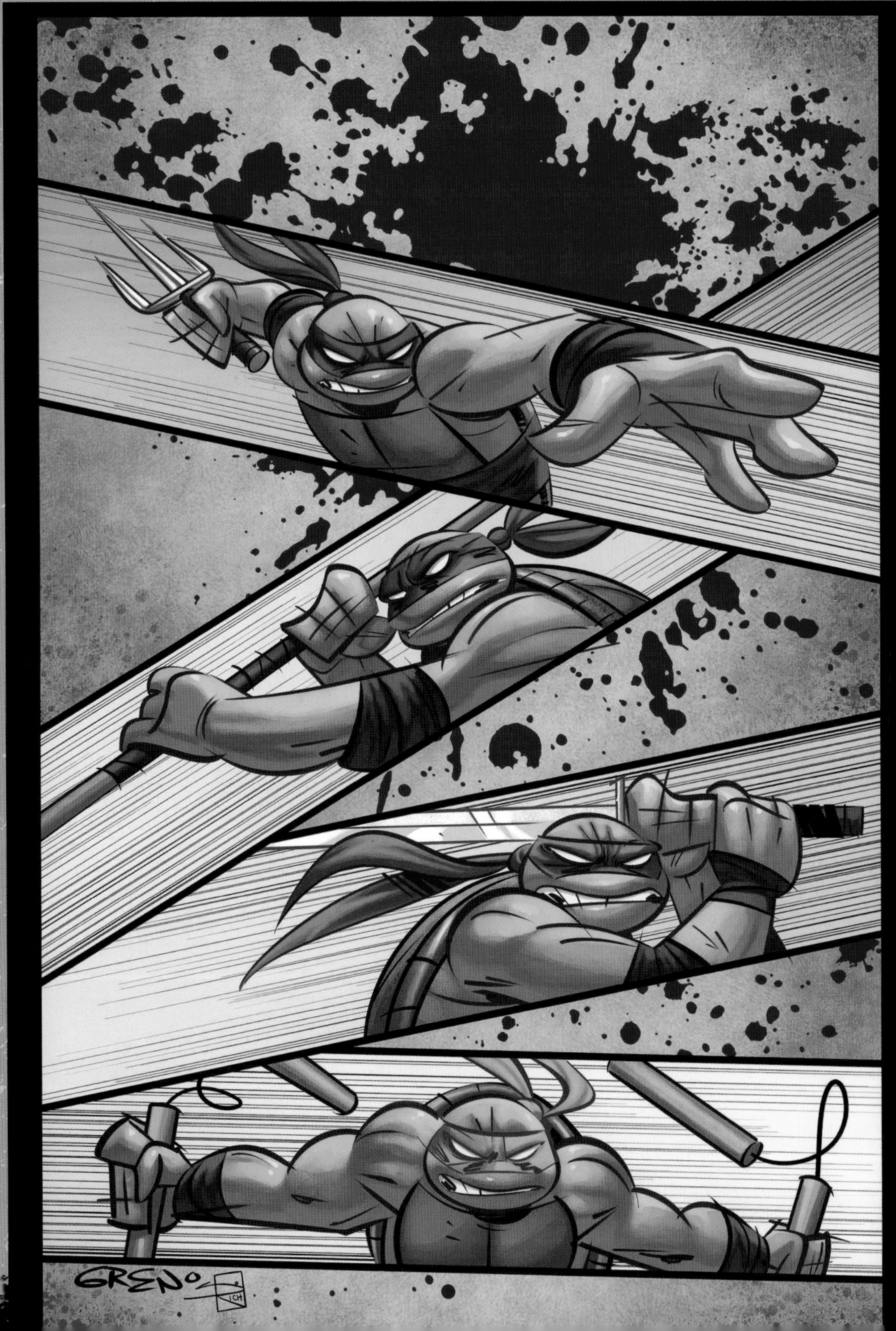
GRENO

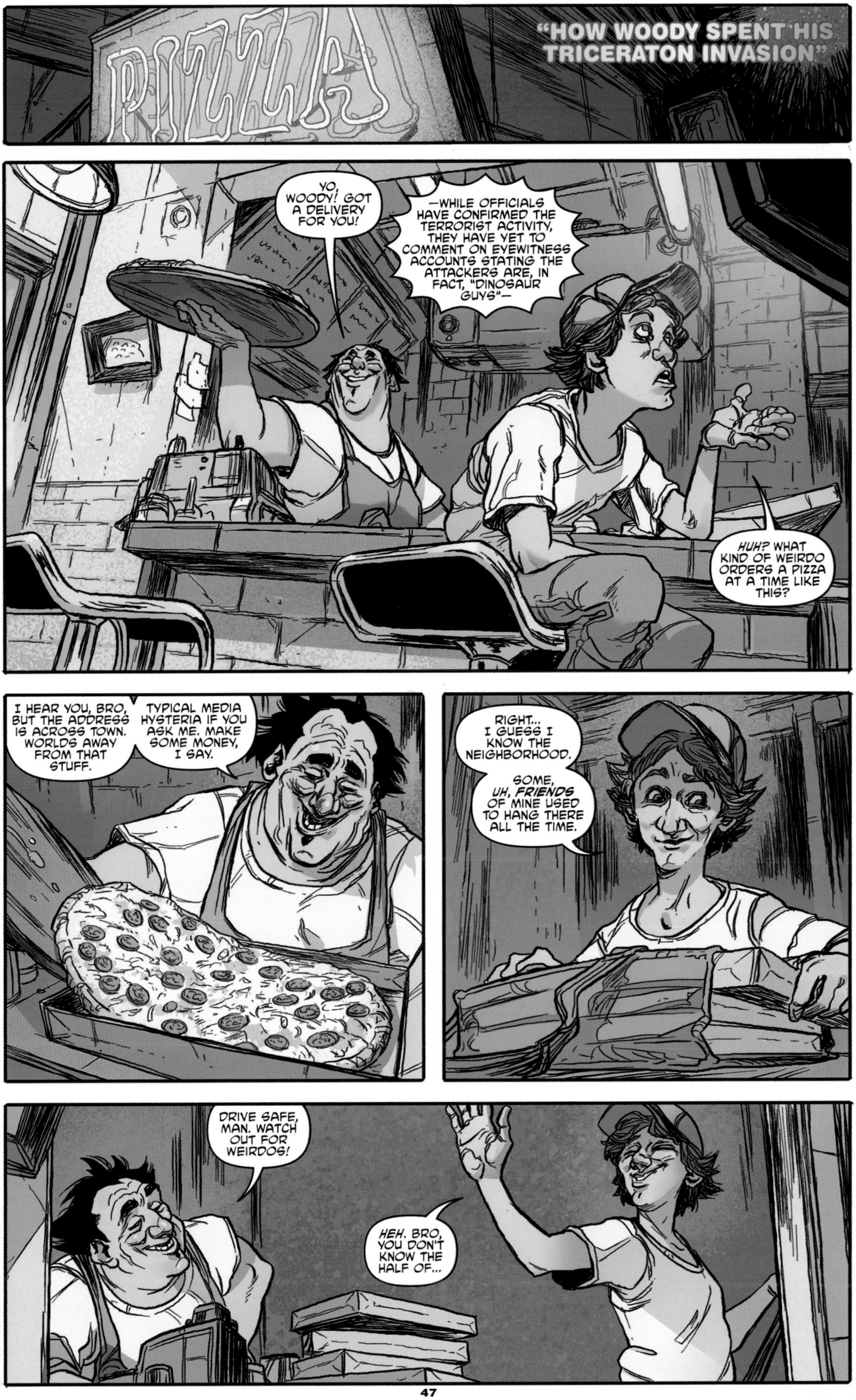
PIZZA
"HOW WOODY SPENT HIS TRICERATON INVASION"
YO, WOODY! GOT A DELIVERY FOR YOU!
—WHILE OFFICIALS HAVE CONFIRMED THE TERRORIST ACTIVITY, THEY HAVE YET TO COMMENT ON EYEWITNESS ACCOUNTS STATING THE ATTACKERS ARE, IN FACT, "DINOSAUR GUYS"—
HUH? WHAT KIND OF WEIRDO ORDERS A PIZZA AT A TIME LIKE THIS?
I HEAR YOU, BRO, BUT THE ADDRESS IS ACROSS TOWN. WORLDS AWAY FROM THAT STUFF.
TYPICAL MEDIA HYSTERIA IF YOU ASK ME. MAKE SOME MONEY, I SAY.
RIGHT... I GUESS I KNOW THE NEIGHBORHOOD.
SOME, UH, FRIENDS OF MINE USED TO HANG THERE ALL THE TIME.
DRIVE SAFE, MAN. WATCH OUT FOR WEIRDOS!
HEH. BRO, YOU DON'T KNOW THE HALF OF...

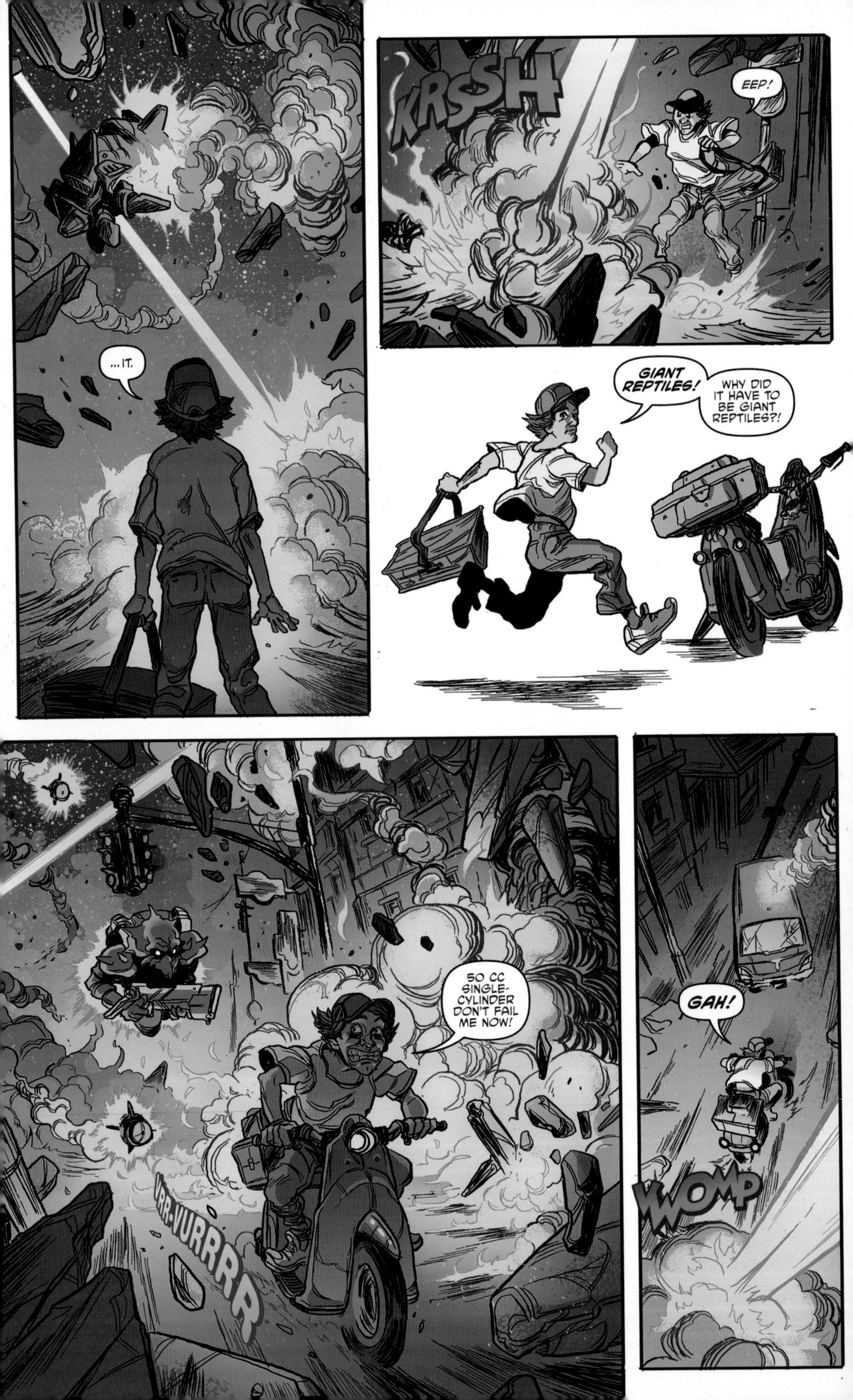
KRSSH
EEP!
...IT.
GIANT REPTILES!
WHY DID IT HAVE TO BE GIANT REPTILES?!
50 CC SINGLE-CYLINDER DON'T FAIL ME NOW!
VRR-VURRRRR
GAH!
WOMP

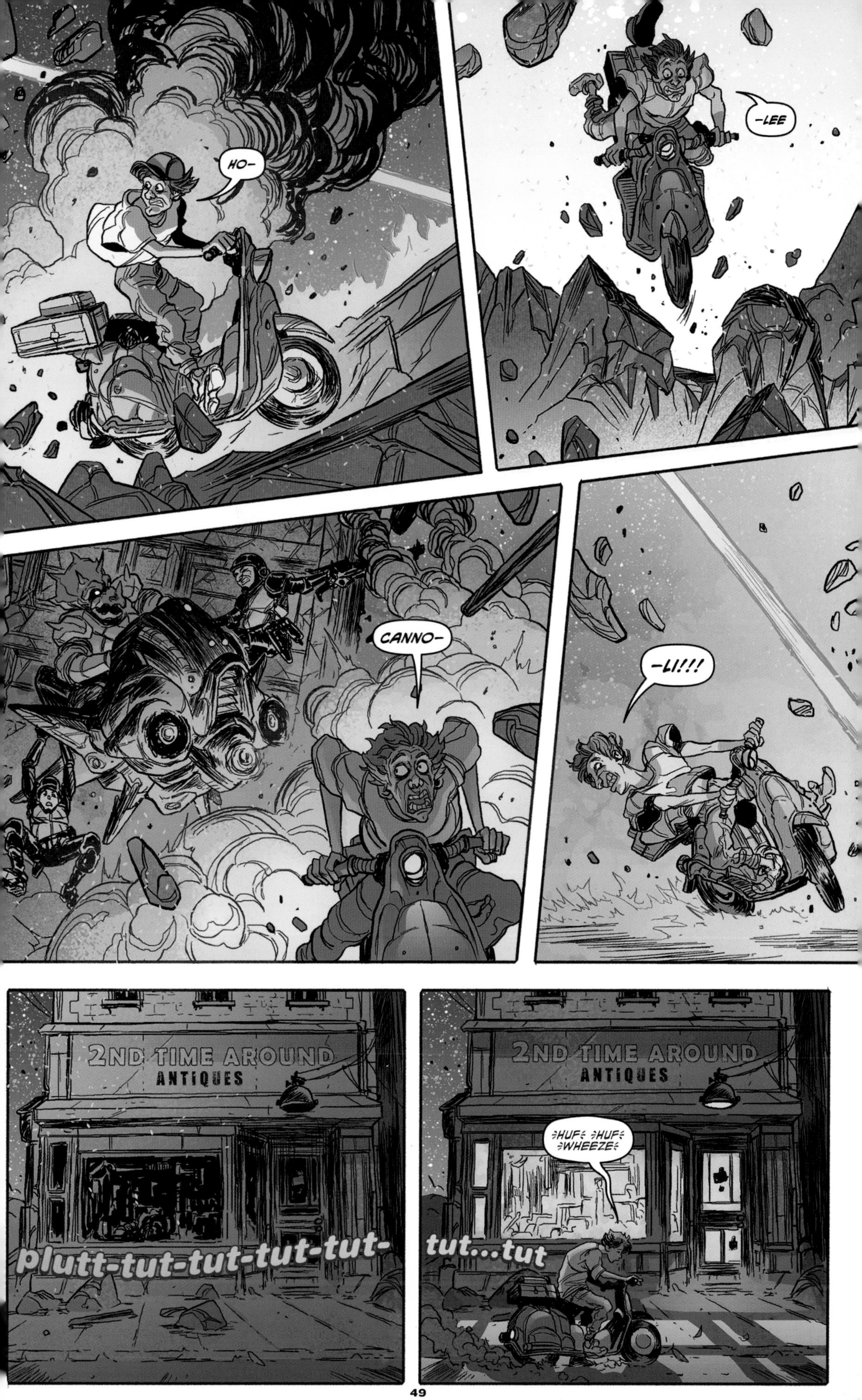
HO-
-LEE
CANNO-
-LI!!!
2ND TIME AROUND
ANTIQUES
plutt-tut-tut-tut-tut-
2ND TIME AROUND
ANTIQUES
HUF HUF
WHEEZE
tut...tut

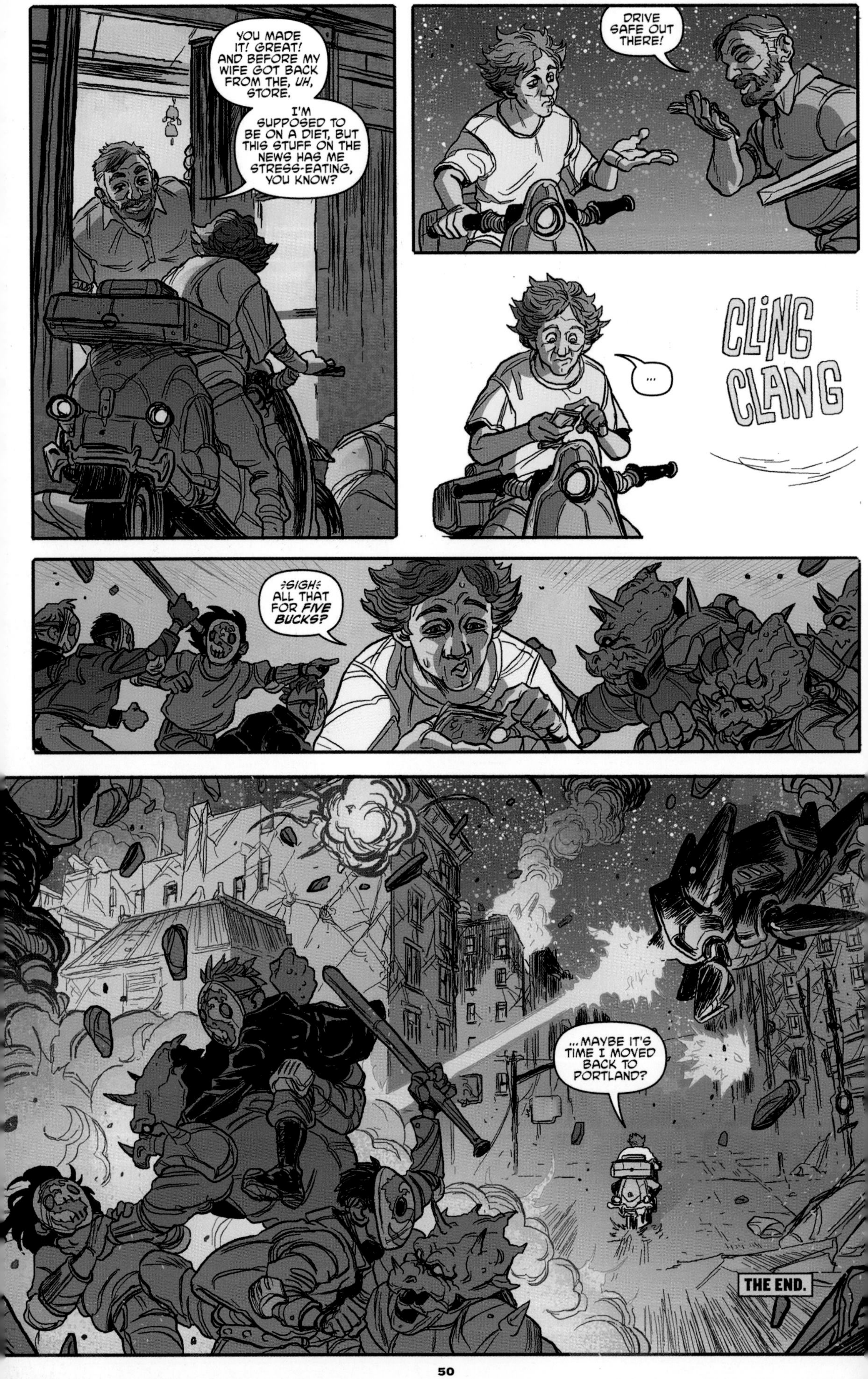

YOU MADE IT! GREAT! AND BEFORE MY WIFE GOT BACK FROM THE, *UH*, STORE.
I'M SUPPOSED TO BE ON A DIET, BUT THIS STUFF ON THE NEWS HAS ME STRESS-EATING, YOU KNOW?
DRIVE SAFE OUT THERE!
...
CLING
CLANG
SIGH ALL THAT FOR *FIVE BUCKS?*
...MAYBE IT'S TIME I MOVED BACK TO PORTLAND?
THE END.

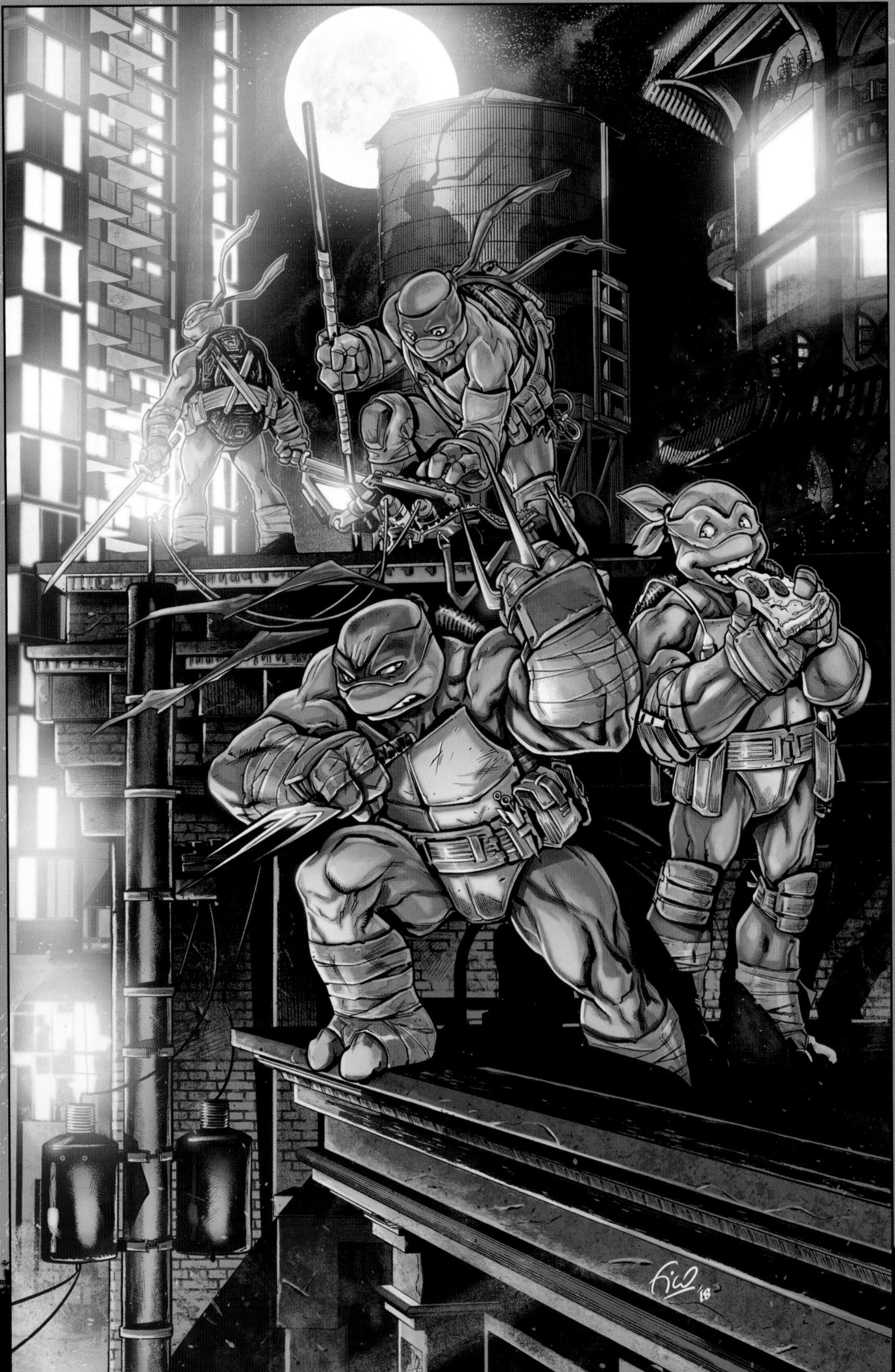

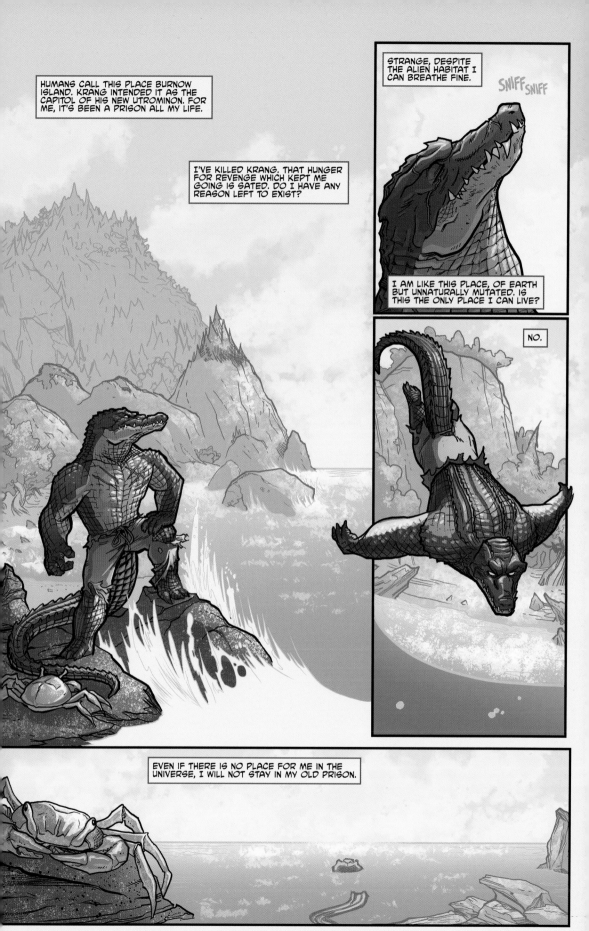

HUMANS CALL THIS PLACE BURNOW ISLAND. KRANG INTENDED IT AS THE CAPITOL OF HIS NEW UTROMINON. FOR ME, IT'S BEEN A PRISON ALL MY LIFE.

I'VE KILLED KRANG. THAT HUNGER FOR REVENGE WHICH KEPT ME GOING IS SATED. DO I HAVE ANY REASON LEFT TO EXIST?

STRANGE, DESPITE THE ALIEN HABITAT I CAN BREATHE FINE.

SNIFF SNIFF

I AM LIKE THIS PLACE, OF EARTH BUT UNNATURALLY MUTATED. IS THIS THE ONLY PLACE I CAN LIVE?

NO.

EVEN IF THERE IS NO PLACE FOR ME IN THE UNIVERSE, I WILL NOT STAY IN MY OLD PRISON.

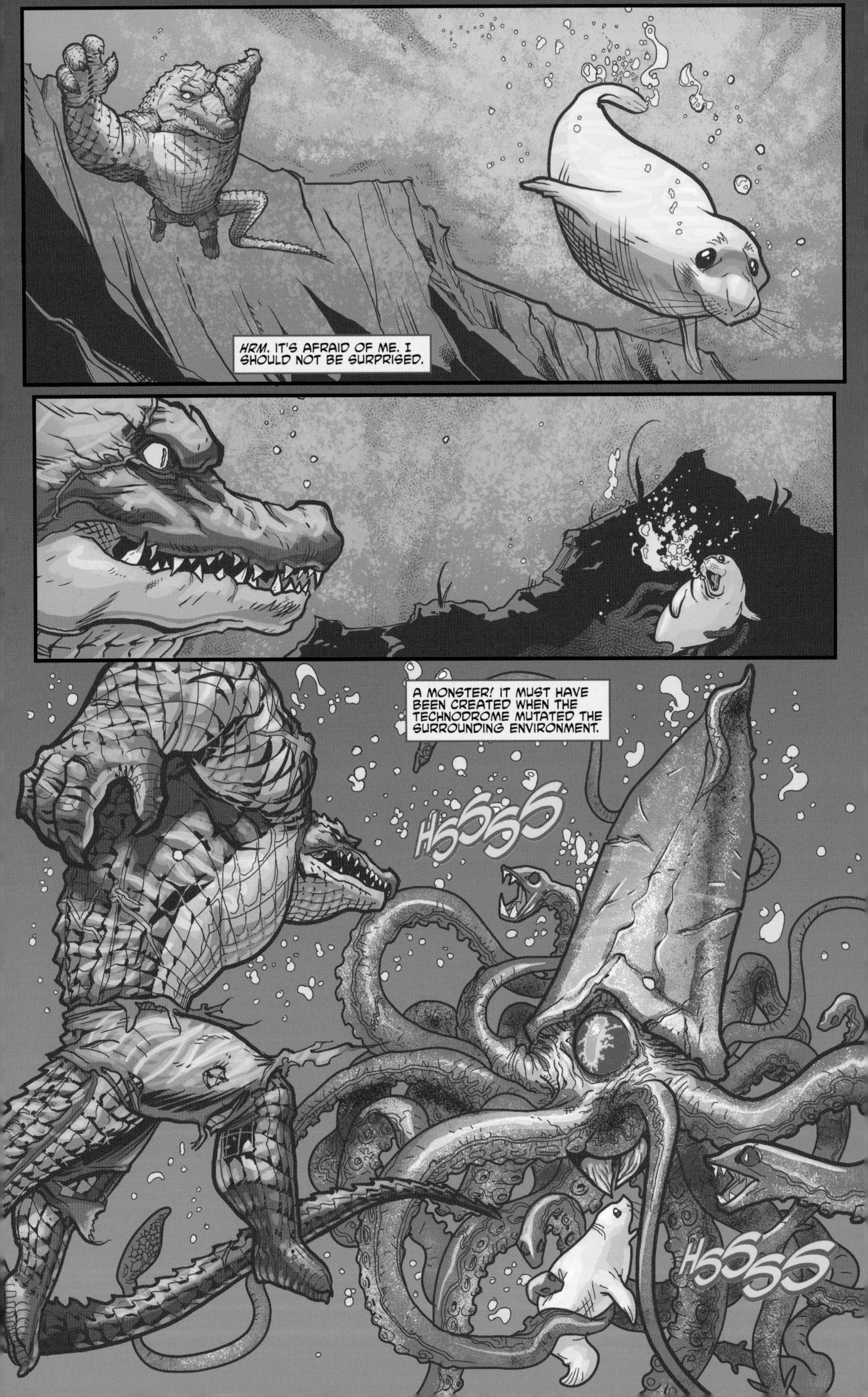
HRM. IT'S AFRAID OF ME. I SHOULD NOT BE SURPRISED.
A MONSTER! IT MUST HAVE BEEN CREATED WHEN THE TECHNODROME MUTATED THE SURROUNDING ENVIRONMENT.
HSSSS
HSSSS

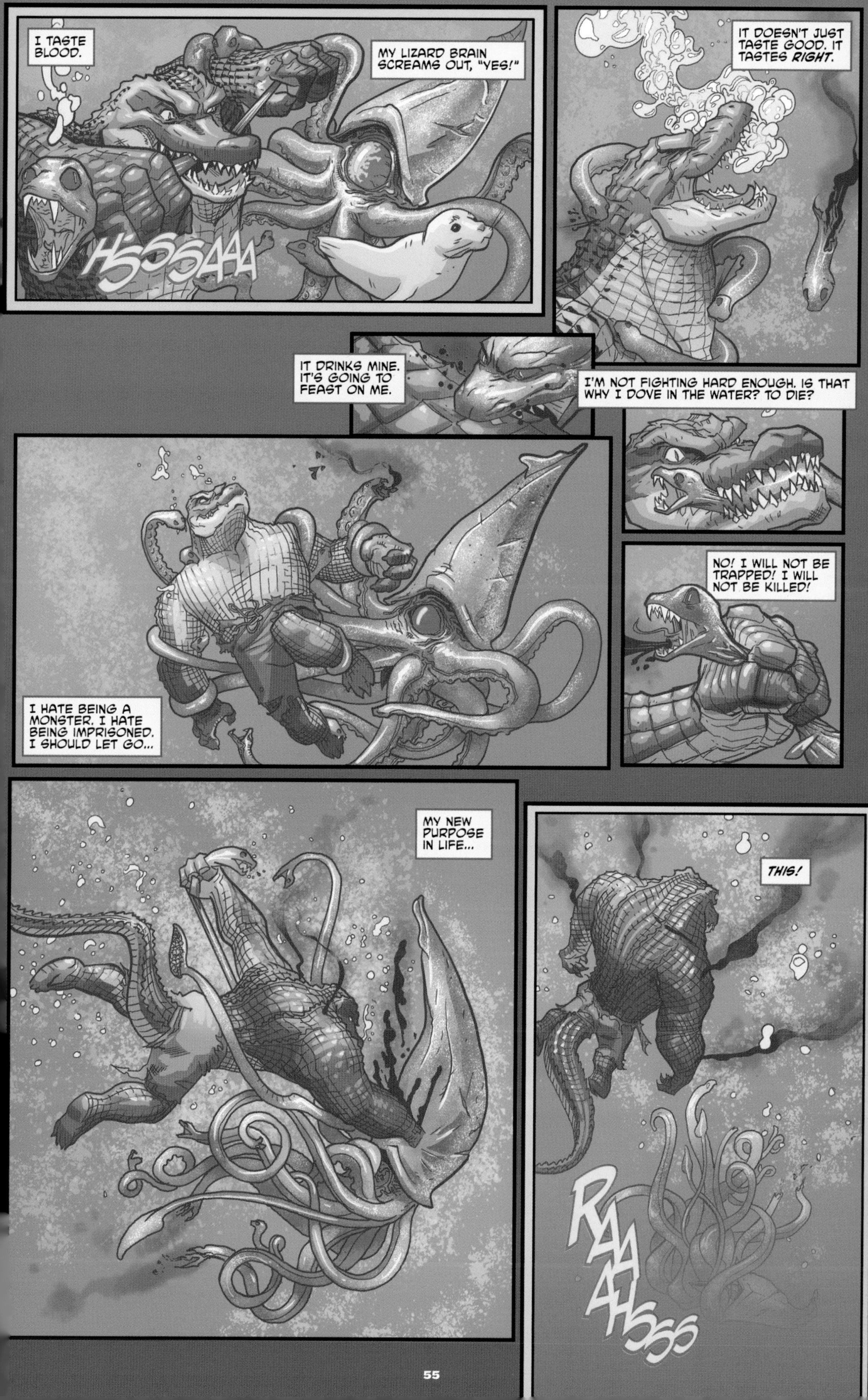
I TASTE BLOOD.
MY LIZARD BRAIN SCREAMS OUT, "YES!"
HSSSAAA
IT DOESN'T JUST TASTE GOOD. IT TASTES *RIGHT*.
IT DRINKS MINE. IT'S GOING TO FEAST ON ME.
I'M NOT FIGHTING HARD ENOUGH. IS THAT WHY I DOVE IN THE WATER? TO DIE?
I HATE BEING A MONSTER. I HATE BEING IMPRISONED. I SHOULD LET GO...
NO! I WILL NOT BE TRAPPED! I WILL NOT BE KILLED!
MY NEW PURPOSE IN LIFE...
THIS!
RAAAHSSS

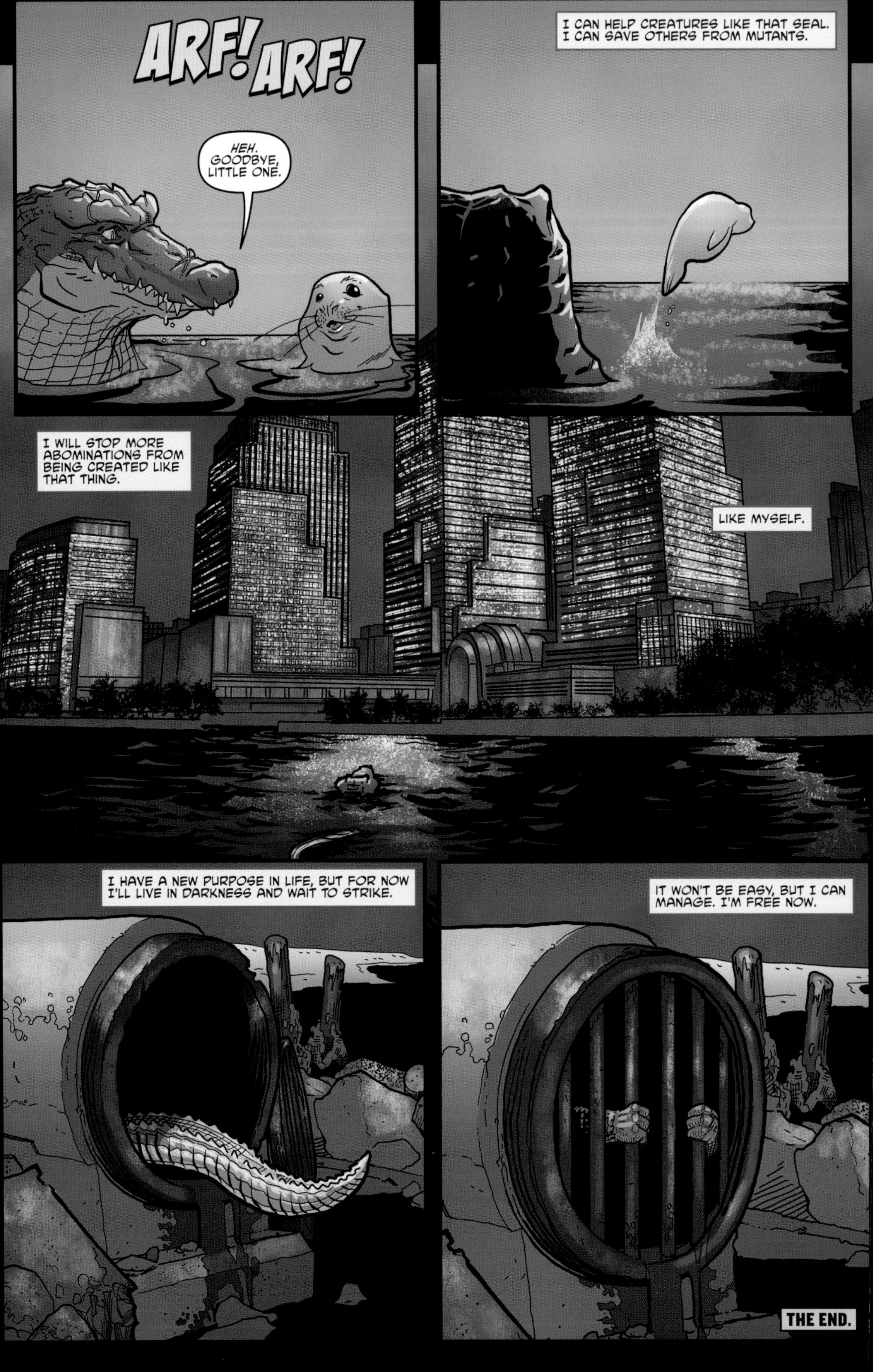
ARF! ARF!
HEH. GOODBYE, LITTLE ONE.
I CAN HELP CREATURES LIKE THAT SEAL. I CAN SAVE OTHERS FROM MUTANTS.
I WILL STOP MORE ABOMINATIONS FROM BEING CREATED LIKE THAT THING.
LIKE MYSELF.
I HAVE A NEW PURPOSE IN LIFE, BUT FOR NOW I'LL LIVE IN DARKNESS AND WAIT TO STRIKE.
IT WON'T BE EASY, BUT I CAN MANAGE. I'M FREE NOW.
THE END.

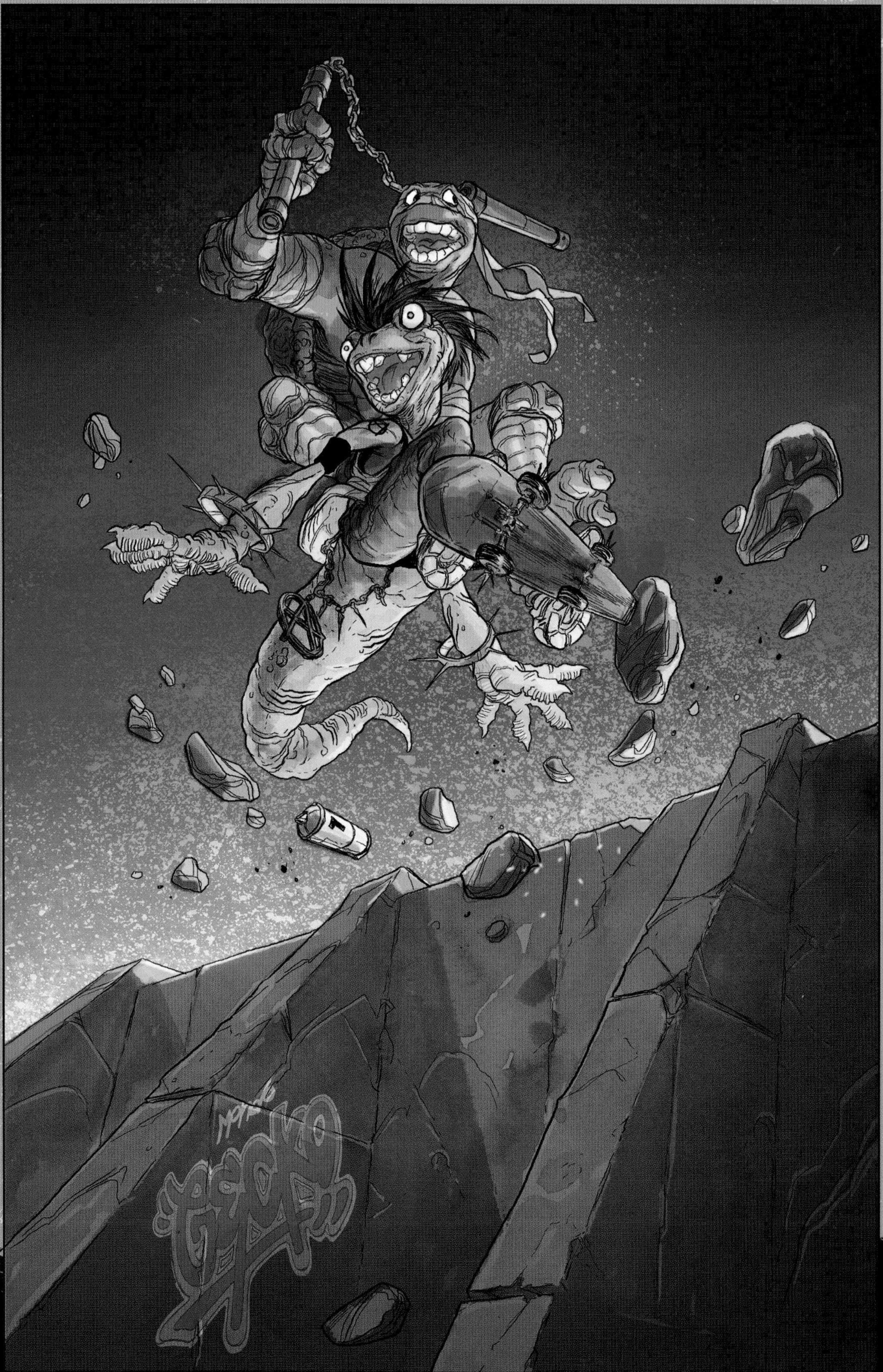

ART BY PABLO TUNICA

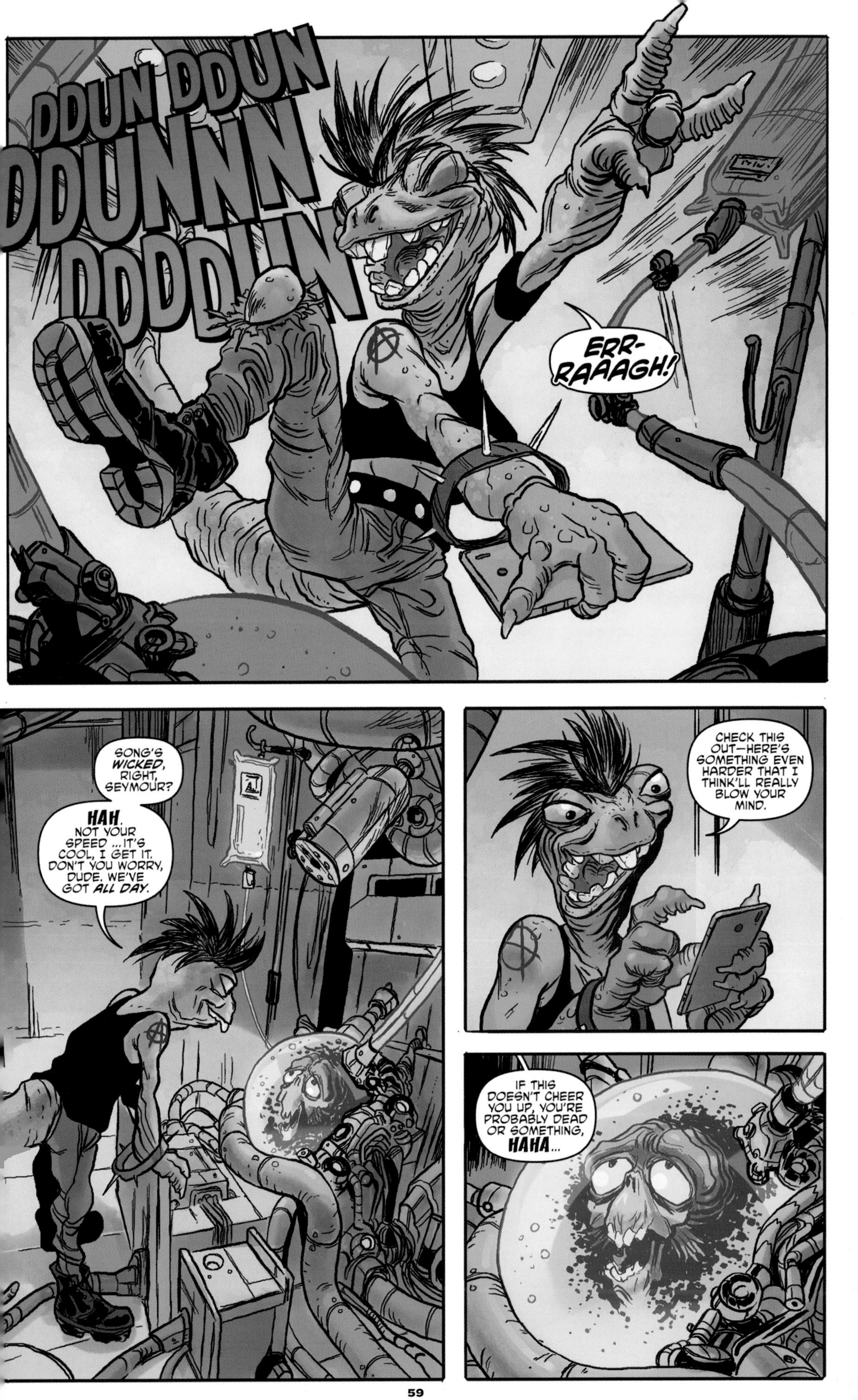
DDUN DDUN DDUNNN DDDDUN
ERR-RAAAGH!
SONG'S WICKED, RIGHT, SEYMOUR?
HAH. NOT YOUR SPEED ...IT'S COOL, I GET IT. DON'T YOU WORRY, DUDE. WE'VE GOT ALL DAY.
CHECK THIS OUT—HERE'S SOMETHING EVEN HARDER THAT I THINK'LL REALLY BLOW YOUR MIND.
IF THIS DOESN'T CHEER YOU UP, YOU'RE PROBABLY DEAD OR SOMETHING, HAHA...

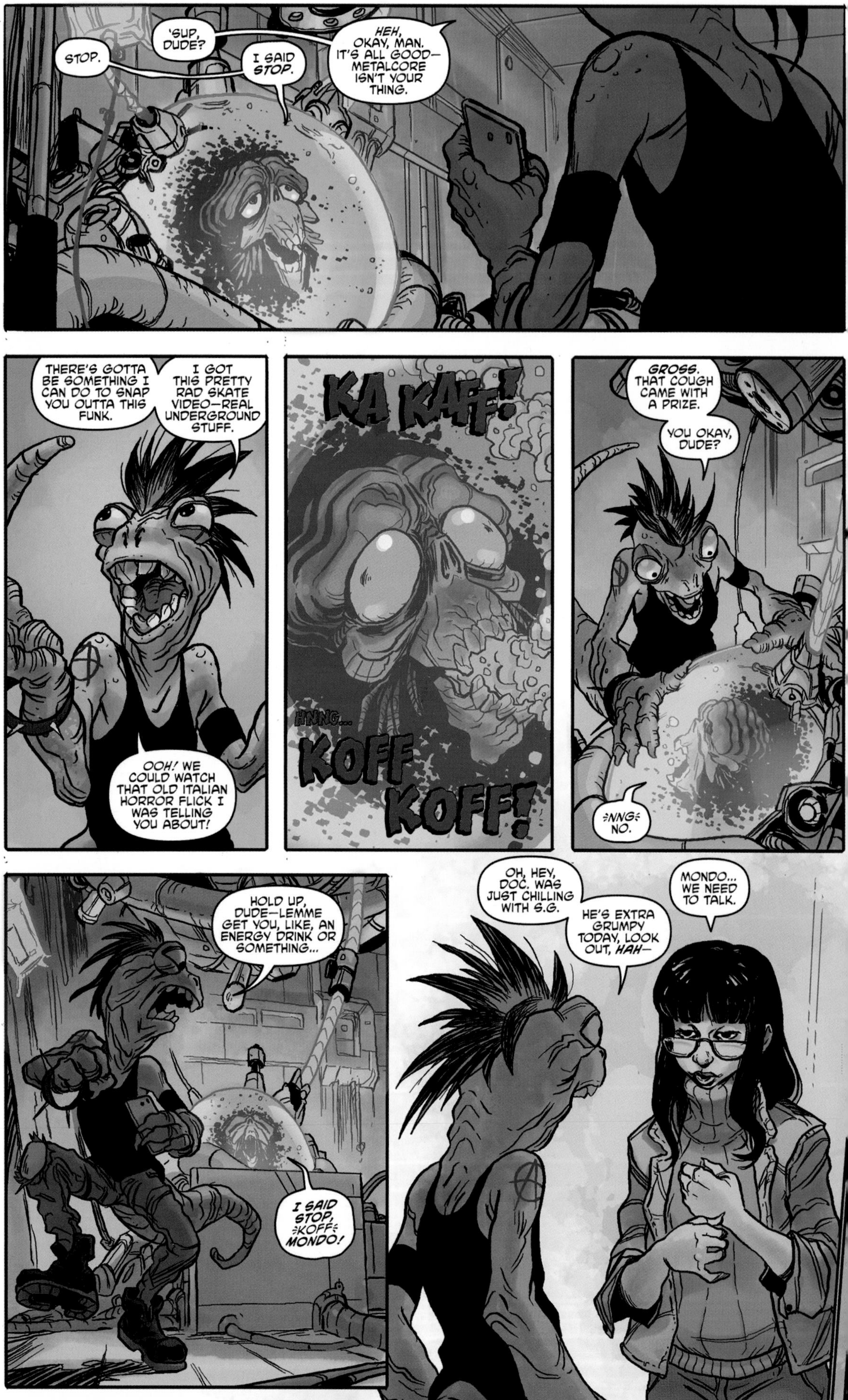
STOP.
'SUP, DUDE?
I SAID STOP.
HEH, OKAY, MAN. IT'S ALL GOOD— METALCORE ISN'T YOUR THING.
THERE'S GOTTA BE SOMETHING I CAN DO TO SNAP YOU OUTTA THIS FUNK.
I GOT THIS PRETTY RAD SKATE VIDEO—REAL UNDERGROUND STUFF.
OOH! WE COULD WATCH THAT OLD ITALIAN HORROR FLICK I WAS TELLING YOU ABOUT!
KA KAFF!
HNNG...
KOFF KOFF!
GROSS. THAT COUGH CAME WITH A PRIZE.
YOU OKAY, DUDE?
NNG NO.
HOLD UP, DUDE—LEMME GET YOU, LIKE, AN ENERGY DRINK OR SOMETHING...
I SAID STOP, KOFF MONDO!
OH, HEY, DOC. WAS JUST CHILLING WITH S.G.
HE'S EXTRA GRUMPY TODAY, LOOK OUT, HAH—
MONDO... WE NEED TO TALK.

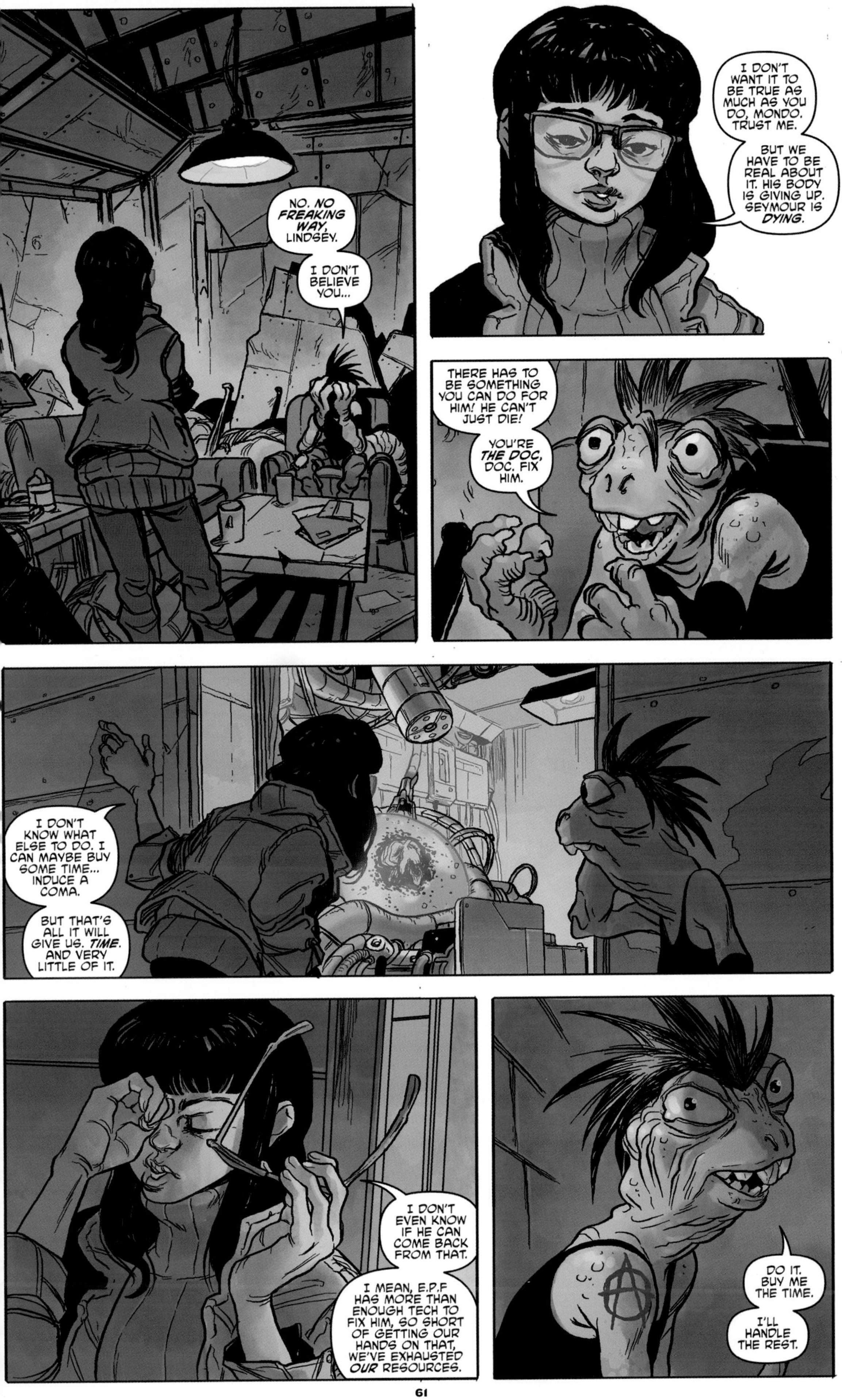
NO. NO FREAKING WAY, LINDSEY.
I DON'T BELIEVE YOU...
I DON'T WANT IT TO BE TRUE AS MUCH AS YOU DO, MONDO. TRUST ME.
BUT WE HAVE TO BE REAL ABOUT IT. HIS BODY IS GIVING UP. SEYMOUR IS DYING.
THERE HAS TO BE SOMETHING YOU CAN DO FOR HIM! HE CAN'T JUST DIE!
YOU'RE THE DOC, DOC. FIX HIM.
I DON'T KNOW WHAT ELSE TO DO. I CAN MAYBE BUY SOME TIME... INDUCE A COMA.
BUT THAT'S ALL IT WILL GIVE US. TIME. AND VERY LITTLE OF IT.
I DON'T EVEN KNOW IF HE CAN COME BACK FROM THAT.
I MEAN, E.P.F HAS MORE THAN ENOUGH TECH TO FIX HIM, SO SHORT OF GETTING OUR HANDS ON THAT, WE'VE EXHAUSTED OUR RESOURCES.
DO IT. BUY ME THE TIME.
I'LL HANDLE THE REST.

SEYMOUR IS—FOR A LACK OF BETTER WORDS—*MESSED UP.*

NOT AT ALL HUMAN, BUT NOT FAR FROM IT EITHER.

I'M GIVING HIM SOME PROPOFOL.

ONCE HE'S OUT I'LL HAVE TO MONITOR HIS VITALS AND FIGURE IT OUT AS I GO.

A TIGHT ROPE BETWEEN TOO MUCH AND TOO LITTLE... LEANING ON THE LATTER.

WHATEVER YOU GOTTA DO, DOC.

HE DOESN'T DESERVE THIS. NO ONE DOES.

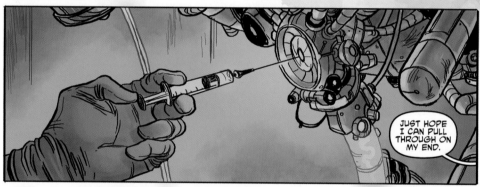

JUST HOPE I CAN PULL THROUGH ON MY END.

THERE. SHOULDN'T TAKE LONG TO KICK IN. HE'LL JUST GO TO SLEEP UNTIL WE WAKE HIM UP. HOPEFULLY.

DON'T SWEAT IT, PAL. JUST CATCH SOME ZZZ'S FOR NOW, AIGHT?

OL' MONDO'S GONNA GET YOU SOME NEW—

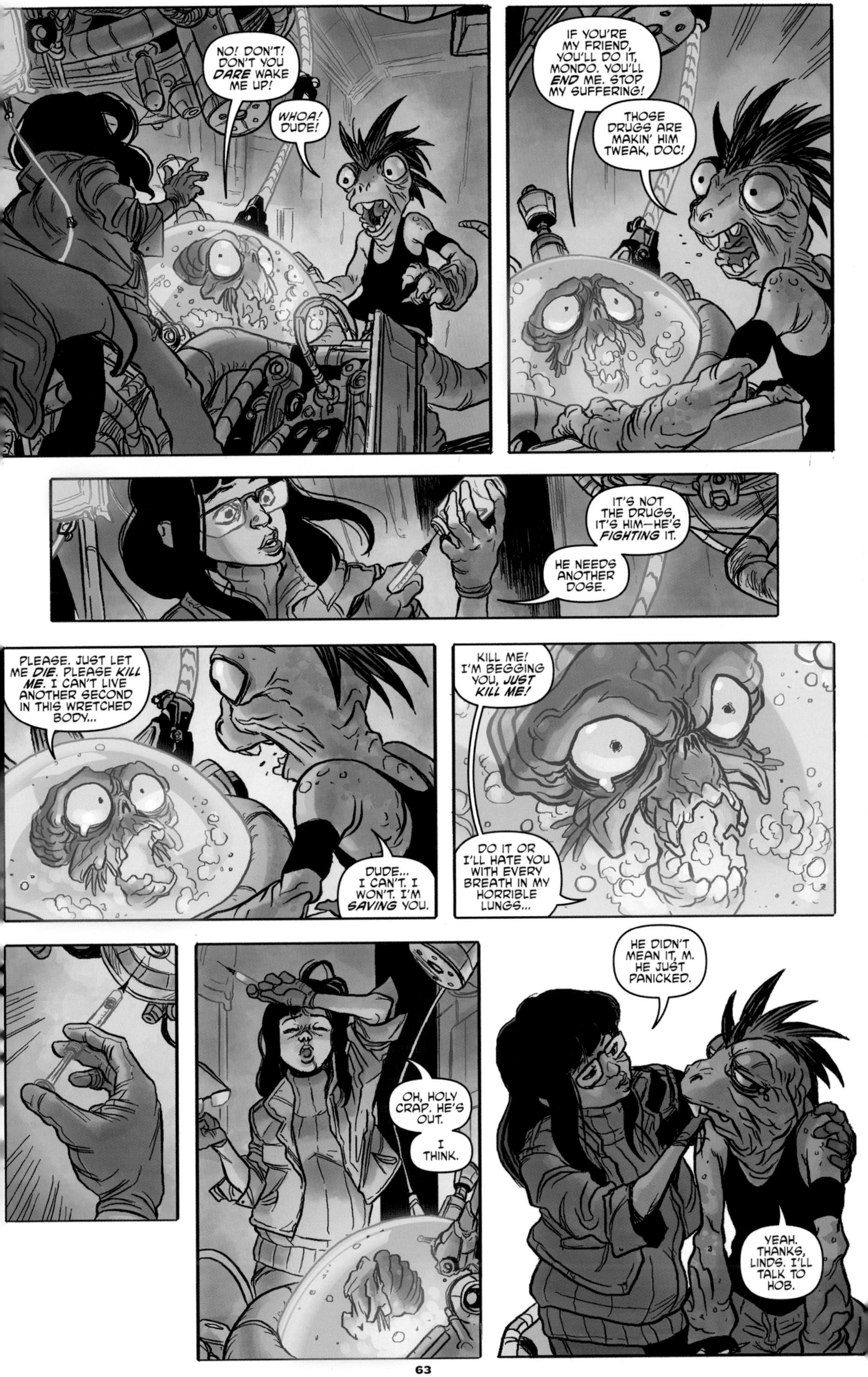
NO! DON'T! DON'T YOU DARE WAKE ME UP!
WHOA! DUDE!
IF YOU'RE MY FRIEND, YOU'LL DO IT, MONDO. YOU'LL END ME. STOP MY SUFFERING!
THOSE DRUGS ARE MAKIN' HIM TWEAK, DOC!
IT'S NOT THE DRUGS, IT'S HIM—HE'S FIGHTING IT.
HE NEEDS ANOTHER DOSE.
PLEASE. JUST LET ME DIE. PLEASE KILL ME. I CAN'T LIVE ANOTHER SECOND IN THIS WRETCHED BODY...
DUDE... I CAN'T. I WON'T. I'M SAVING YOU.
KILL ME! I'M BEGGING YOU, JUST KILL ME!
DO IT OR I'LL HATE YOU WITH EVERY BREATH IN MY HORRIBLE LUNGS...
OH, HOLY CRAP. HE'S OUT.
I THINK.
HE DIDN'T MEAN IT, M. HE JUST PANICKED.
YEAH. THANKS, LINDS. I'LL TALK TO HOB.

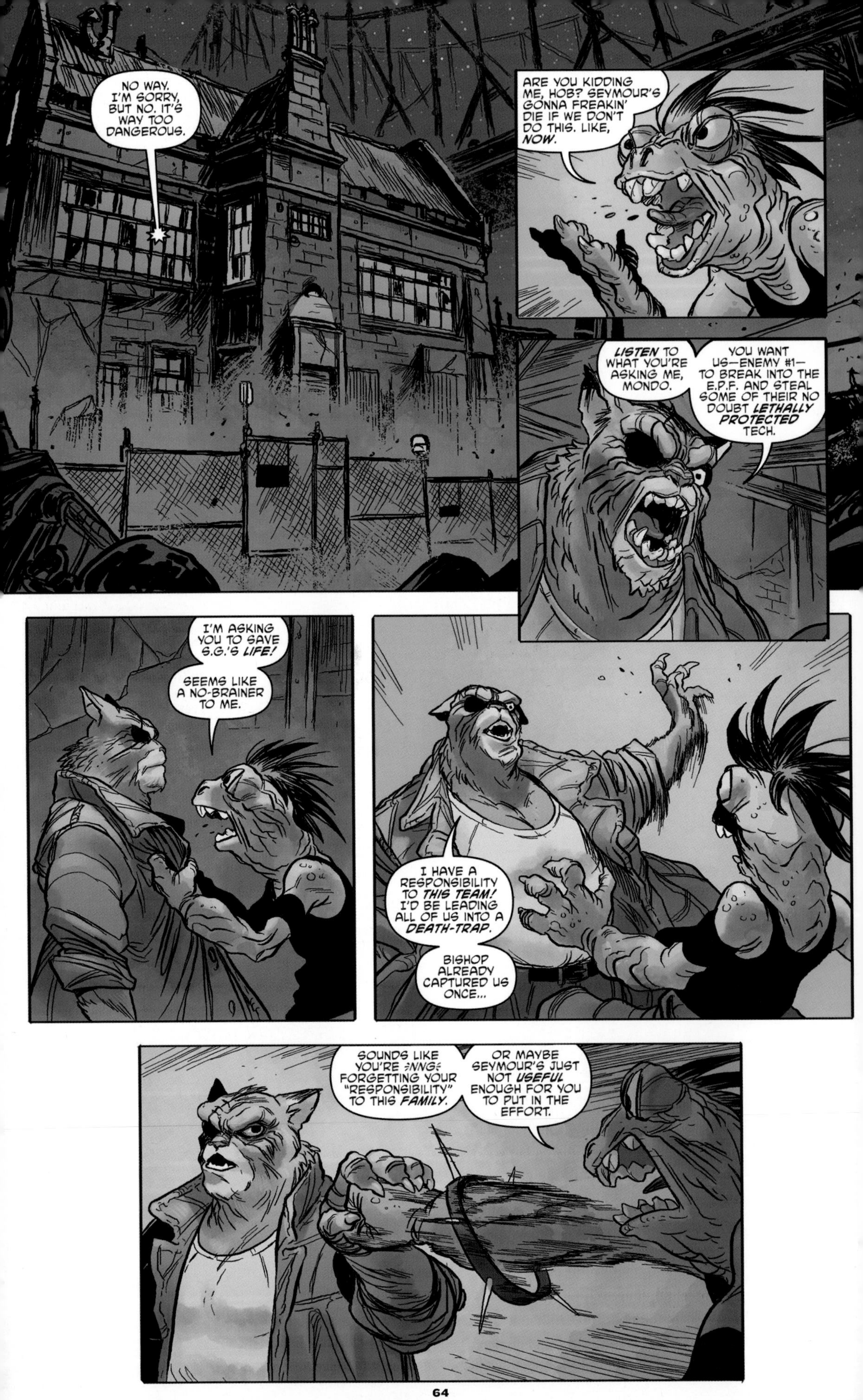
NO WAY. I'M SORRY, BUT NO. IT'S WAY TOO DANGEROUS.
ARE YOU KIDDING ME, HOB? SEYMOUR'S GONNA FREAKIN' DIE IF WE DON'T DO THIS. LIKE, *NOW*.
LISTEN TO WHAT YOU'RE ASKING ME, MONDO.
YOU WANT US—ENEMY #1—TO BREAK INTO THE E.P.F. AND STEAL SOME OF THEIR NO DOUBT *LETHALLY PROTECTED* TECH.
I'M ASKING YOU TO SAVE S.G.'S *LIFE!*
SEEMS LIKE A NO-BRAINER TO ME.
I HAVE A RESPONSIBILITY TO *THIS TEAM!* I'D BE LEADING ALL OF US INTO A *DEATH-TRAP*.
BISHOP ALREADY CAPTURED US ONCE...
SOUNDS LIKE YOU'RE ~NNG~ FORGETTING YOUR "RESPONSIBILITY" TO THIS *FAMILY*.
OR MAYBE SEYMOUR'S JUST NOT *USEFUL* ENOUGH FOR YOU TO PUT IN THE EFFORT.

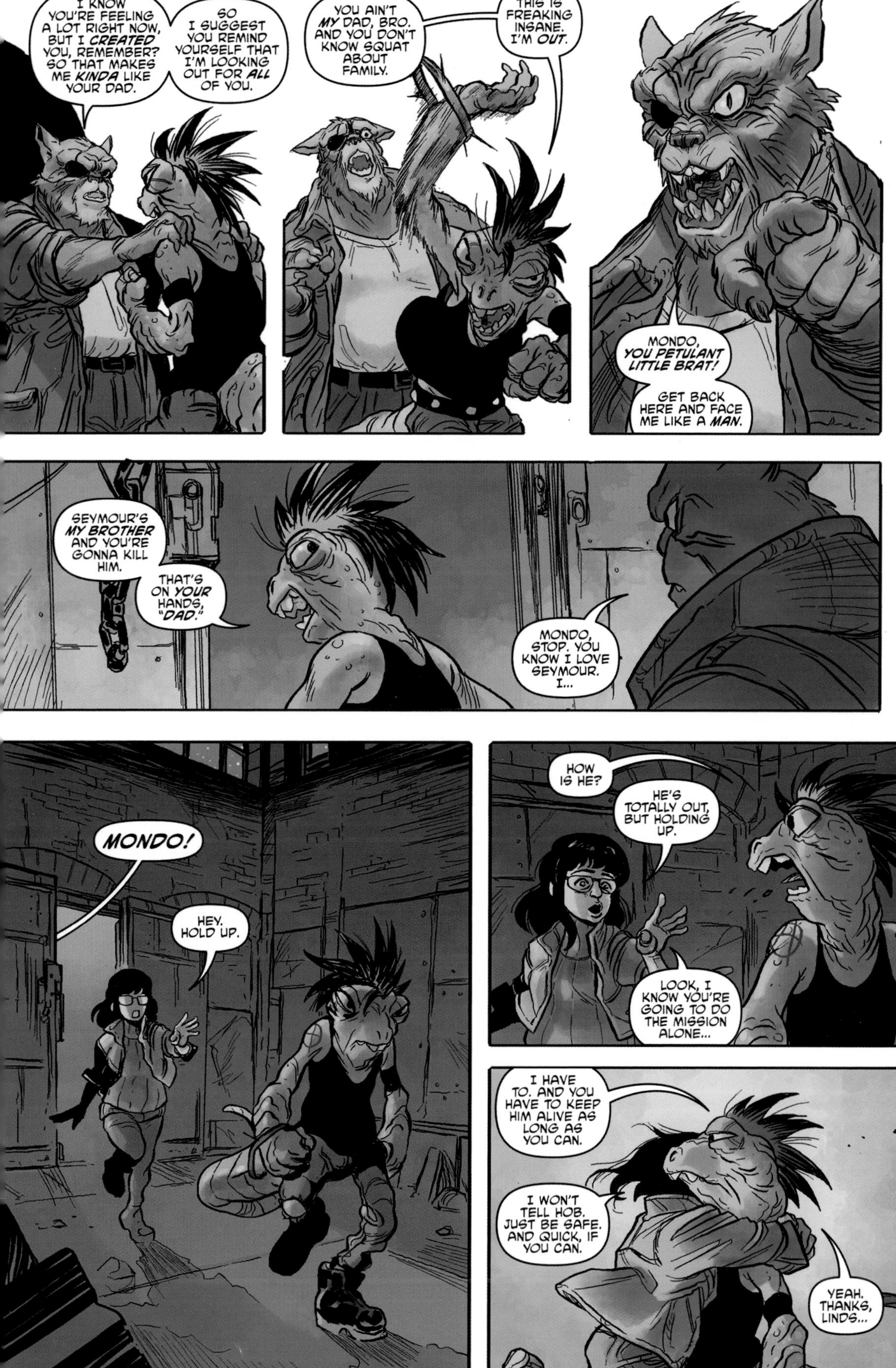

I KNOW YOU'RE FEELING A LOT RIGHT NOW, BUT I *CREATED* YOU, REMEMBER? SO THAT MAKES ME *KINDA* LIKE YOUR DAD.
SO I SUGGEST YOU REMIND YOURSELF THAT I'M LOOKING OUT FOR *ALL* OF YOU.
YOU AIN'T *MY* DAD, BRO. AND YOU DON'T KNOW SQUAT ABOUT FAMILY.
THIS IS FREAKING INSANE. I'M *OUT*.
MONDO, ***YOU PETULANT LITTLE BRAT!***
GET BACK HERE AND FACE ME LIKE A ***MAN***.
SEYMOUR'S ***MY BROTHER*** AND YOU'RE GONNA KILL HIM.
THAT'S ON ***YOUR*** HANDS, *"DAD."*
MONDO, STOP. YOU KNOW I LOVE SEYMOUR. I...
MONDO!
HEY. HOLD UP.
HOW IS HE?
HE'S TOTALLY OUT, BUT HOLDING UP.
LOOK, I KNOW YOU'RE GOING TO DO THE MISSION ALONE...
I HAVE TO. AND YOU HAVE TO KEEP HIM ALIVE AS LONG AS YOU CAN.
I WON'T TELL HOB. JUST BE SAFE. AND QUICK, IF YOU CAN.
YEAH. THANKS, LINDS...

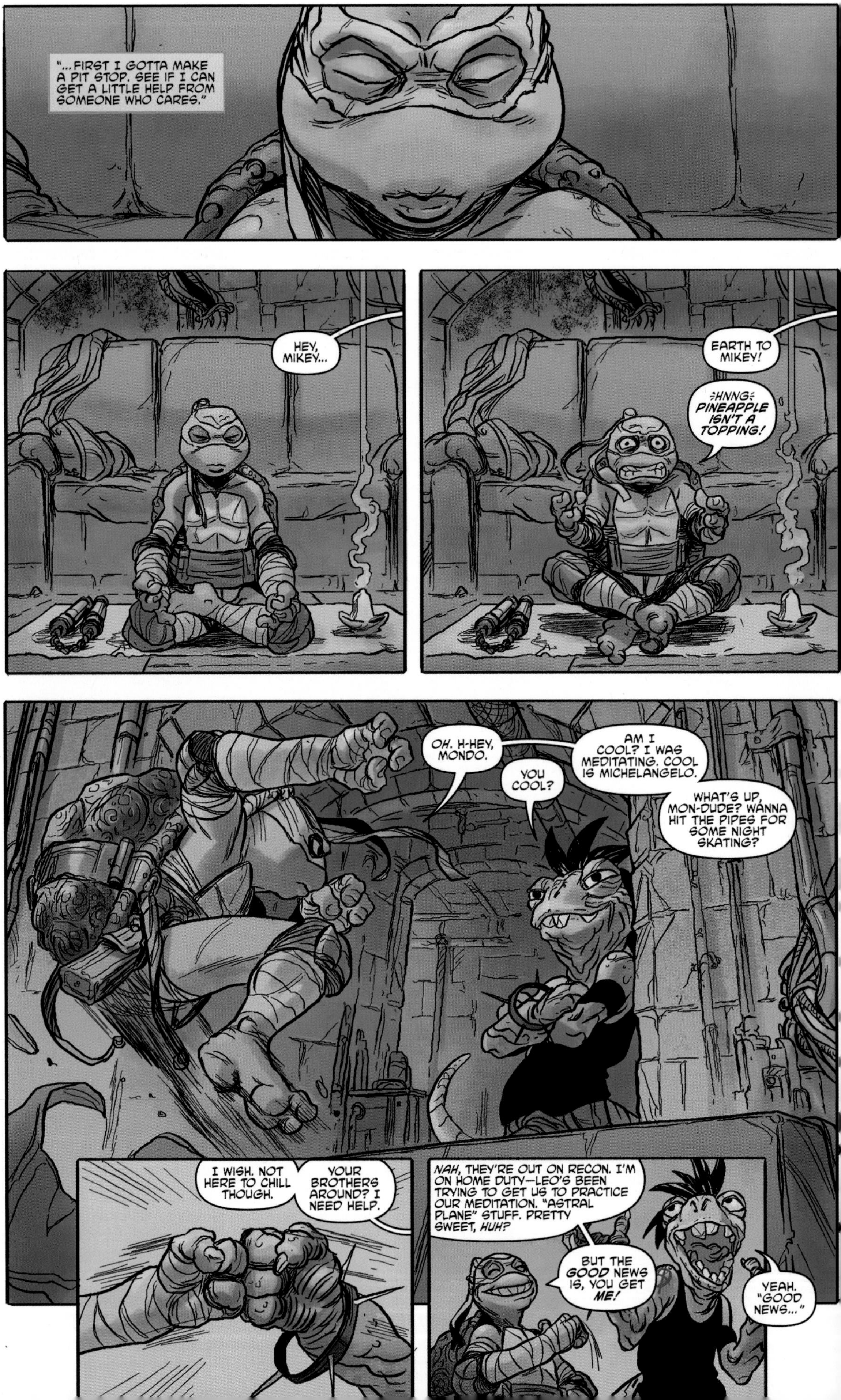
"...FIRST I GOTTA MAKE A PIT STOP. SEE IF I CAN GET A LITTLE HELP FROM SOMEONE WHO CARES."
HEY, MIKEY...
EARTH TO MIKEY!
HNNG PINEAPPLE ISN'T A TOPPING!
OH. H-HEY, MONDO.
YOU COOL?
AM I COOL? I WAS MEDITATING. COOL IS MICHELANGELO.
WHAT'S UP, MON-DUDE? WANNA HIT THE PIPES FOR SOME NIGHT SKATING?
I WISH. NOT HERE TO CHILL THOUGH.
YOUR BROTHERS AROUND? I NEED HELP.
NAH, THEY'RE OUT ON RECON. I'M ON HOME DUTY—LEO'S BEEN TRYING TO GET US TO PRACTICE OUR MEDITATION. "ASTRAL PLANE" STUFF. PRETTY SWEET, HUH?
BUT THE GOOD NEWS IS, YOU GET ME!
YEAH. "GOOD NEWS..."

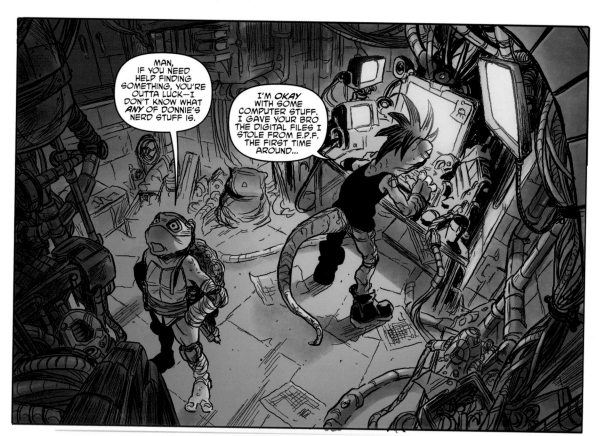

MAN, IF YOU NEED HELP FINDING SOMETHING, YOU'RE OUTTA LUCK—I DON'T KNOW WHAT *ANY* OF DONNIE'S NERD STUFF IS.

I'M *OKAY* WITH SOME COMPUTER STUFF. I GAVE YOUR BRO THE DIGITAL FILES I STOLE FROM E.P.F. THE FIRST TIME AROUND...

BINGO. GOT 'EM.

THAT'S GOING TO GET YOU INTO THE BASE? IT'S JUST WORDS AND NUMBERS.

OOH— IS IT, LIKE, A SECRET PASSWORD?

IF ONLY IT WERE THAT EASY. THE FILES ARE STAFF CONTACT INFO FOR E.P.F. AGENTS...

...AND *PERSONAL ADDRESSES.*

OH! I KNOW WHAT YOU'RE THINKING. PIZZA DELIVERY BOMB! E.P.F. WON'T KNOW WHO HIT 'EM.

NAH, I'M GOING TO BREAK INTO ONE OF THESE PUNK'S *HOUSES* AND TEAR IT APART UNTIL I FIND OUT HOW TO GET INTO THEIR BASE.

OH. THAT'S... ACTUALLY *REALLY* DARK, DUDE.

MONDO, WAIT! THIS ISN'T LIKE YOU. I'M WORRIED. I'M COMING WITH.

DON'T GOTTA DO THAT, BRO. THIS COULD GET GNARLY.

EXACTLY! WHO *ELSE* WOULD YOU RATHER HAVE WITH YOU?

I'M VERY WELL KNOWN FOR MY HIGH GNAR-POTENCY.

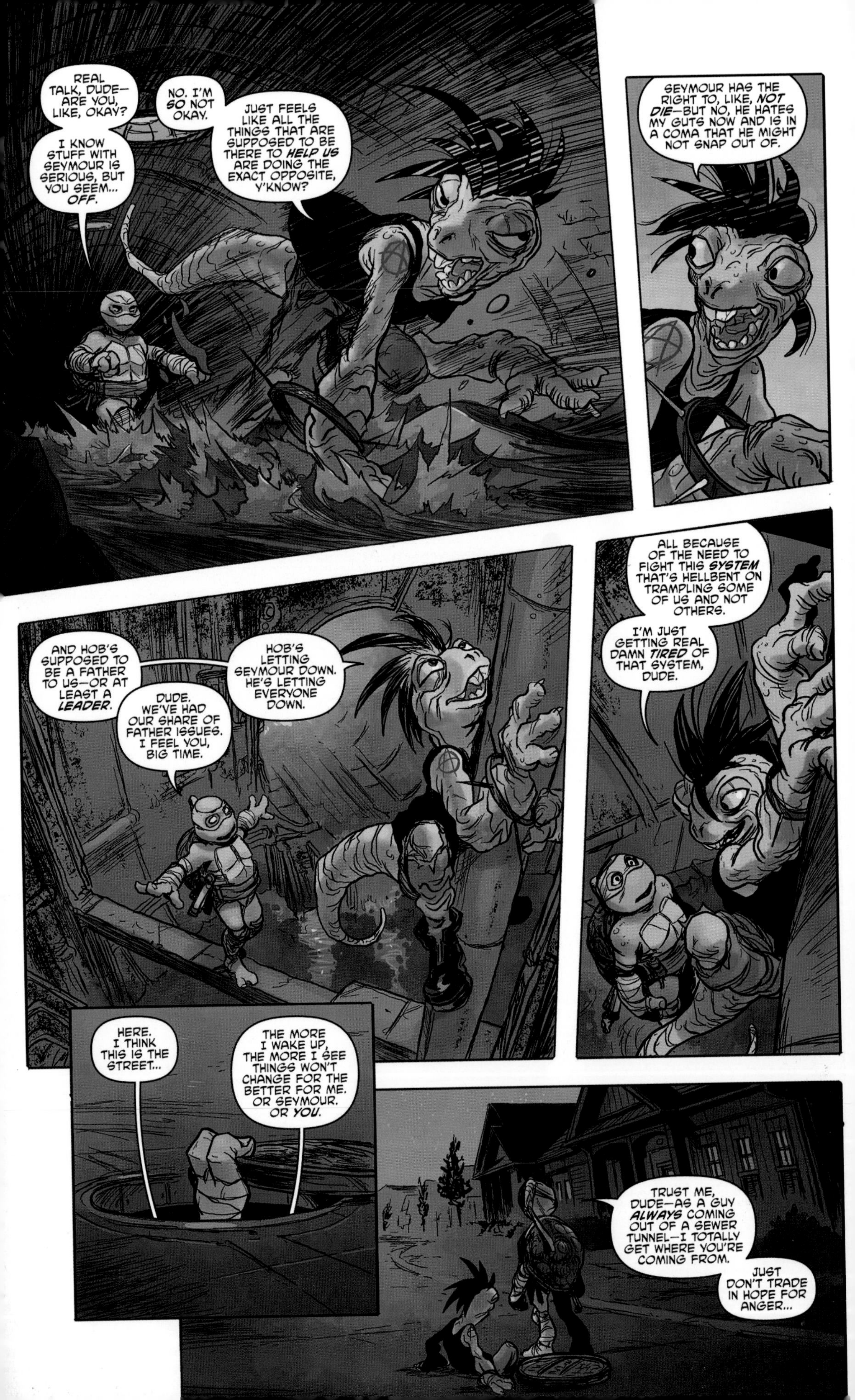

REAL TALK, DUDE—ARE YOU, LIKE, OKAY?
I KNOW STUFF WITH SEYMOUR IS SERIOUS, BUT YOU SEEM... *OFF*.
NO. I'M *SO* NOT OKAY.
JUST FEELS LIKE ALL THE THINGS THAT ARE SUPPOSED TO BE THERE TO *HELP US* ARE DOING THE EXACT OPPOSITE, Y'KNOW?
SEYMOUR HAS THE RIGHT TO, LIKE, *NOT DIE*—BUT NO, HE HATES MY GUTS NOW AND IS IN A COMA THAT HE MIGHT NOT SNAP OUT OF.
AND HOB'S SUPPOSED TO BE A FATHER TO US—OR AT LEAST A *LEADER*.
HOB'S LETTING SEYMOUR DOWN. HE'S LETTING EVERYONE DOWN.
DUDE. WE'VE HAD OUR SHARE OF FATHER ISSUES. I FEEL YOU, BIG TIME.
ALL BECAUSE OF THE NEED TO FIGHT THIS *SYSTEM* THAT'S HELLBENT ON TRAMPLING SOME OF US AND NOT OTHERS.
I'M JUST GETTING REAL DAMN *TIRED* OF THAT SYSTEM, DUDE.
HERE. I THINK THIS IS THE STREET...
THE MORE I WAKE UP, THE MORE I SEE THINGS WON'T CHANGE FOR THE BETTER FOR ME. OR SEYMOUR. *OR YOU*.
TRUST ME, DUDE—AS A GUY *ALWAYS* COMING OUT OF A SEWER TUNNEL—I TOTALLY GET WHERE YOU'RE COMING FROM.
JUST DON'T TRADE IN HOPE FOR ANGER...

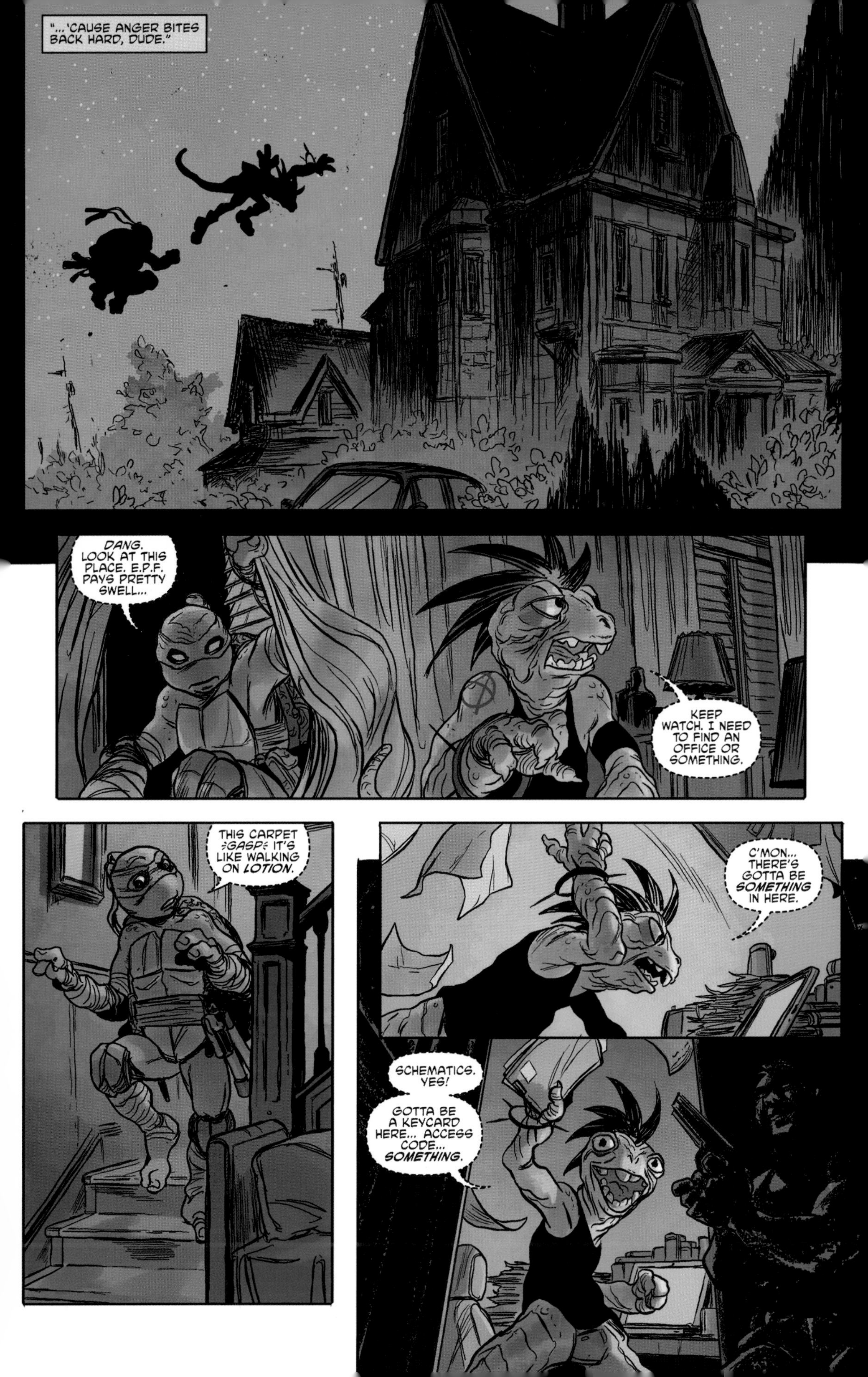

"...'CAUSE ANGER BITES BACK HARD, DUDE."
DANG. LOOK AT THIS PLACE. E.P.F. PAYS PRETTY SWELL...
KEEP WATCH. I NEED TO FIND AN OFFICE OR SOMETHING.
THIS CARPET *GASP* IT'S LIKE WALKING ON *LOTION*.
C'MON... THERE'S GOTTA BE *SOMETHING* IN HERE.
SCHEMATICS. YES!
GOTTA BE A KEYCARD HERE... ACCESS CODE... *SOMETHING*.

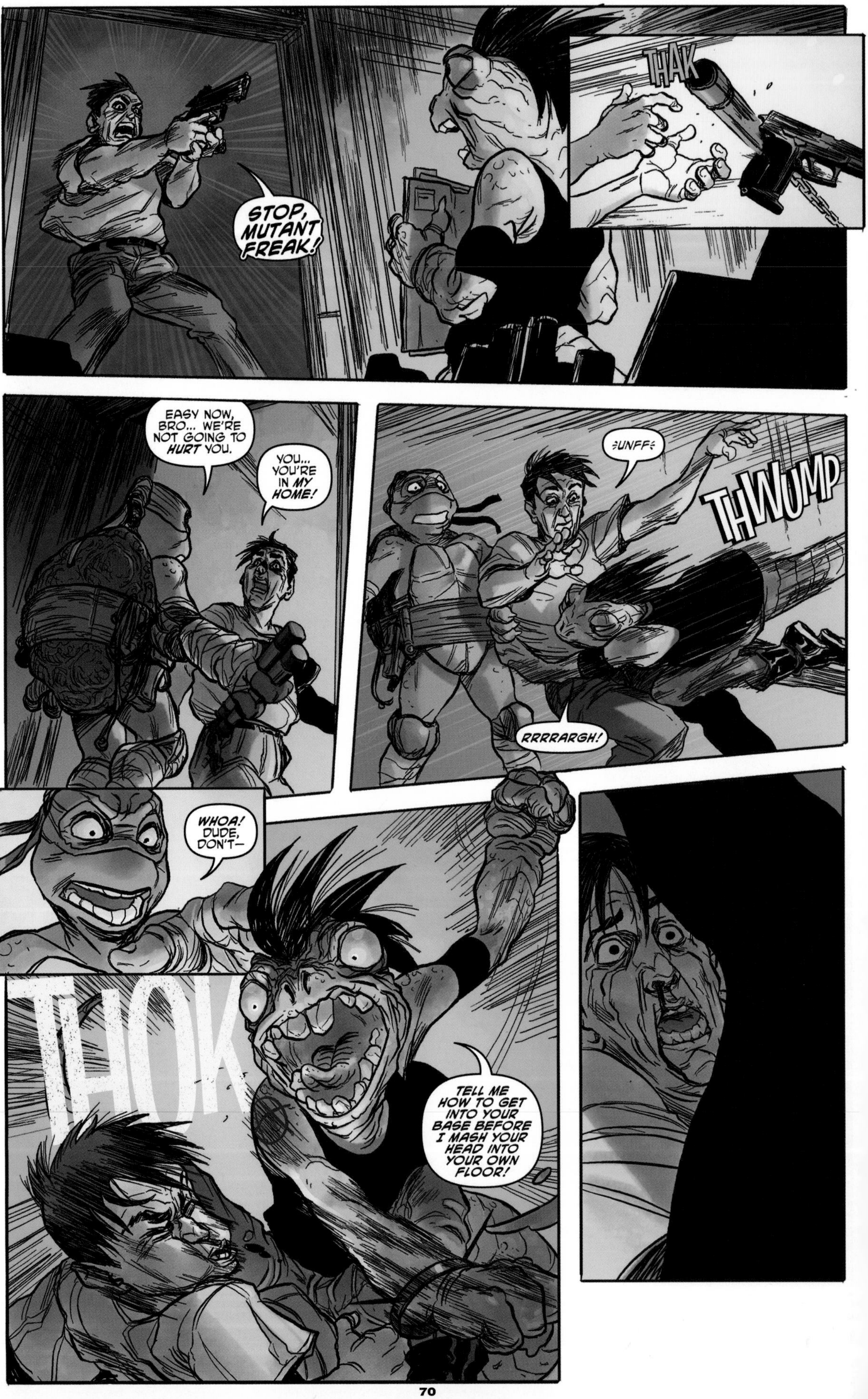
STOP, MUTANT FREAK!
THAK
EASY NOW, BRO... WE'RE NOT GOING TO HURT YOU.
YOU... YOU'RE IN MY HOME!
UNFF
THWUMP
RRRRARGH!
WHOA! DUDE, DON'T—
THOK
TELL ME HOW TO GET INTO YOUR BASE BEFORE I MASH YOUR HEAD INTO YOUR OWN FLOOR!

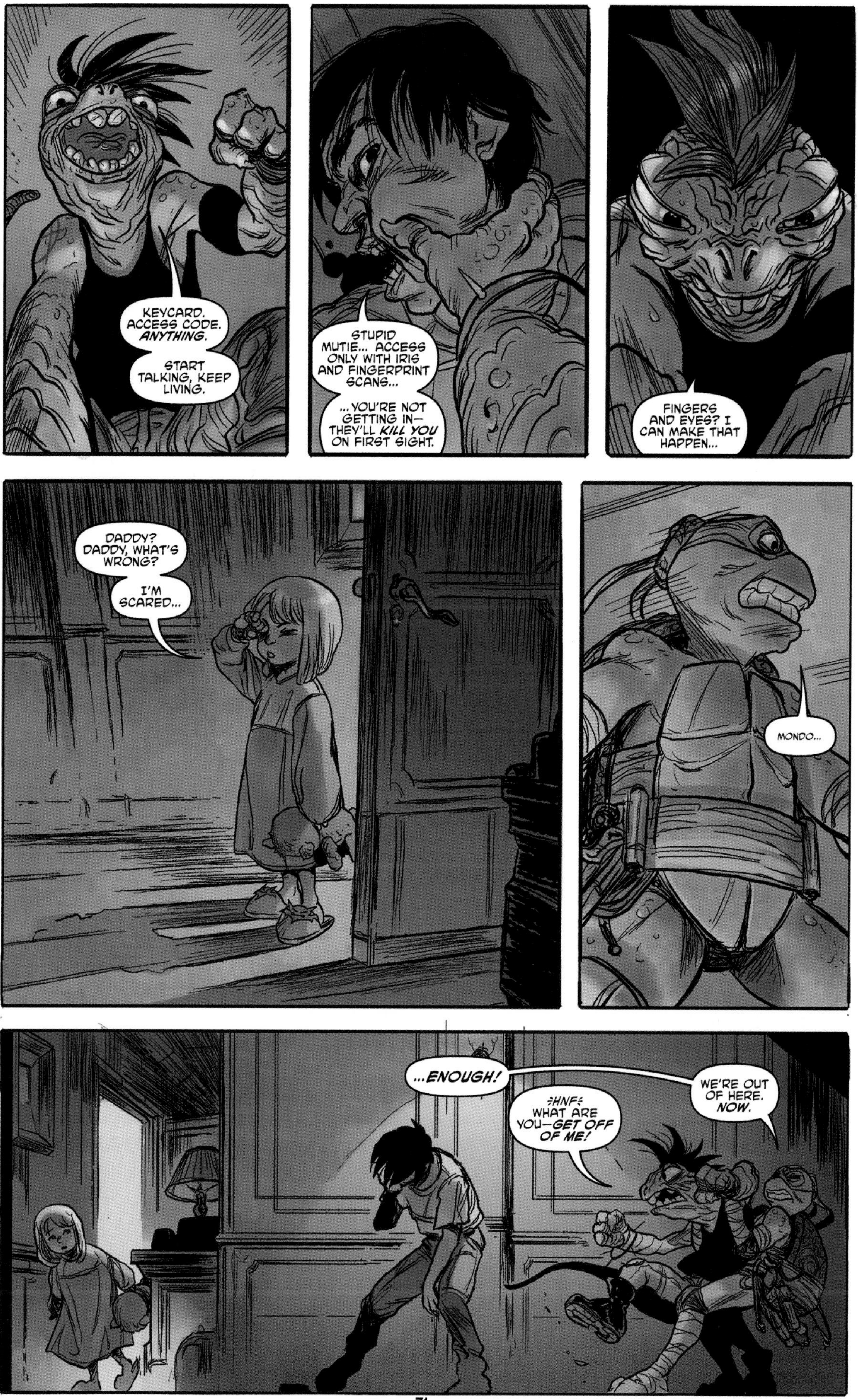
KEYCARD. ACCESS CODE. ANYTHING.
START TALKING, KEEP LIVING.
STUPID MUTIE... ACCESS ONLY WITH IRIS AND FINGERPRINT SCANS...
...YOU'RE NOT GETTING IN— THEY'LL KILL YOU ON FIRST SIGHT.
FINGERS AND EYES? I CAN MAKE THAT HAPPEN...
DADDY? DADDY, WHAT'S WRONG?
I'M SCARED...
MONDO...
...ENOUGH!
WE'RE OUT OF HERE. NOW.
HNF WHAT ARE YOU—GET OFF OF ME!

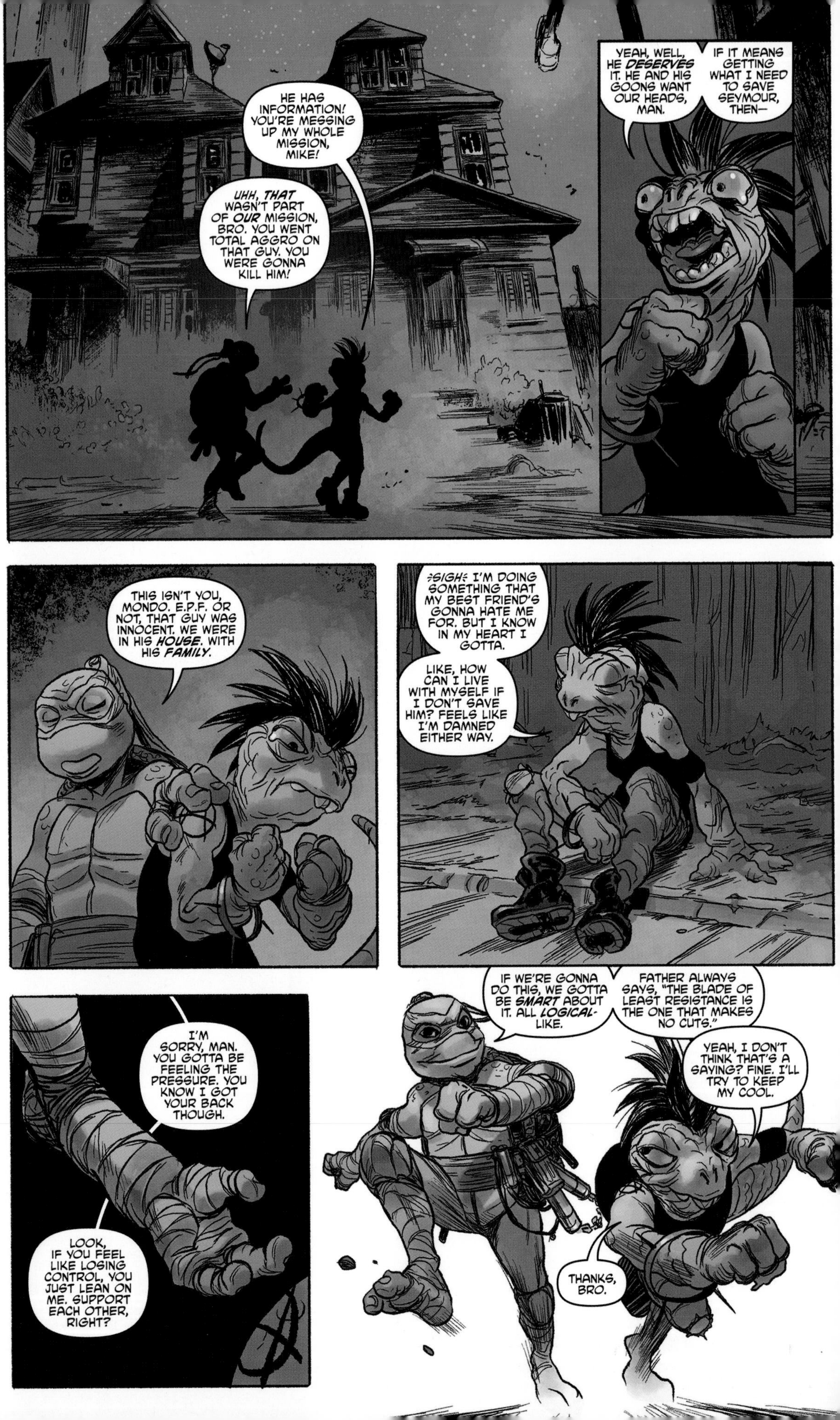
HE HAS INFORMATION! YOU'RE MESSING UP MY WHOLE MISSION, MIKE!
UHH, THAT WASN'T PART OF OUR MISSION, BRO. YOU WENT TOTAL AGGRO ON THAT GUY. YOU WERE GONNA KILL HIM!
YEAH, WELL, HE DESERVES IT. HE AND HIS GOONS WANT OUR HEADS, MAN.
IF IT MEANS GETTING WHAT I NEED TO SAVE SEYMOUR, THEN—
THIS ISN'T YOU, MONDO. E.P.F. OR NOT, THAT GUY WAS INNOCENT. WE WERE IN HIS HOUSE. WITH HIS FAMILY.
SIGH I'M DOING SOMETHING THAT MY BEST FRIEND'S GONNA HATE ME FOR. BUT I KNOW IN MY HEART I GOTTA.
LIKE, HOW CAN I LIVE WITH MYSELF IF I DON'T SAVE HIM? FEELS LIKE I'M DAMNED EITHER WAY.
I'M SORRY, MAN. YOU GOTTA BE FEELING THE PRESSURE. YOU KNOW I GOT YOUR BACK THOUGH.
LOOK, IF YOU FEEL LIKE LOSING CONTROL, YOU JUST LEAN ON ME. SUPPORT EACH OTHER, RIGHT?
IF WE'RE GONNA DO THIS, WE GOTTA BE SMART ABOUT IT. ALL LOGICAL-LIKE.
FATHER ALWAYS SAYS, "THE BLADE OF LEAST RESISTANCE IS THE ONE THAT MAKES NO CUTS."
YEAH, I DON'T THINK THAT'S A SAYING? FINE. I'LL TRY TO KEEP MY COOL.
THANKS, BRO.

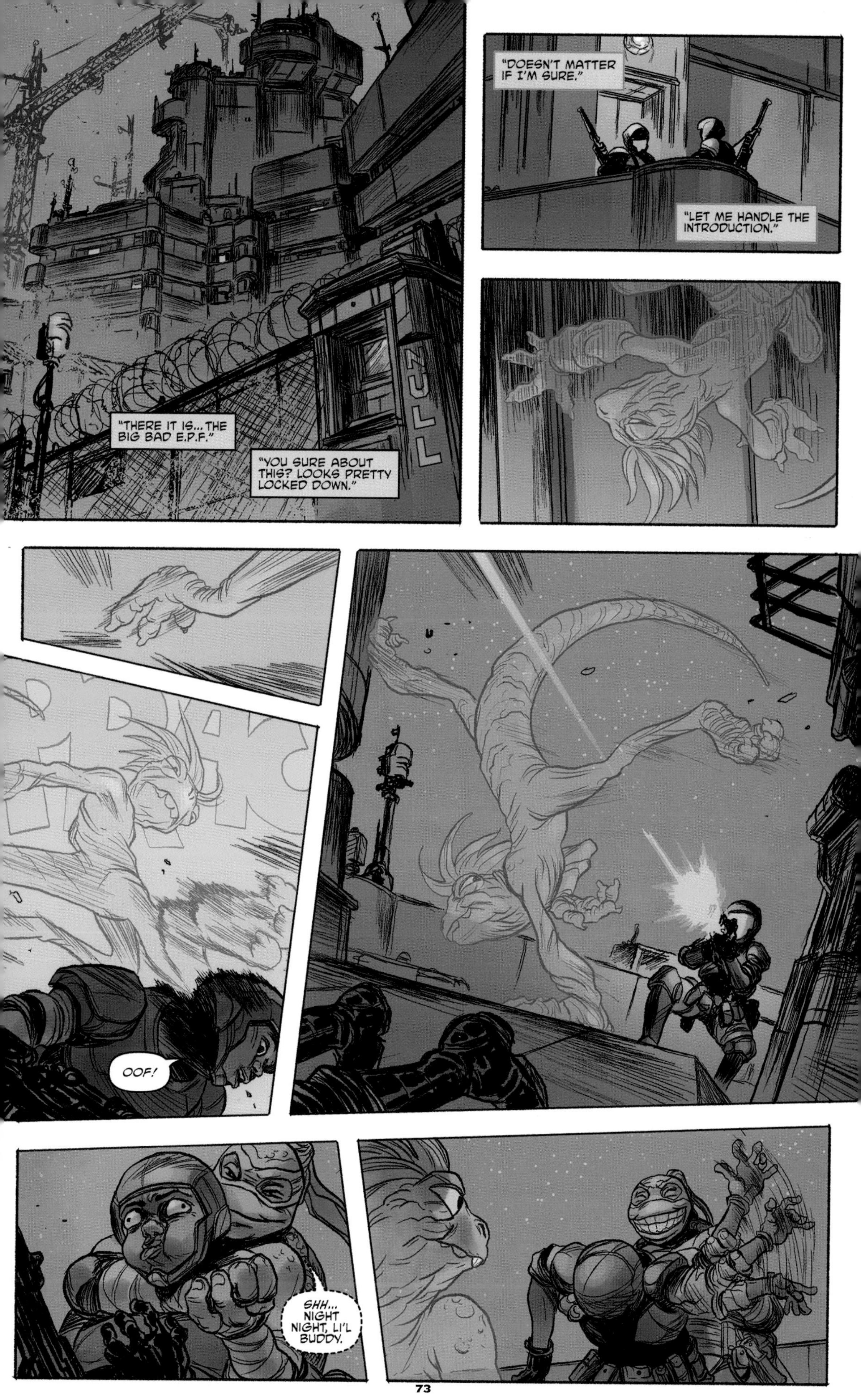
"THERE IT IS... THE BIG BAD E.P.F."
"YOU SURE ABOUT THIS? LOOKS PRETTY LOCKED DOWN."
NULL
"DOESN'T MATTER IF I'M SURE."
"LET ME HANDLE THE INTRODUCTION."
OOF!
SHH... NIGHT NIGHT, LI'L BUDDY.

VEEEP

FSSH!

DEE-DEET

E.P.F. HEADQUARTERS, LEVEL 16.

16

NGLK!

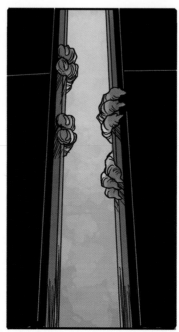

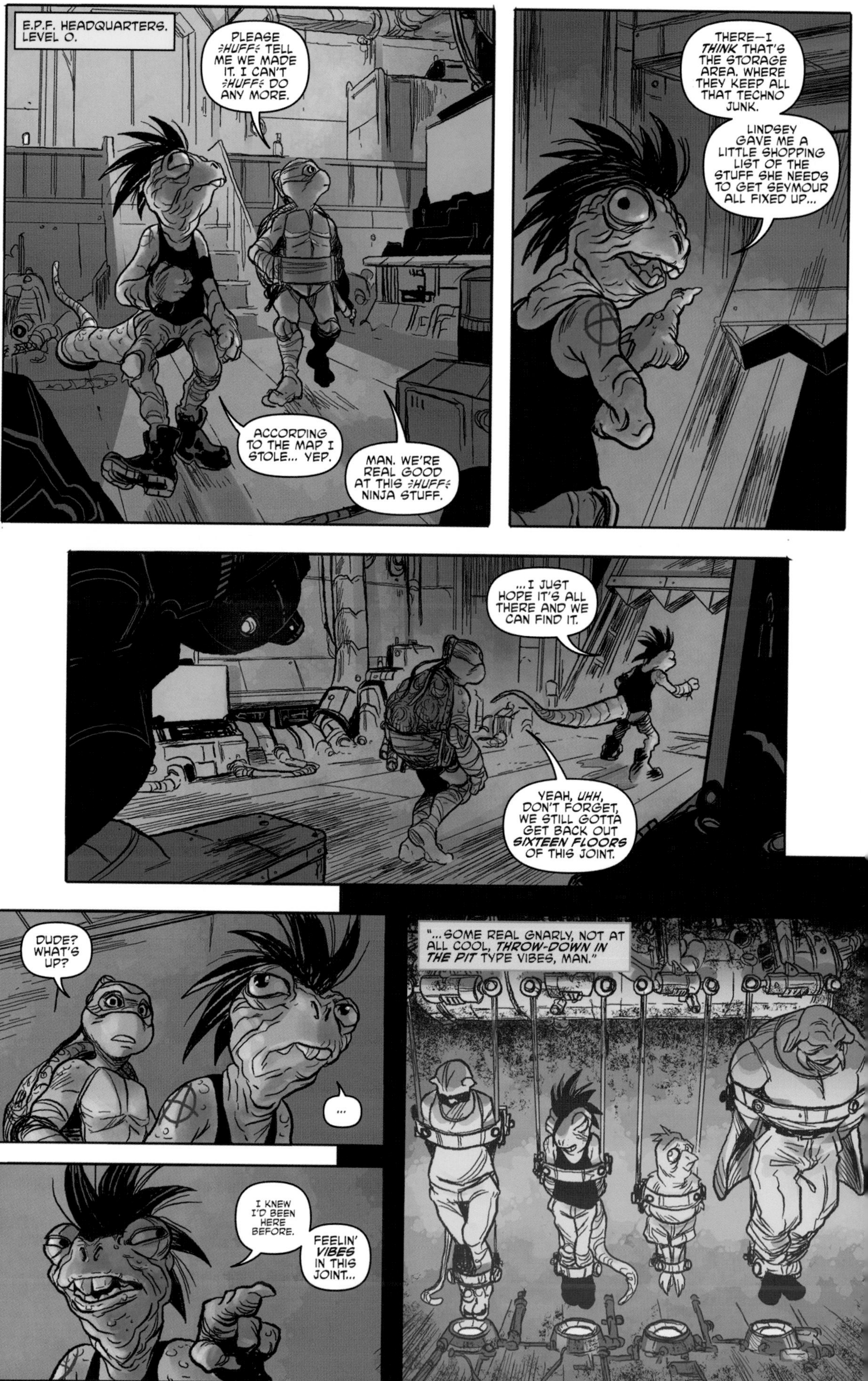
E.P.F. HEADQUARTERS. LEVEL 0.
PLEASE *HUFF* TELL ME WE MADE IT. I CAN'T *HUFF* DO ANY MORE.
ACCORDING TO THE MAP I STOLE... YEP.
MAN. WE'RE REAL GOOD AT THIS *HUFF* NINJA STUFF.
THERE—I *THINK* THAT'S THE STORAGE AREA. WHERE THEY KEEP ALL THAT TECHNO JUNK.
LINDSEY GAVE ME A LITTLE SHOPPING LIST OF THE STUFF SHE NEEDS TO GET SEYMOUR ALL FIXED UP...
...I JUST HOPE IT'S ALL THERE AND WE CAN FIND IT.
YEAH, *UHH*, DON'T FORGET, WE STILL GOTTA GET BACK OUT ***SIXTEEN FLOORS*** OF THIS JOINT.
DUDE? WHAT'S UP?
...
I KNEW I'D BEEN HERE BEFORE.
FEELIN' ***VIBES*** IN THIS JOINT...
"...SOME REAL GNARLY, NOT AT ALL COOL, ***THROW-DOWN IN THE PIT*** TYPE VIBES, MAN."

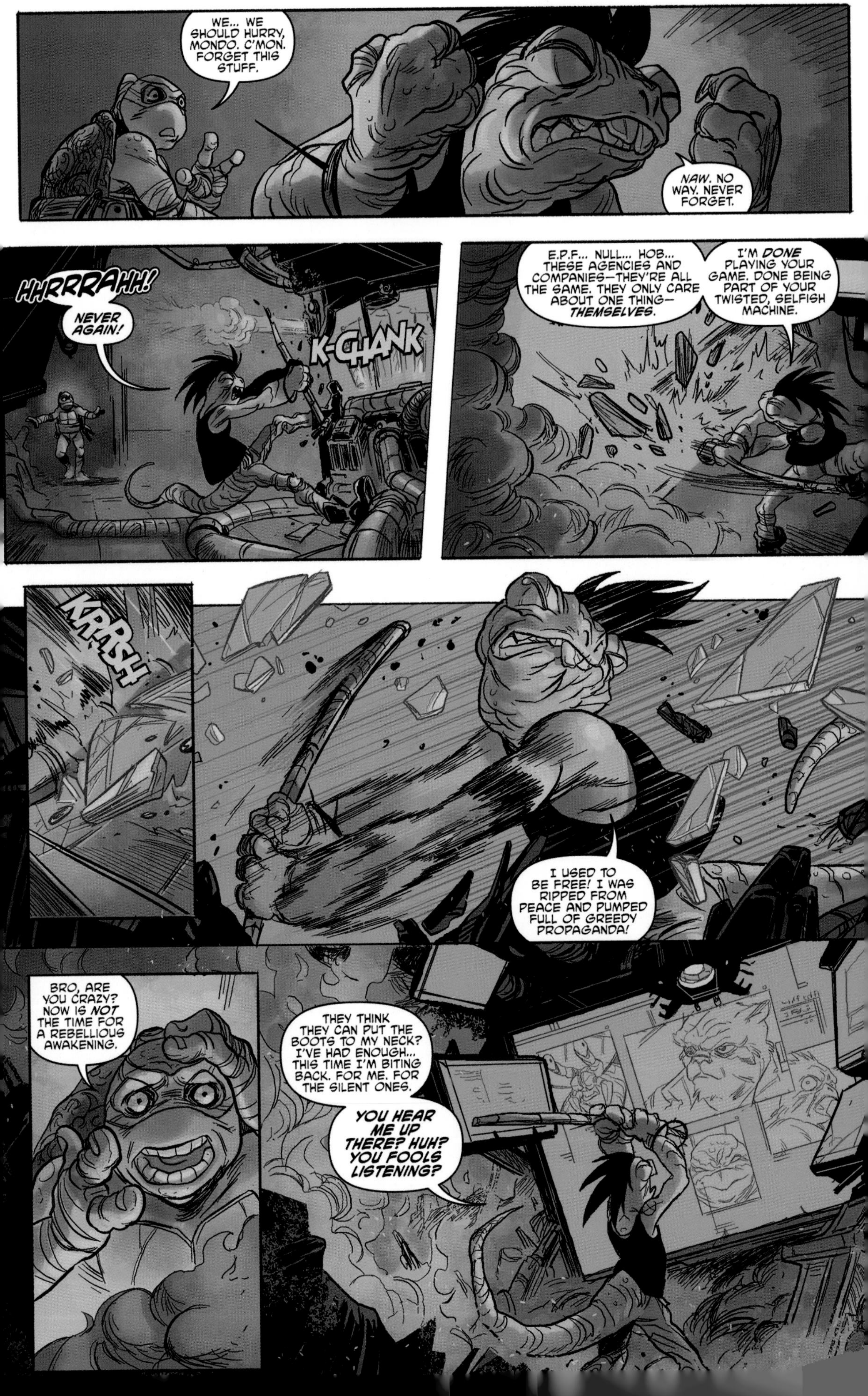
WE... WE SHOULD HURRY, MONDO. C'MON. FORGET THIS STUFF.
NAW. NO WAY. NEVER FORGET.
HHRRRAHH!
NEVER AGAIN!
K-CHANK
E.P.F... NULL... HOB... THESE AGENCIES AND COMPANIES—THEY'RE ALL THE SAME. THEY ONLY CARE ABOUT ONE THING— THEMSELVES.
I'M DONE PLAYING YOUR GAME. DONE BEING PART OF YOUR TWISTED, SELFISH MACHINE.
KRASH
I USED TO BE FREE! I WAS RIPPED FROM PEACE AND PUMPED FULL OF GREEDY PROPAGANDA!
BRO, ARE YOU CRAZY? NOW IS NOT THE TIME FOR A REBELLIOUS AWAKENING.
THEY THINK THEY CAN PUT THE BOOTS TO MY NECK? I'VE HAD ENOUGH... THIS TIME I'M BITING BACK. FOR ME. FOR THE SILENT ONES.
YOU HEAR ME UP THERE? HUH? YOU FOOLS LISTENING?

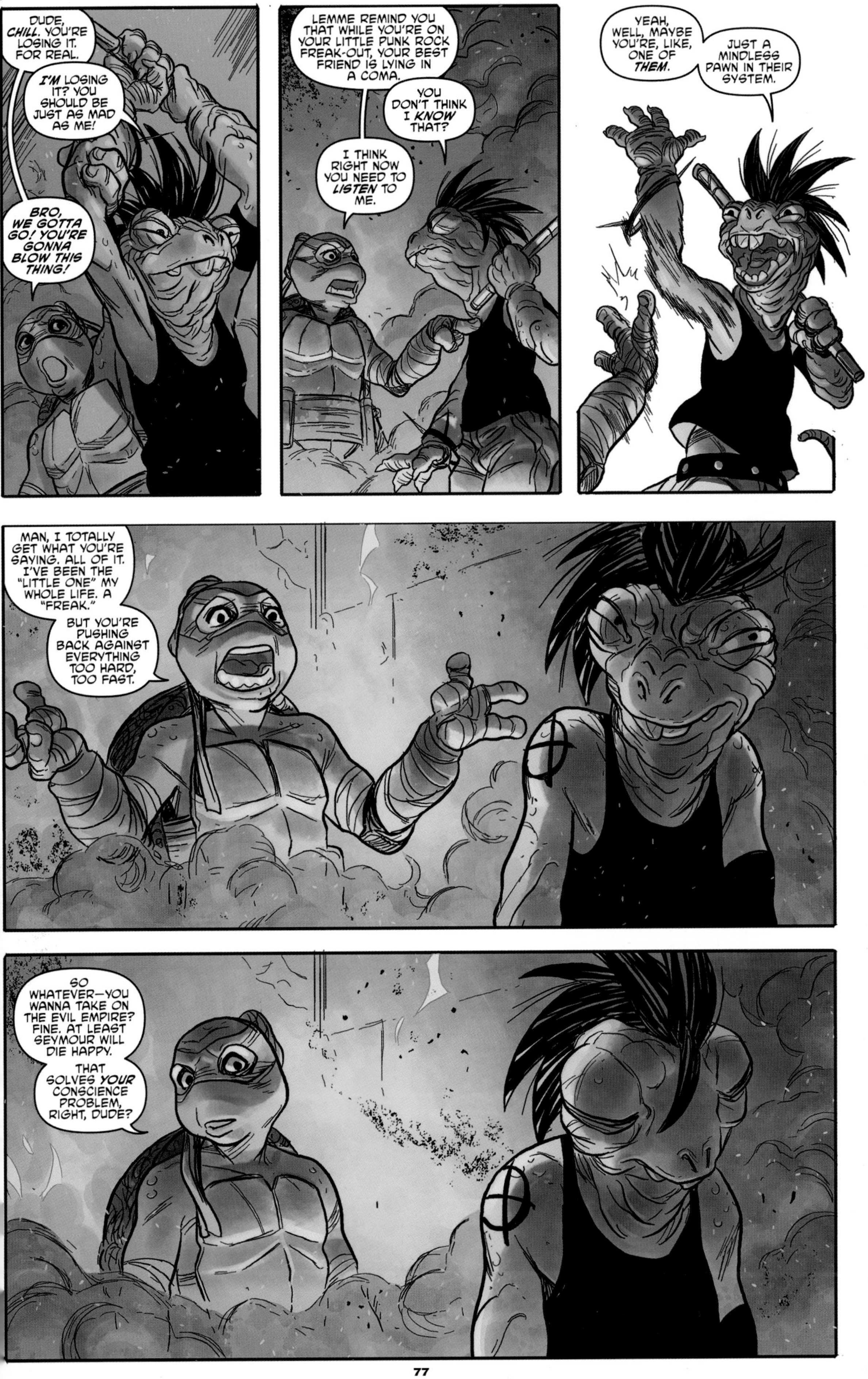
DUDE, CHILL. YOU'RE LOSING IT. FOR REAL.
I'M LOSING IT? YOU SHOULD BE JUST AS MAD AS ME!
BRO, WE GOTTA GO! YOU'RE GONNA BLOW THIS THING!
LEMME REMIND YOU THAT WHILE YOU'RE ON YOUR LITTLE PUNK ROCK FREAK-OUT, YOUR BEST FRIEND IS LYING IN A COMA.
YOU DON'T THINK I KNOW THAT?
I THINK RIGHT NOW YOU NEED TO LISTEN TO ME.
YEAH, WELL, MAYBE YOU'RE, LIKE, ONE OF THEM.
JUST A MINDLESS PAWN IN THEIR SYSTEM.
MAN, I TOTALLY GET WHAT YOU'RE SAYING. ALL OF IT. I'VE BEEN THE "LITTLE ONE" MY WHOLE LIFE. A "FREAK."
BUT YOU'RE PUSHING BACK AGAINST EVERYTHING TOO HARD, TOO FAST.
SO WHATEVER—YOU WANNA TAKE ON THE EVIL EMPIRE? FINE. AT LEAST SEYMOUR WILL DIE HAPPY.
THAT SOLVES YOUR CONSCIENCE PROBLEM, RIGHT, DUDE?

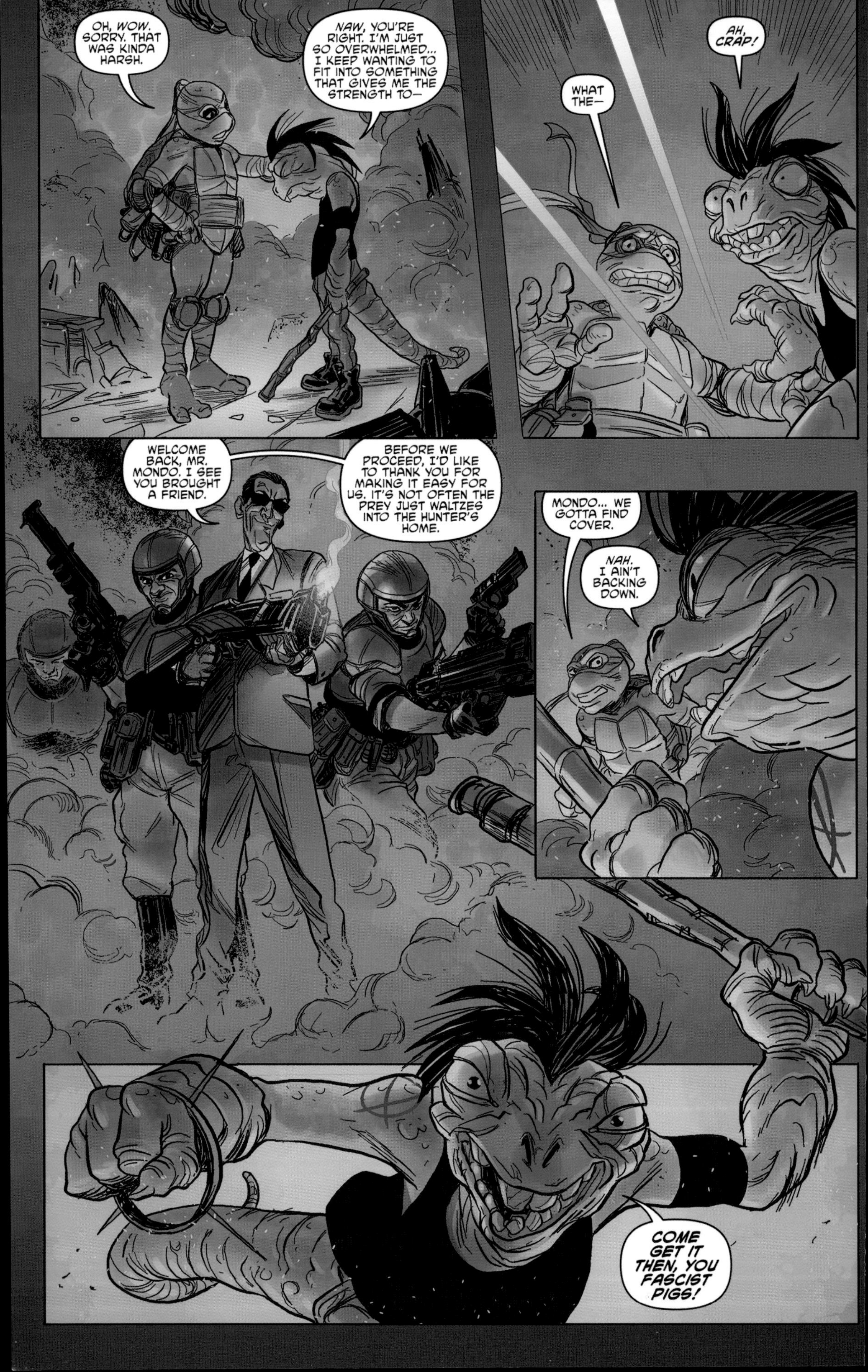
OH, *WOW*. SORRY. THAT WAS KINDA HARSH.
NAW, YOU'RE RIGHT. I'M JUST SO OVERWHELMED... I KEEP WANTING TO FIT INTO SOMETHING THAT GIVES ME THE STRENGTH TO—
AH, CRAP!
WHAT THE—
WELCOME BACK, MR. MONDO. I SEE YOU BROUGHT A FRIEND.
BEFORE WE PROCEED, I'D LIKE TO THANK YOU FOR MAKING IT EASY FOR US. IT'S NOT OFTEN THE PREY JUST WALTZES INTO THE HUNTER'S HOME.
MONDO... WE GOTTA FIND COVER.
NAH. I AIN'T BACKING DOWN.
COME GET IT THEN, YOU FASCIST PIGS!

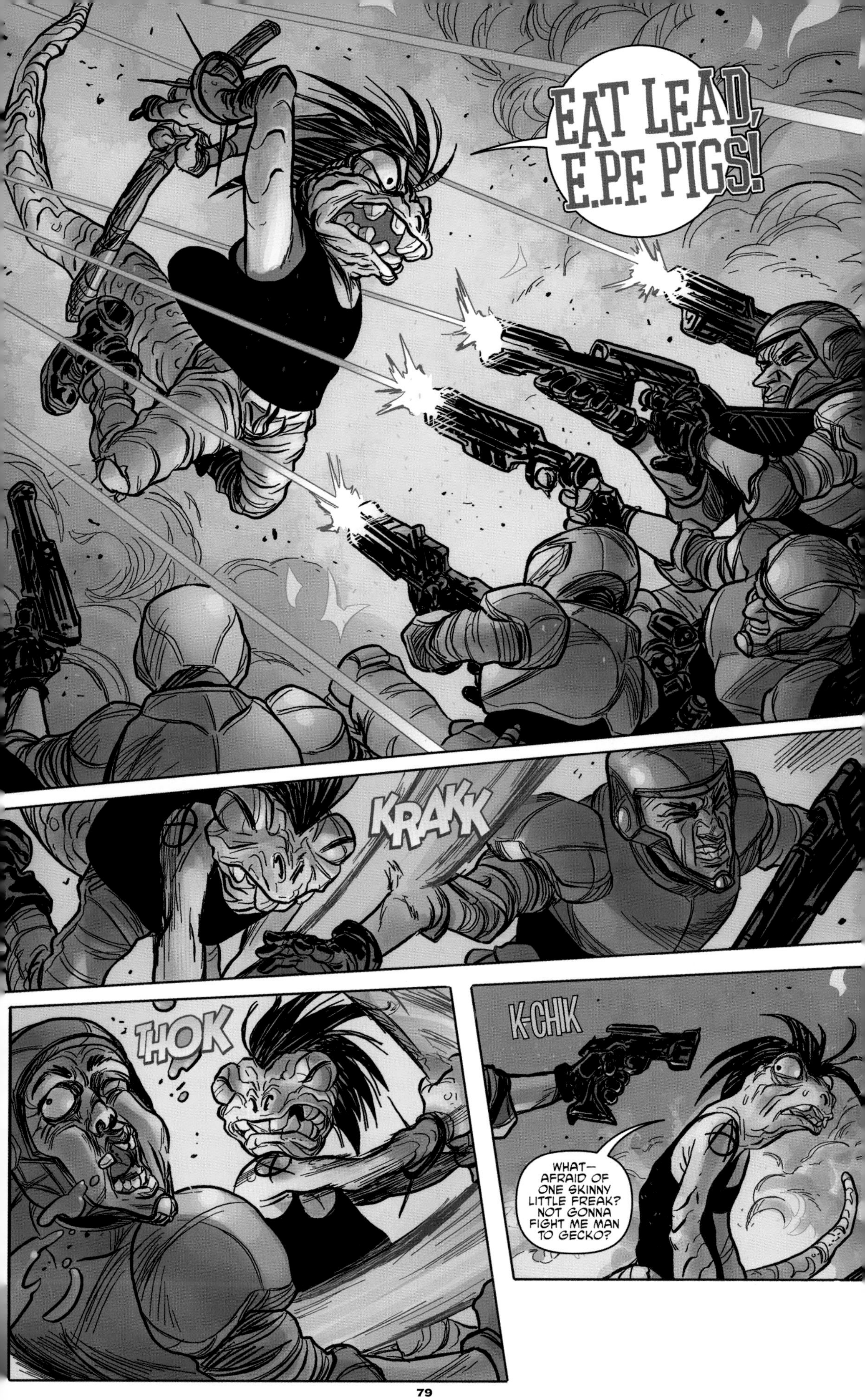
EAT LEAD, E.P.F PIGS!
KRAKK
THOK
K-CHIK
WHAT— AFRAID OF ONE SKINNY LITTLE FREAK? NOT GONNA FIGHT ME MAN TO GECKO?

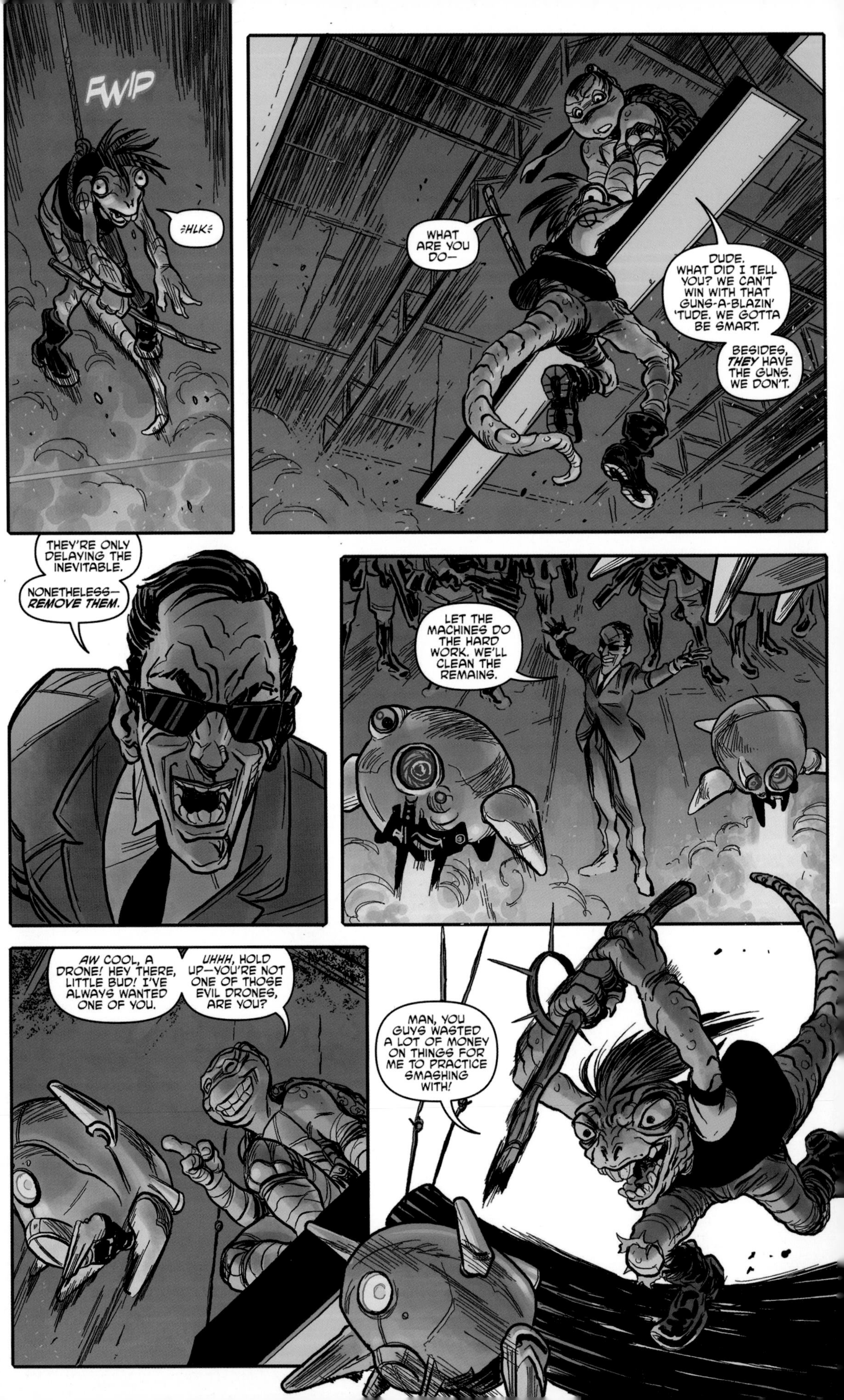
FWIP
HLK
WHAT ARE YOU DO—
DUDE. WHAT DID I TELL YOU? WE CAN'T WIN WITH THAT GUNS-A-BLAZIN' 'TUDE. WE GOTTA BE SMART.
BESIDES, THEY HAVE THE GUNS. WE DON'T.
THEY'RE ONLY DELAYING THE INEVITABLE.
NONETHELESS— REMOVE THEM.
LET THE MACHINES DO THE HARD WORK. WE'LL CLEAN THE REMAINS.
AW COOL, A DRONE! HEY THERE, LITTLE BUD! I'VE ALWAYS WANTED ONE OF YOU.
UHHH, HOLD UP—YOU'RE NOT ONE OF THOSE EVIL DRONES, ARE YOU?
MAN, YOU GUYS WASTED A LOT OF MONEY ON THINGS FOR ME TO PRACTICE SMASHING WITH!

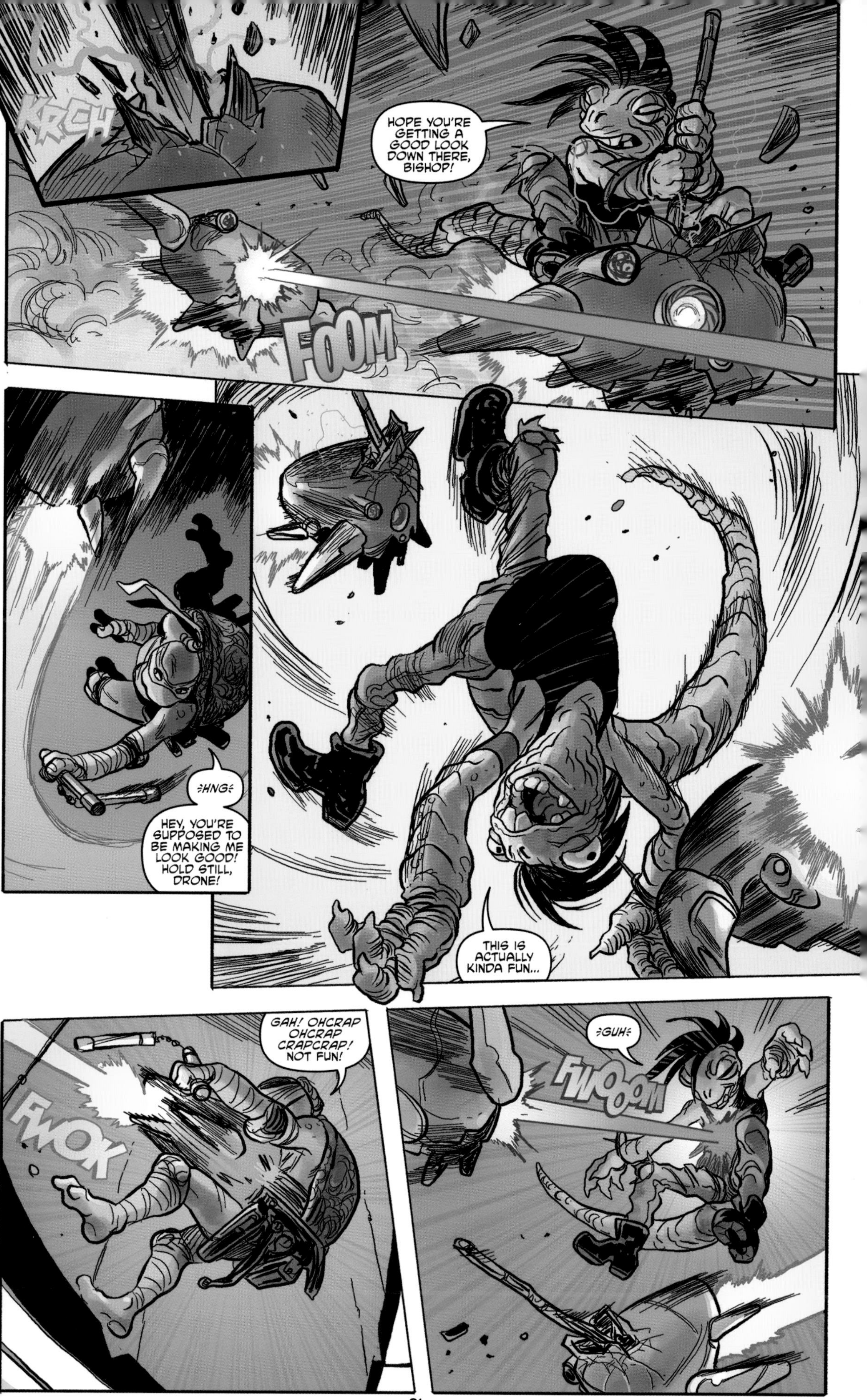
KRCH
HOPE YOU'RE GETTING A GOOD LOOK DOWN THERE, BISHOP!
FOOM
⚡HNG⚡
HEY, YOU'RE SUPPOSED TO BE MAKING ME LOOK GOOD! HOLD STILL, DRONE!
THIS IS ACTUALLY KINDA FUN...
GAH! OHCRAP OHCRAP CRAPCRAP! NOT FUN!
FWOK
⚡GUH⚡
FWOOOOM

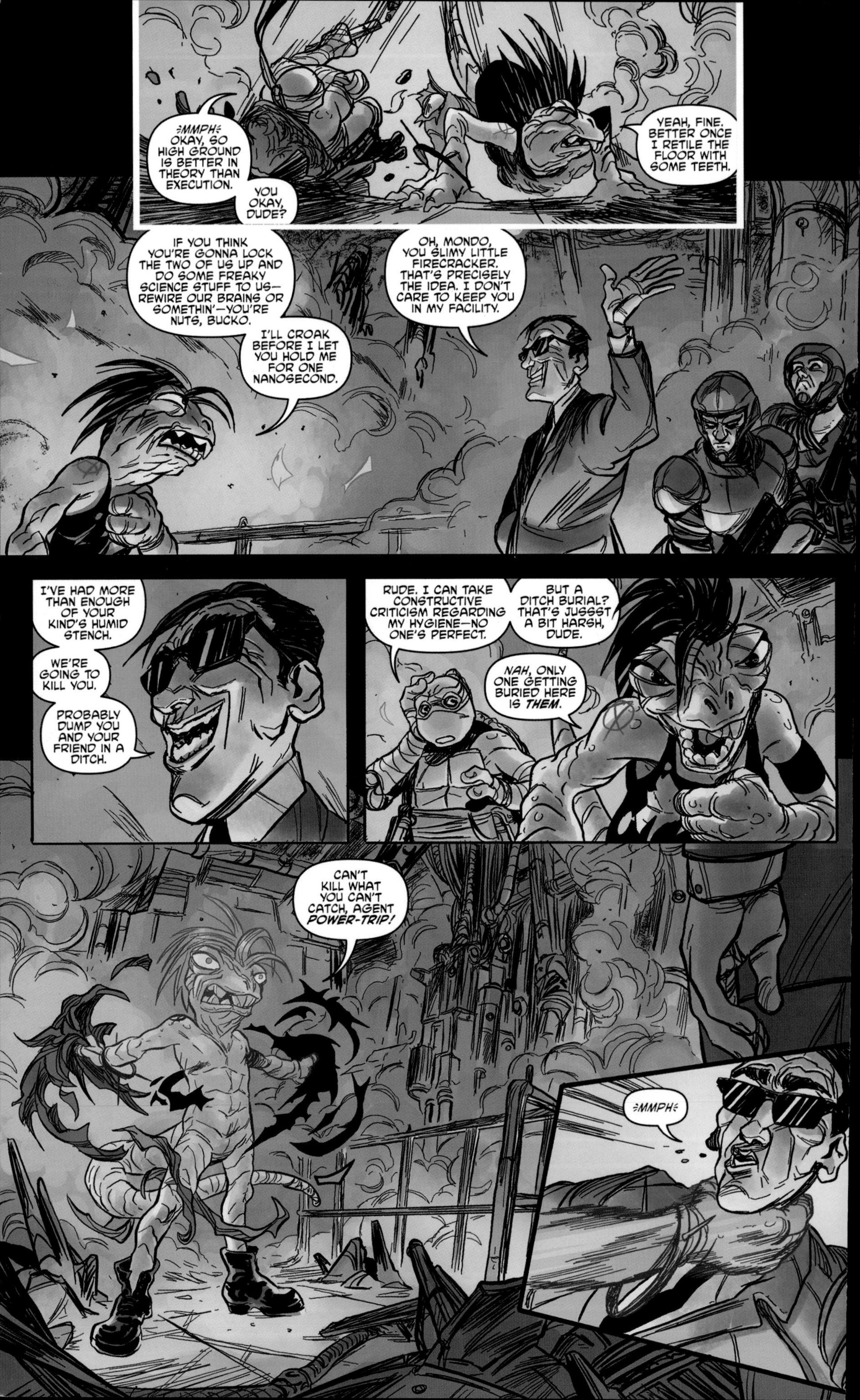

=MMPH= OKAY, SO HIGH GROUND IS BETTER IN THEORY THAN EXECUTION.
YOU OKAY, DUDE?
YEAH, FINE. BETTER ONCE I RETILE THE FLOOR WITH SOME TEETH.
IF YOU THINK YOU'RE GONNA LOCK THE TWO OF US UP AND DO SOME FREAKY SCIENCE STUFF TO US—REWIRE OUR BRAINS OR SOMETHIN'—YOU'RE NUTS, BUCKO.
I'LL CROAK BEFORE I LET YOU HOLD ME FOR ONE NANOSECOND.
OH, MONDO, YOU SLIMY LITTLE FIRECRACKER. THAT'S PRECISELY THE IDEA. I DON'T CARE TO KEEP YOU IN MY FACILITY.
I'VE HAD MORE THAN ENOUGH OF YOUR KIND'S HUMID STENCH.
WE'RE GOING TO KILL YOU.
PROBABLY DUMP YOU AND YOUR FRIEND IN A DITCH.
RUDE. I CAN TAKE CONSTRUCTIVE CRITICISM REGARDING MY HYGIENE—NO ONE'S PERFECT.
BUT A DITCH BURIAL? THAT'S JUSSST A BIT HARSH, DUDE.
NAH, ONLY ONE GETTING BURIED HERE IS THEM.
CAN'T KILL WHAT YOU CAN'T CATCH, AGENT POWER-TRIP!
=MMPH=

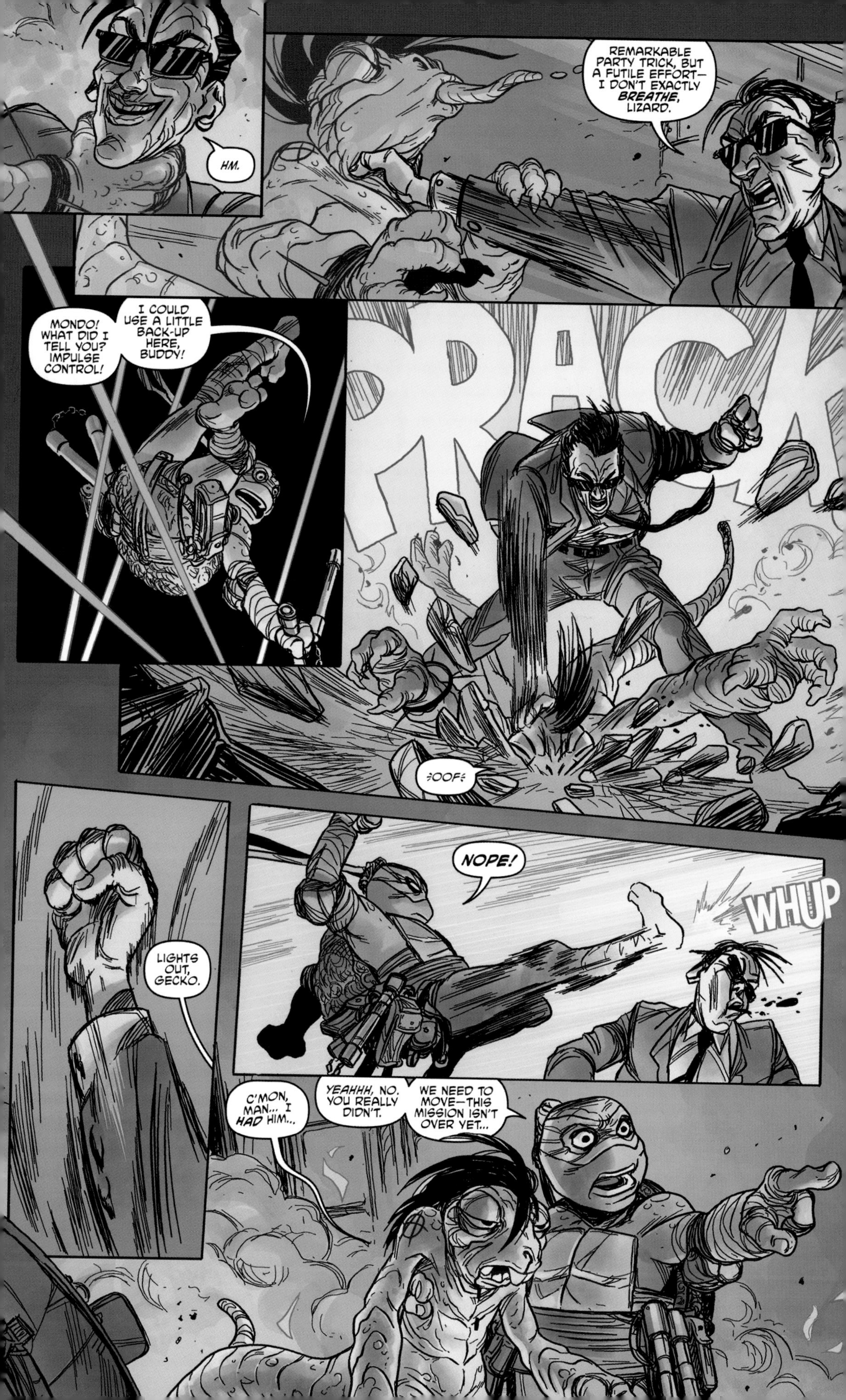
HM.
REMARKABLE PARTY TRICK, BUT A FUTILE EFFORT— I DON'T EXACTLY BREATHE, LIZARD.
MONDO! WHAT DID I TELL YOU? IMPULSE CONTROL!
I COULD USE A LITTLE BACK-UP HERE, BUDDY!
CRACK
OOF
LIGHTS OUT, GECKO.
NOPE!
WHUP
C'MON, MAN... I HAD HIM...
YEAHHH, NO. YOU REALLY DIDN'T.
WE NEED TO MOVE—THIS MISSION ISN'T OVER YET...

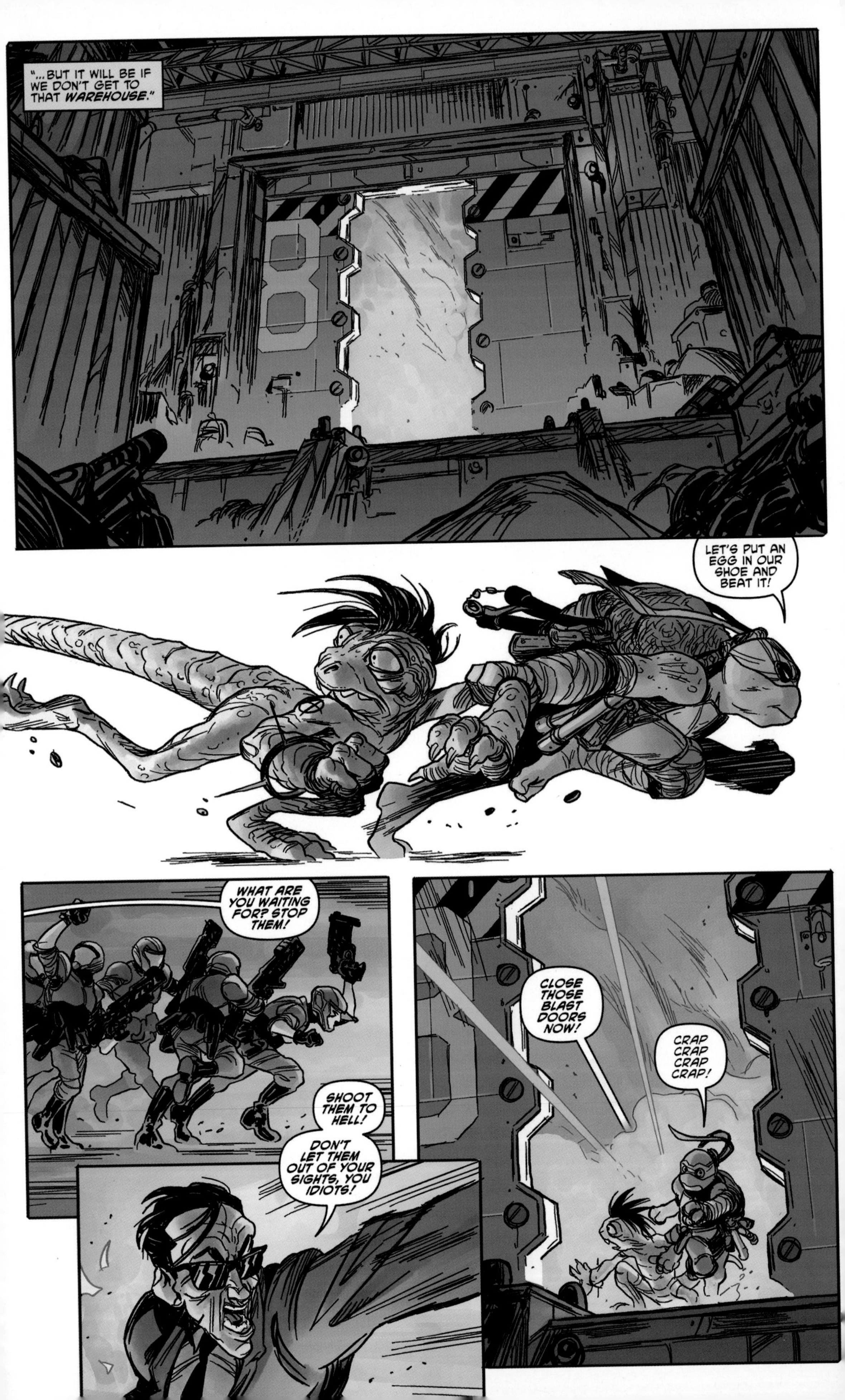
"...BUT IT WILL BE IF WE DON'T GET TO THAT WAREHOUSE."
LET'S PUT AN EGG IN OUR SHOE AND BEAT IT!
WHAT ARE YOU WAITING FOR? STOP THEM!
SHOOT THEM TO HELL!
DON'T LET THEM OUT OF YOUR SIGHTS, YOU IDIOTS!
CLOSE THOSE BLAST DOORS NOW!
CRAP CRAP CRAP CRAP!

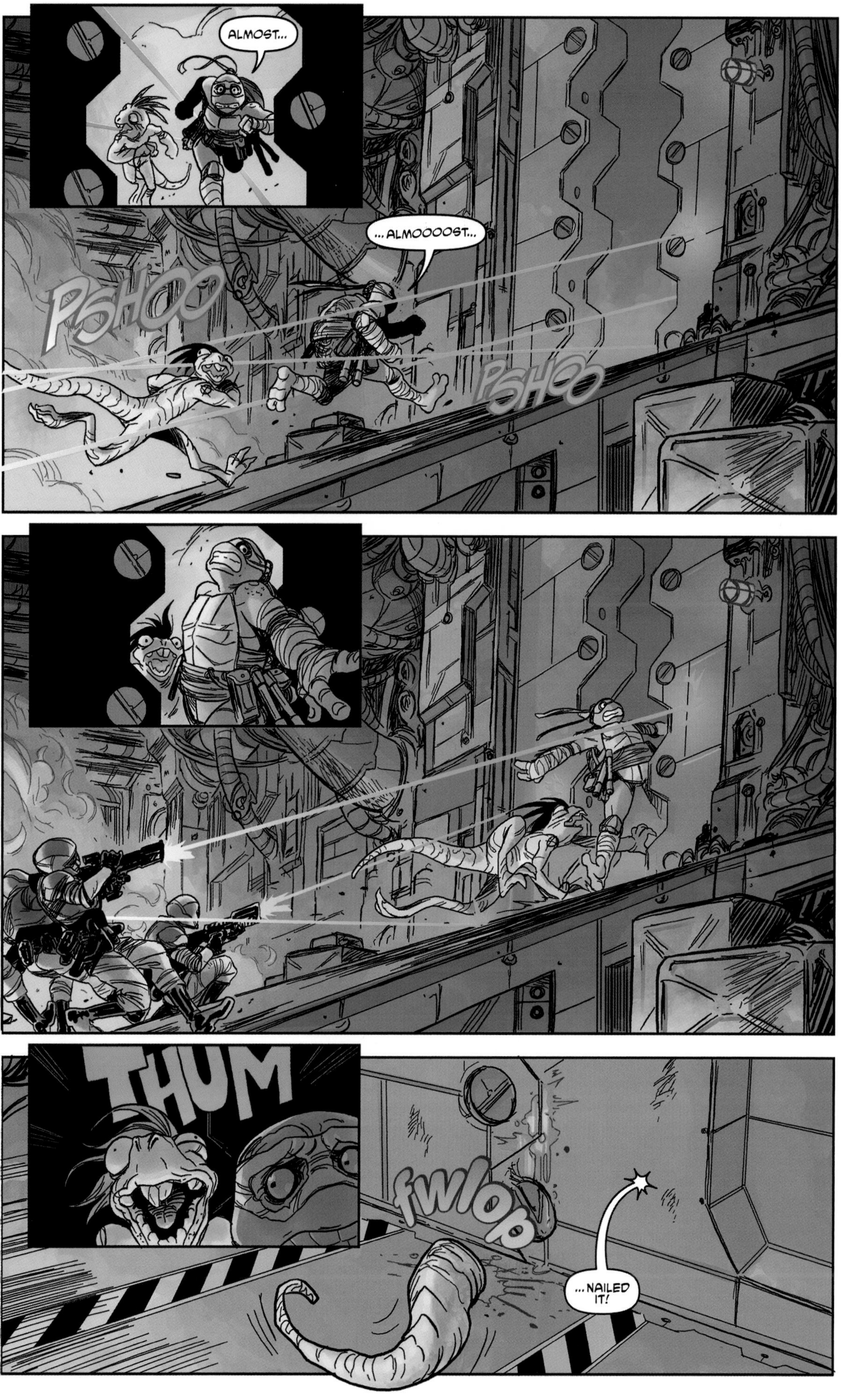
ALMOST...
...ALMOOOOST...
PSHOO
PSHOO
THUM
fwlop
...NAILED IT!

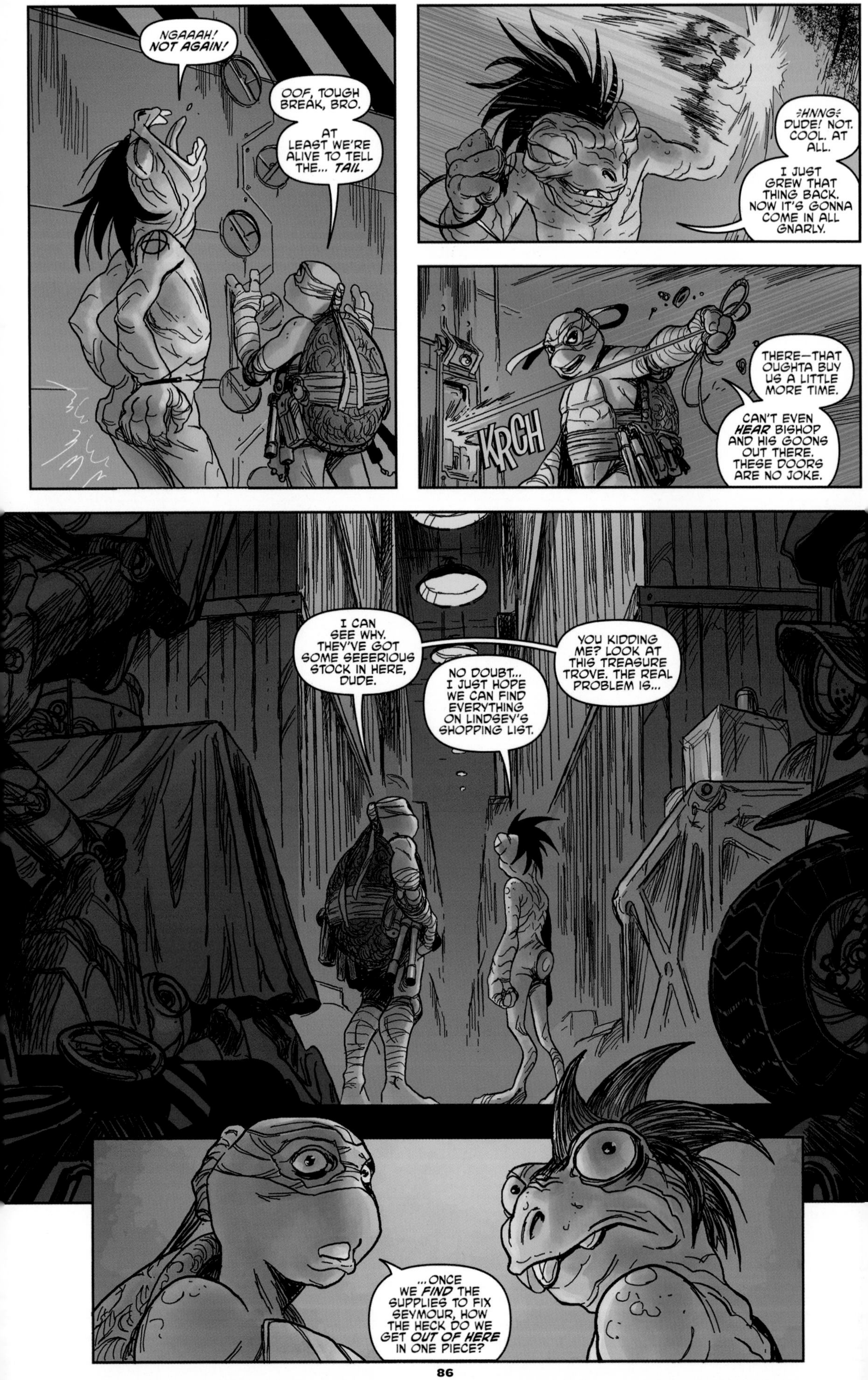
NGAAAH! NOT AGAIN!
OOF, TOUGH BREAK, BRO.
AT LEAST WE'RE ALIVE TO TELL THE... TAIL.
HNNG DUDE! NOT. COOL. AT ALL.
I JUST GREW THAT THING BACK. NOW IT'S GONNA COME IN ALL GNARLY.
KRCH
THERE—THAT OUGHTA BUY US A LITTLE MORE TIME.
CAN'T EVEN HEAR BISHOP AND HIS GOONS OUT THERE. THESE DOORS ARE NO JOKE.
I CAN SEE WHY. THEY'VE GOT SOME SEEERIOUS STOCK IN HERE, DUDE.
NO DOUBT... I JUST HOPE WE CAN FIND EVERYTHING ON LINDSEY'S SHOPPING LIST.
YOU KIDDING ME? LOOK AT THIS TREASURE TROVE. THE REAL PROBLEM IS...
...ONCE WE FIND THE SUPPLIES TO FIX SEYMOUR, HOW THE HECK DO WE GET OUT OF HERE IN ONE PIECE?

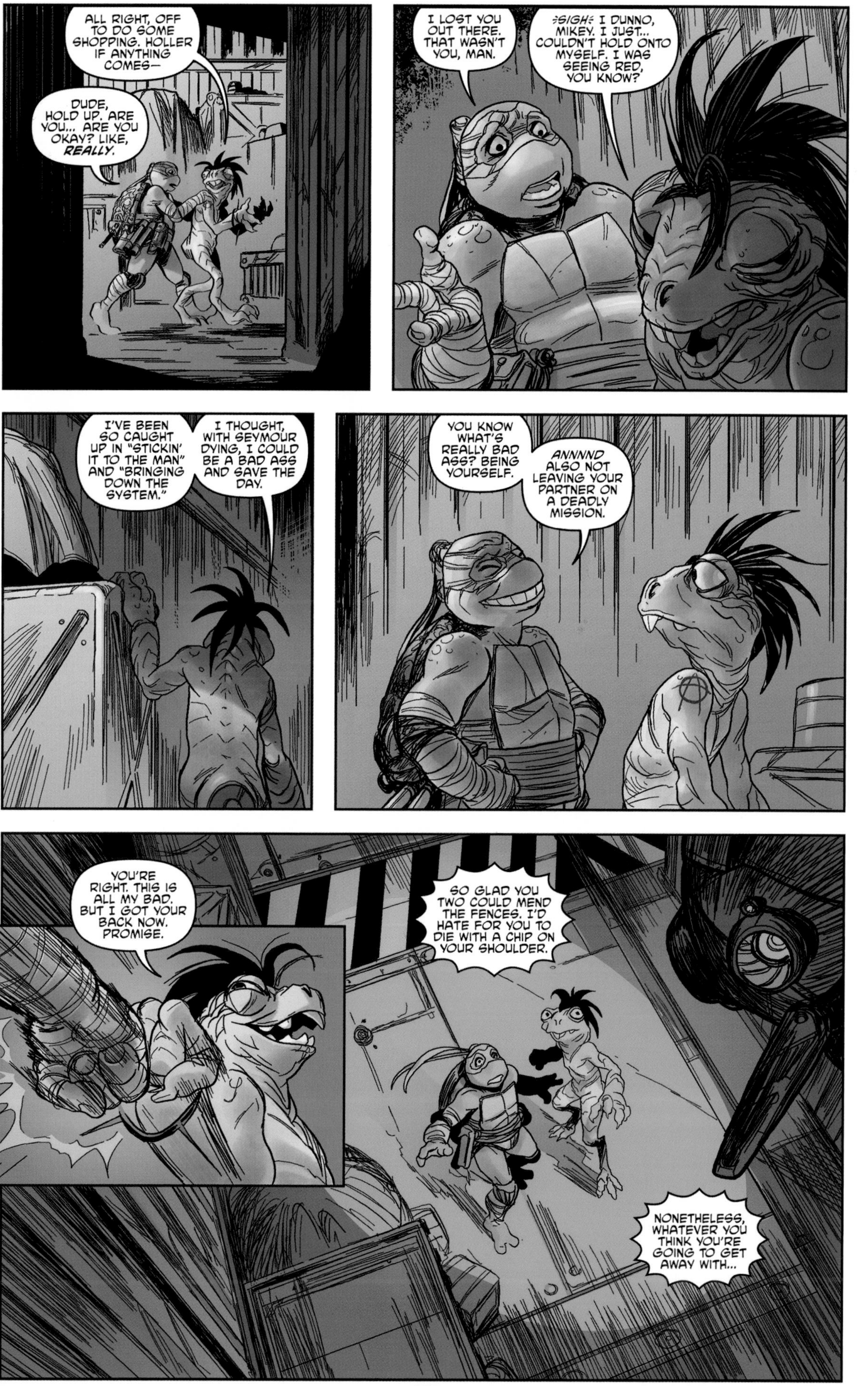
ALL RIGHT, OFF TO DO SOME SHOPPING. HOLLER IF ANYTHING COMES—
DUDE, HOLD UP. ARE YOU... ARE YOU OKAY? LIKE, *REALLY*.
I LOST YOU OUT THERE. THAT WASN'T YOU, MAN.
=SIGH= I DUNNO, MIKEY. I JUST... COULDN'T HOLD ONTO MYSELF. I WAS SEEING RED, YOU KNOW?
I'VE BEEN SO CAUGHT UP IN "STICKIN' IT TO THE MAN" AND "BRINGING DOWN THE SYSTEM."
I THOUGHT, WITH SEYMOUR DYING, I COULD BE A BAD ASS AND SAVE THE DAY.
YOU KNOW WHAT'S REALLY BAD ASS? BEING YOURSELF.
ANNNND ALSO NOT LEAVING YOUR PARTNER ON A DEADLY MISSION.
YOU'RE RIGHT. THIS IS ALL MY BAD. BUT I GOT YOUR BACK NOW. PROMISE.
SO GLAD YOU TWO COULD MEND THE FENCES. I'D HATE FOR YOU TO DIE WITH A CHIP ON YOUR SHOULDER.
NONETHELESS, WHATEVER YOU THINK YOU'RE GOING TO GET AWAY WITH...

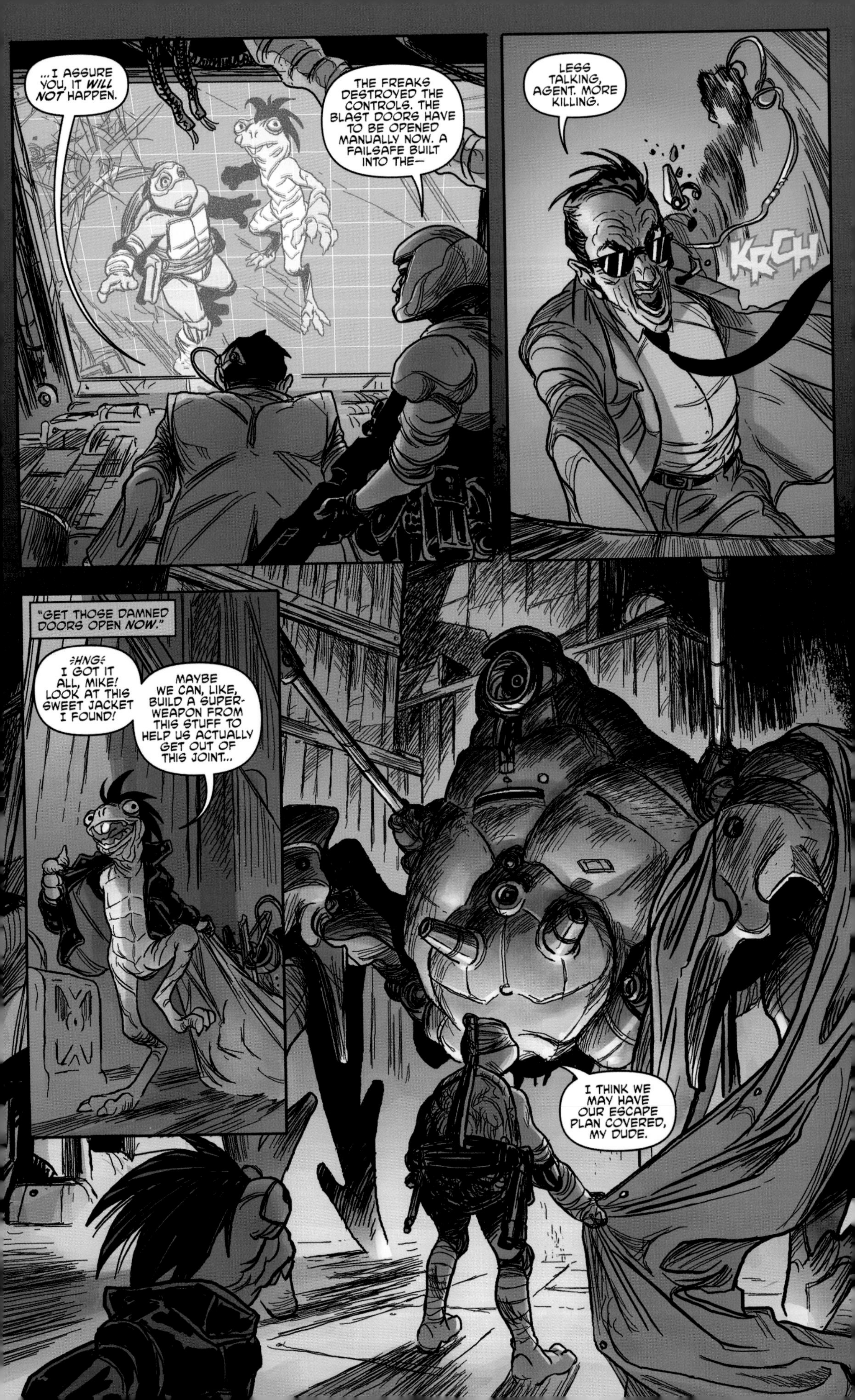
...I ASSURE YOU, IT *WILL NOT* HAPPEN.
THE FREAKS DESTROYED THE CONTROLS. THE BLAST DOORS HAVE TO BE OPENED MANUALLY NOW. A FAILSAFE BUILT INTO THE—
LESS TALKING, AGENT. MORE KILLING.
KRCH
"GET THOSE DAMNED DOORS OPEN *NOW*."
HNG I GOT IT ALL, MIKE! LOOK AT THIS SWEET JACKET I FOUND!
MAYBE WE CAN, LIKE, BUILD A SUPER-WEAPON FROM THIS STUFF TO HELP US ACTUALLY GET OUT OF THIS JOINT...
I THINK WE MAY HAVE OUR ESCAPE PLAN COVERED, MY DUDE.

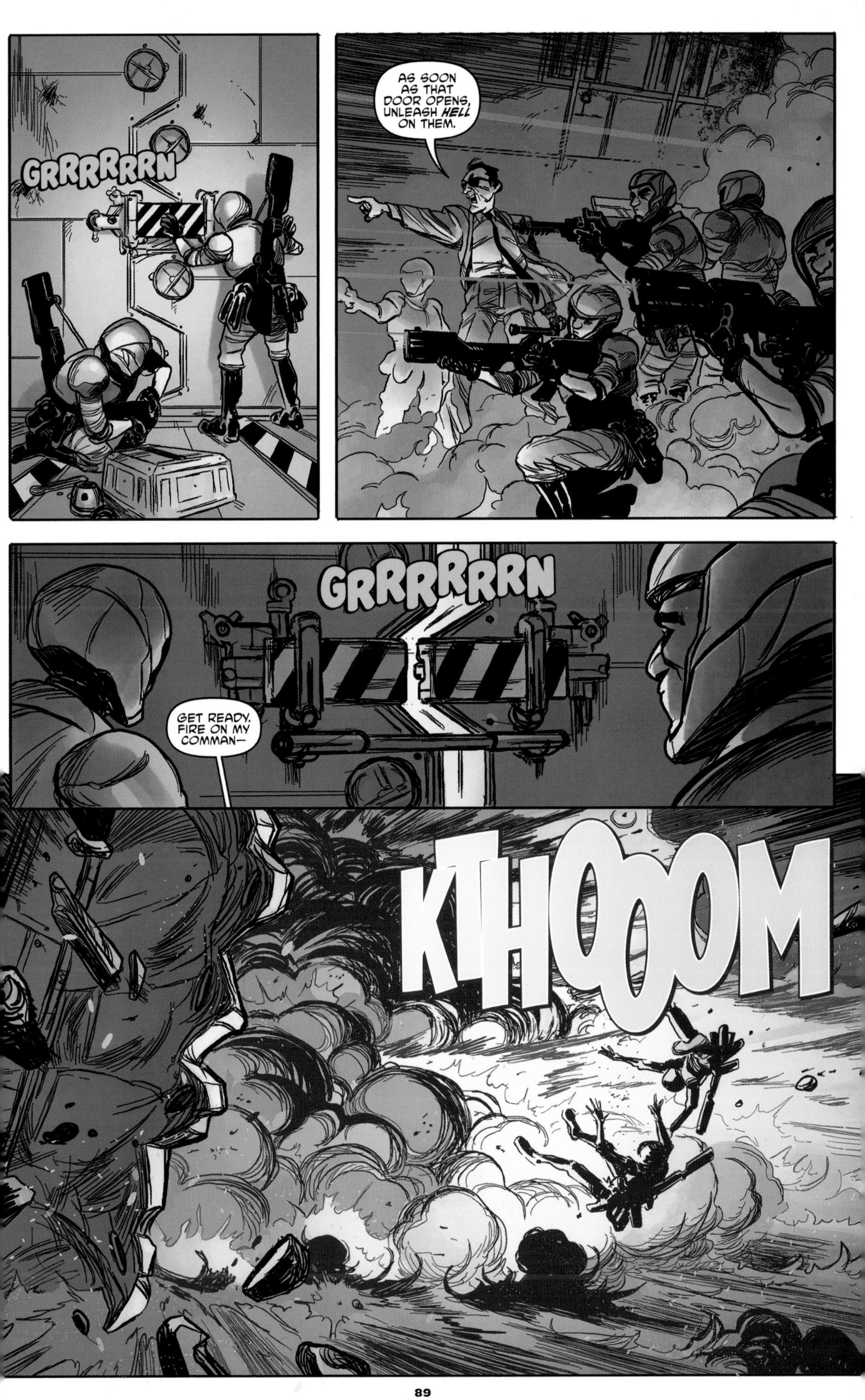
GRRRRRRN
AS SOON AS THAT DOOR OPENS, UNLEASH HELL ON THEM.
GRRRRRRN
GET READY. FIRE ON MY COMMAN—
KTHOOOM

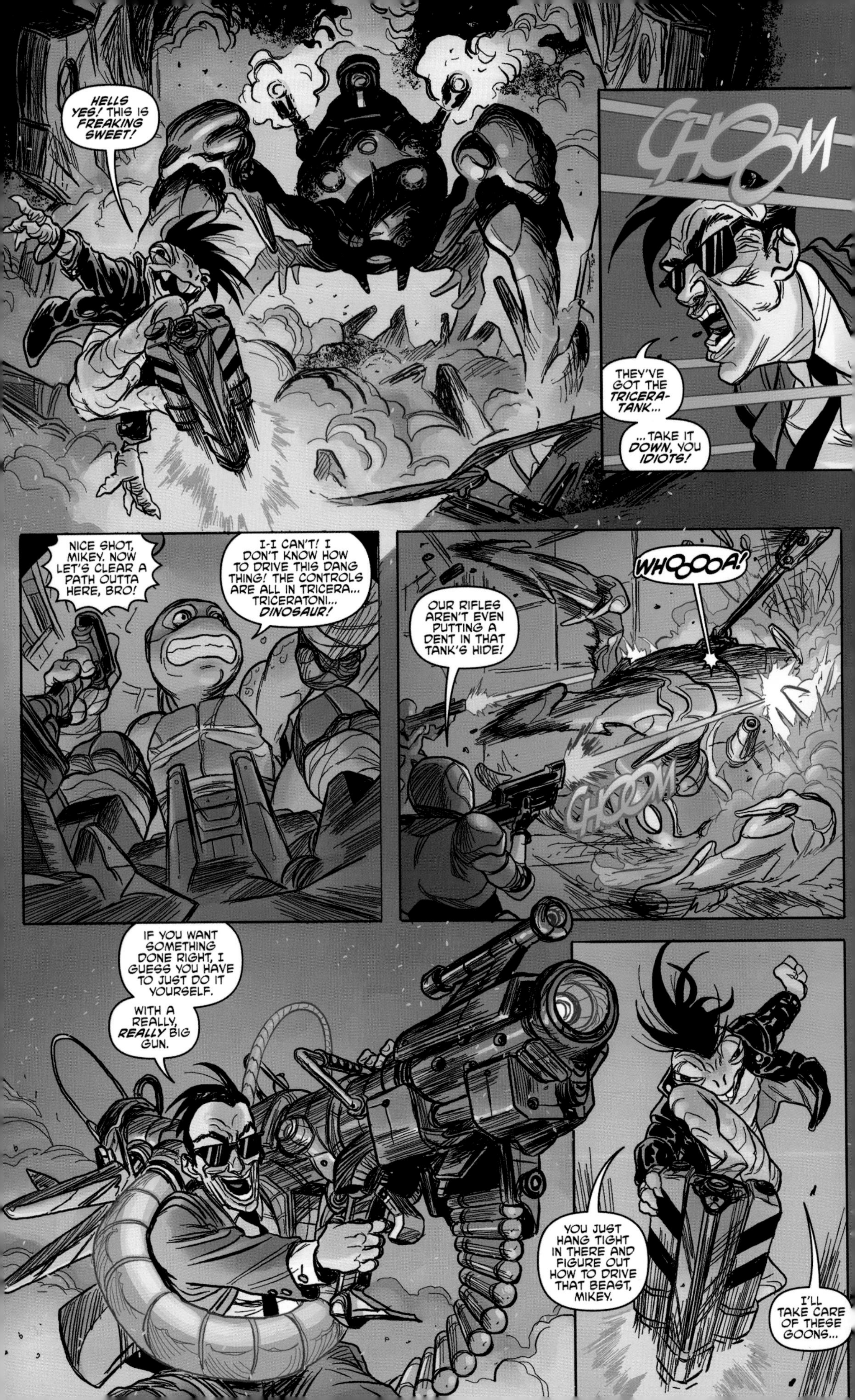
HELLS YES! THIS IS FREAKING SWEET!
CHOOM
THEY'VE GOT THE TRICERA-TANK...
...TAKE IT DOWN, YOU IDIOTS!
NICE SHOT, MIKEY. NOW LET'S CLEAR A PATH OUTTA HERE, BRO!
I-I CAN'T! I DON'T KNOW HOW TO DRIVE THIS DANG THING! THE CONTROLS ARE ALL IN TRICERA... TRICERATONI... DINOSAUR!
WHOOOOA!
OUR RIFLES AREN'T EVEN PUTTING A DENT IN THAT TANK'S HIDE!
CHOOM
IF YOU WANT SOMETHING DONE RIGHT, I GUESS YOU HAVE TO JUST DO IT YOURSELF.
WITH A REALLY, REALLY BIG GUN.
YOU JUST HANG TIGHT IN THERE AND FIGURE OUT HOW TO DRIVE THAT BEAST, MIKEY.
I'LL TAKE CARE OF THESE GOONS...

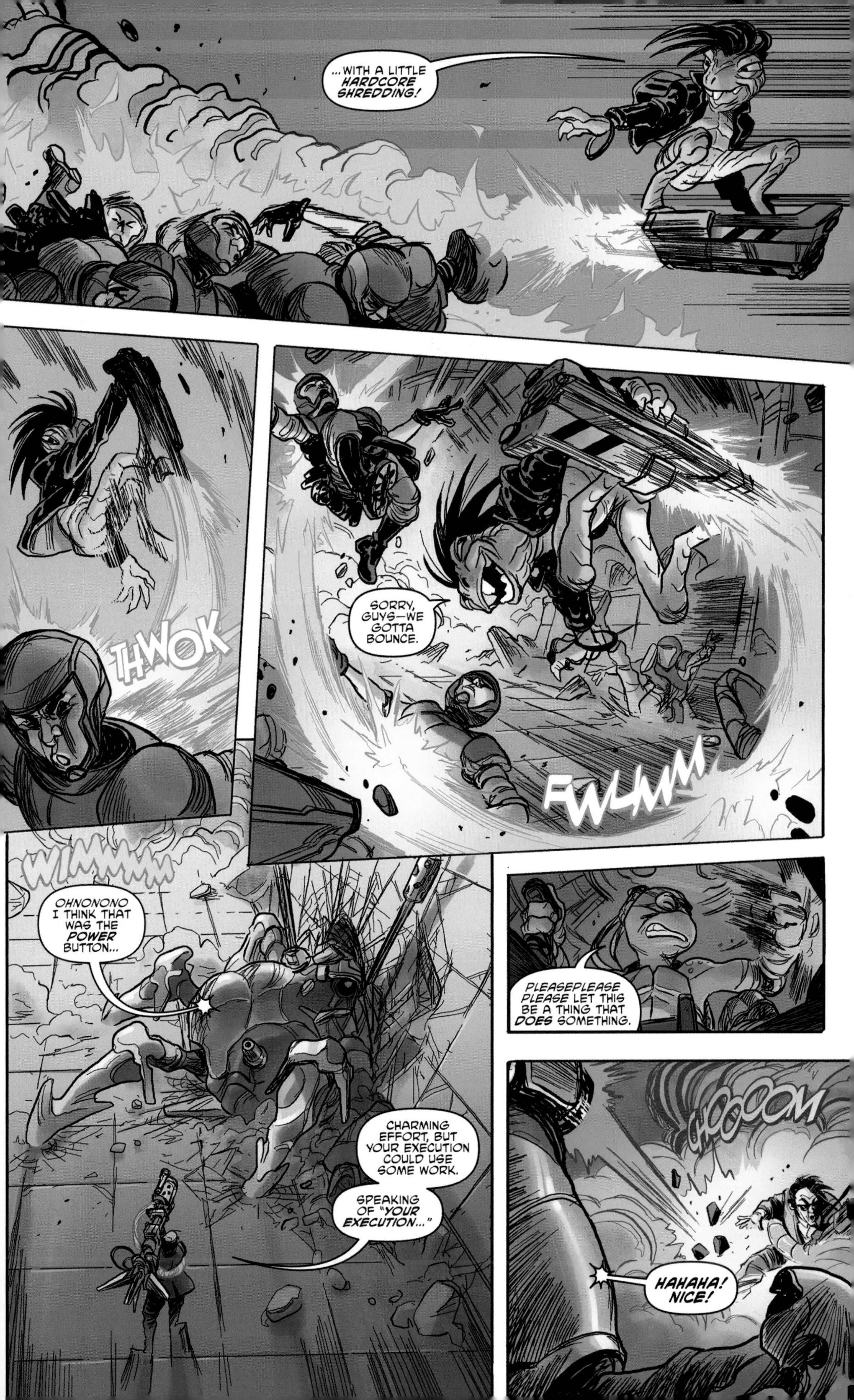
...WITH A LITTLE HARDCORE SHREDDING!
THWOK
SORRY, GUYS—WE GOTTA BOUNCE.
FWUMM
WIMMMM
OHNONONO I THINK THAT WAS THE POWER BUTTON...
PLEASEPLEASE PLEASE LET THIS BE A THING THAT DOES SOMETHING.
CHARMING EFFORT, BUT YOUR EXECUTION COULD USE SOME WORK.
SPEAKING OF "YOUR EXECUTION..."
CHOOOOM
HAHAHA! NICE!

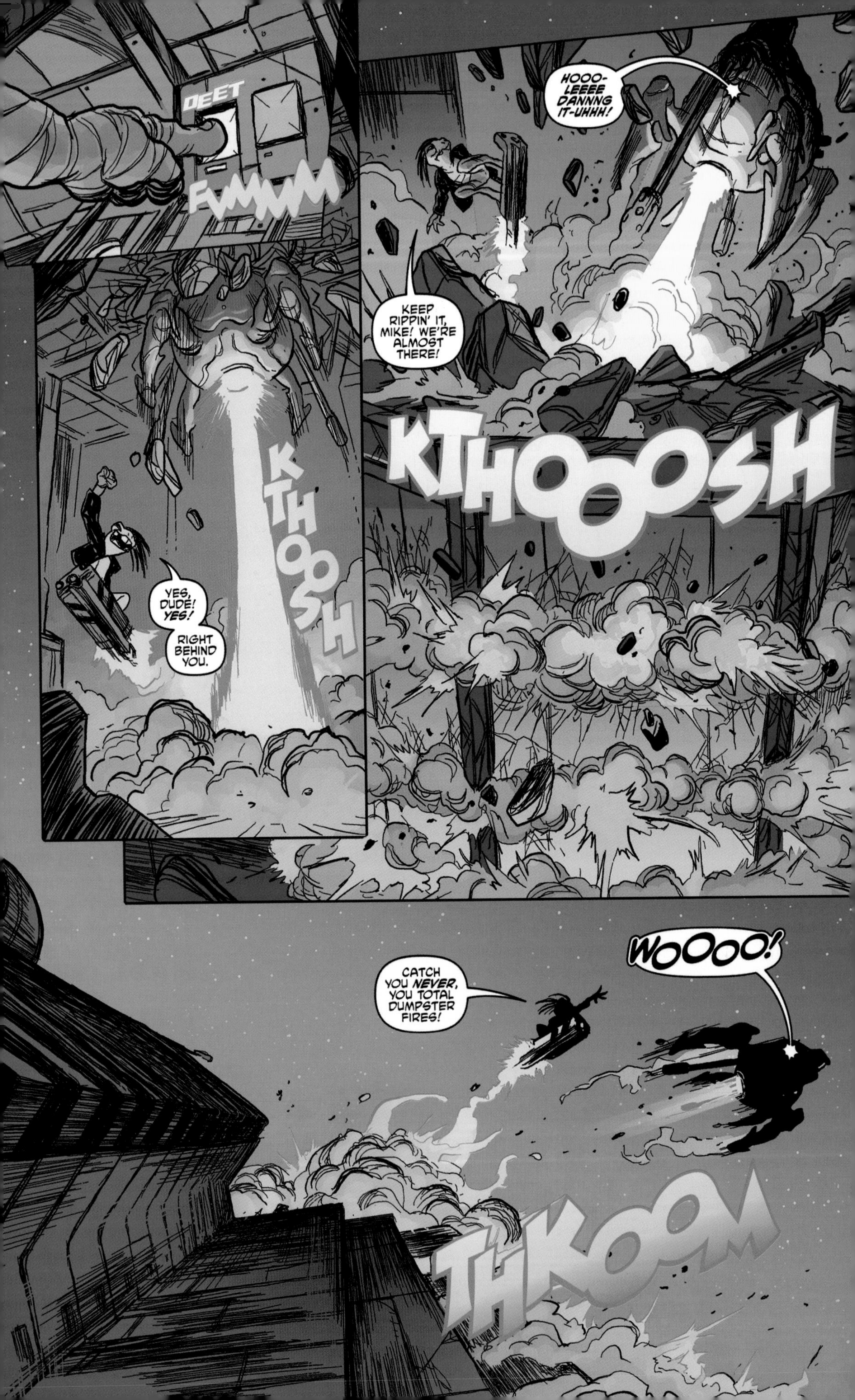
DEET
FWMM
KTHOOSH
YES, DUDE! YES!
RIGHT BEHIND YOU.
HOOO-LEEEE DANNNG IT-UHHH!
KEEP RIPPIN' IT, MIKE! WE'RE ALMOST THERE!
KTHOOOOSH
CATCH YOU NEVER, YOU TOTAL DUMPSTER FIRES!
WOOOO!
THKOOM

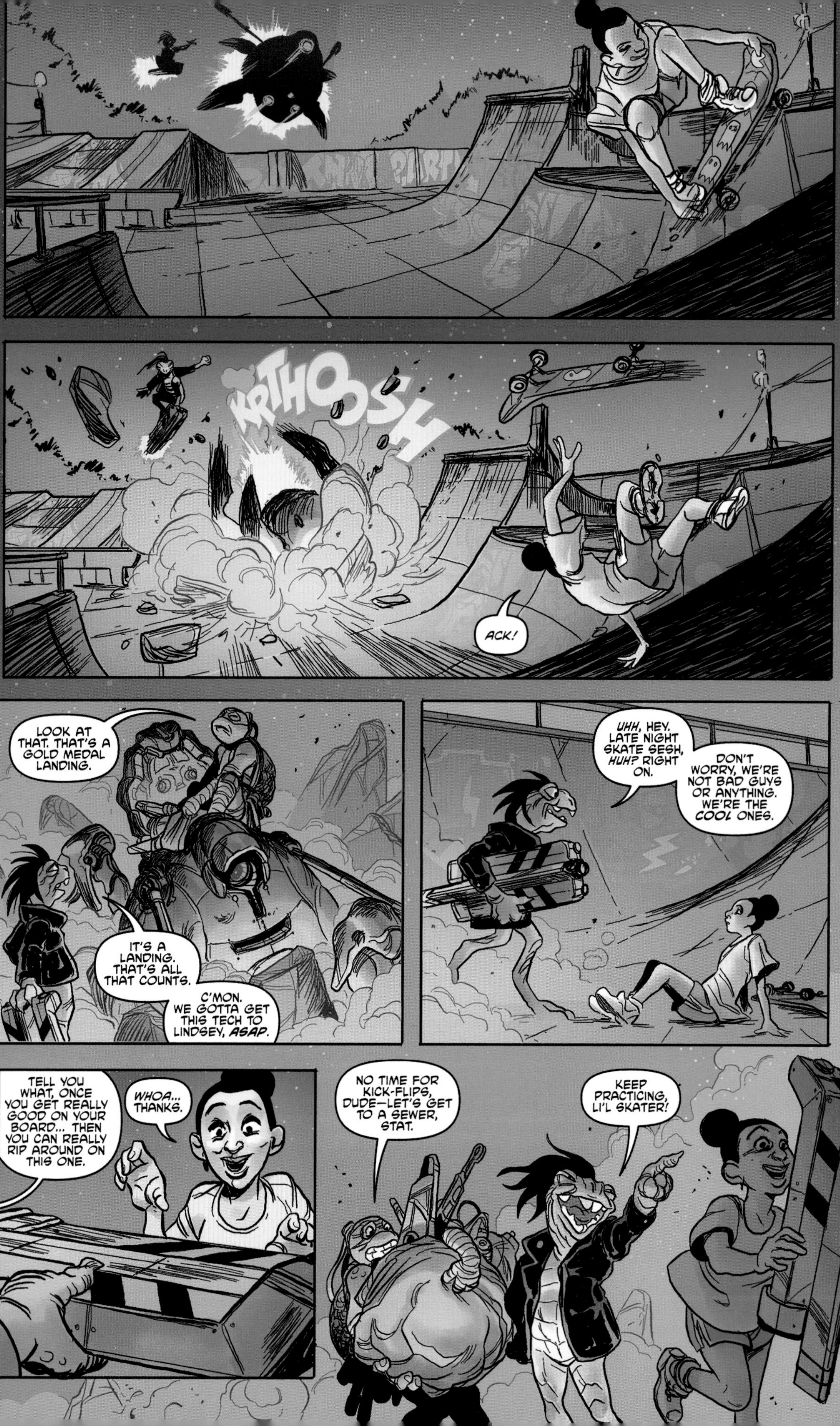
KRTHOOSH
ACK!
LOOK AT THAT. THAT'S A GOLD MEDAL LANDING.
IT'S A LANDING. THAT'S ALL THAT COUNTS.
C'MON. WE GOTTA GET THIS TECH TO LINDSEY, ASAP.
UHH, HEY. LATE NIGHT SKATE SESH, HUH? RIGHT ON.
DON'T WORRY, WE'RE NOT BAD GUYS OR ANYTHING. WE'RE THE COOL ONES.
TELL YOU WHAT, ONCE YOU GET REALLY GOOD ON YOUR BOARD... THEN YOU CAN REALLY RIP AROUND ON THIS ONE.
WHOA... THANKS.
NO TIME FOR KICK-FLIPS, DUDE—LET'S GET TO A SEWER, STAT.
KEEP PRACTICING, LI'L SKATER!

I CAN'T BELIEVE YOU ACTUALLY DID IT.

GOOD TIMING— SEYMOUR DOESN'T HAVE A LOT OF FIGHT IN HIM.

IS HE GONNA...?

I DON'T KNOW. I'LL TRY.

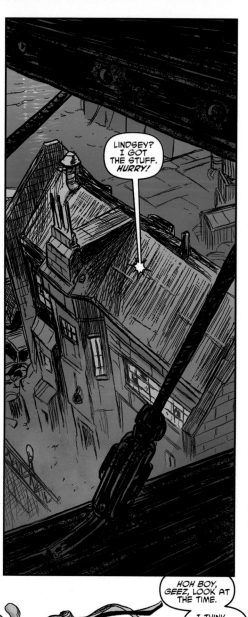

LINDSEY? I GOT THE STUFF. *HURRY!*

WELCOME BACK.

I SEE YOU DID THE *EXACT THING* I TOLD YOU *NOT* TO DO.

HOH BOY, GEEZ, LOOK AT THE TIME.

I THINK... I'LL SEE IF LINDS NEEDS A HAND.

LOOK, HOB. I DON'T WANNA FIGHT WITH YOU ANYMORE.

I GOT THE SUPPLIES. SEYMOUR'S GETTING FIXED.

PROBLEM SOLVED, MAN.

YOU'RE UNDER *MY* ROOF. YOU'LL DO WHAT I SAY OR BEAT YOUR FEET.

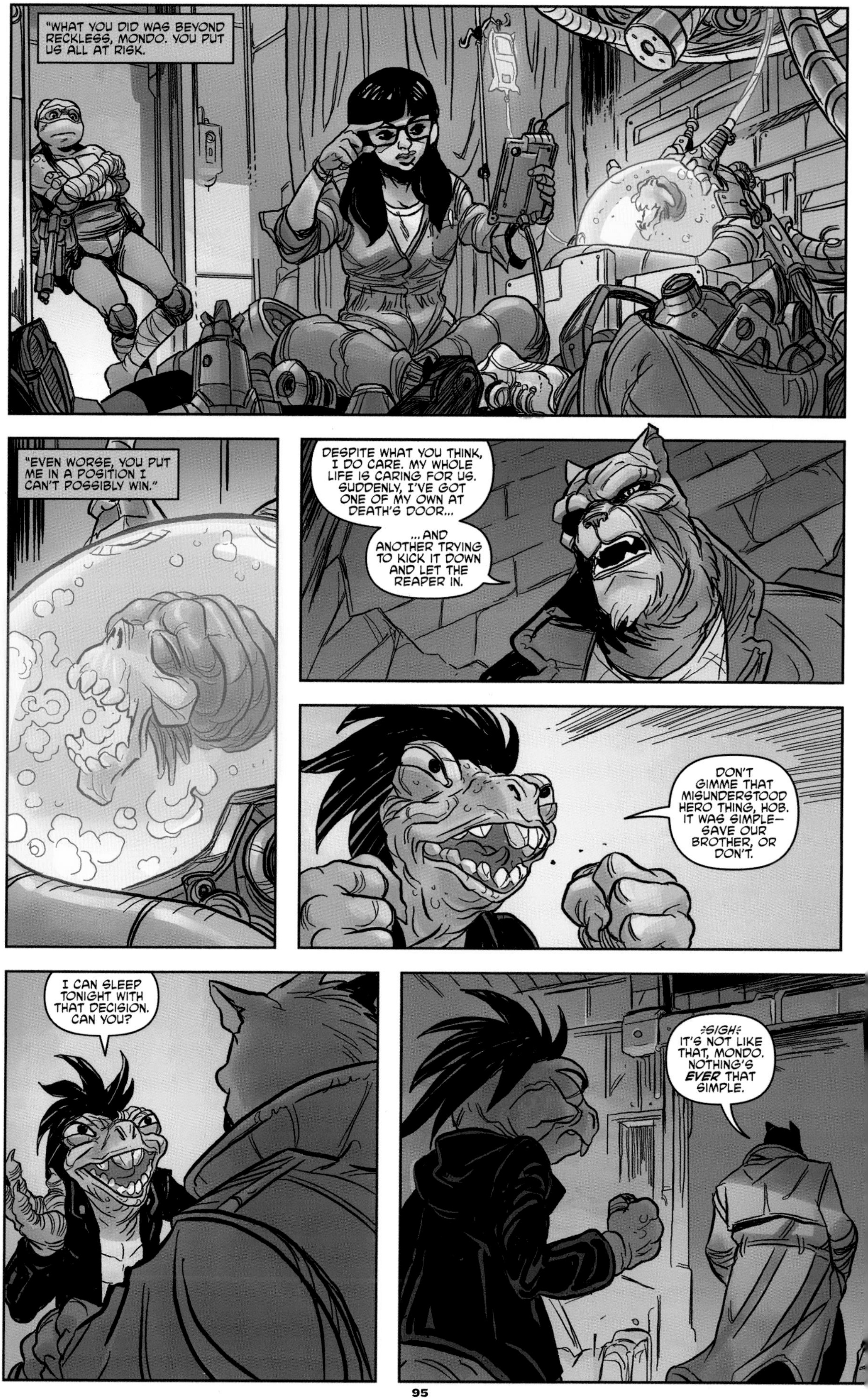
"WHAT YOU DID WAS BEYOND RECKLESS, MONDO. YOU PUT US ALL AT RISK.
"EVEN WORSE, YOU PUT ME IN A POSITION I CAN'T POSSIBLY WIN."
DESPITE WHAT YOU THINK, I DO CARE. MY WHOLE LIFE IS CARING FOR US. SUDDENLY, I'VE GOT ONE OF MY OWN AT DEATH'S DOOR...
...AND ANOTHER TRYING TO KICK IT DOWN AND LET THE REAPER IN.
DON'T GIMME THAT MISUNDERSTOOD HERO THING, HOB. IT WAS SIMPLE— SAVE OUR BROTHER, OR DON'T.
I CAN SLEEP TONIGHT WITH THAT DECISION. CAN YOU?
SIGH
IT'S NOT LIKE THAT, MONDO. NOTHING'S *EVER* THAT SIMPLE.

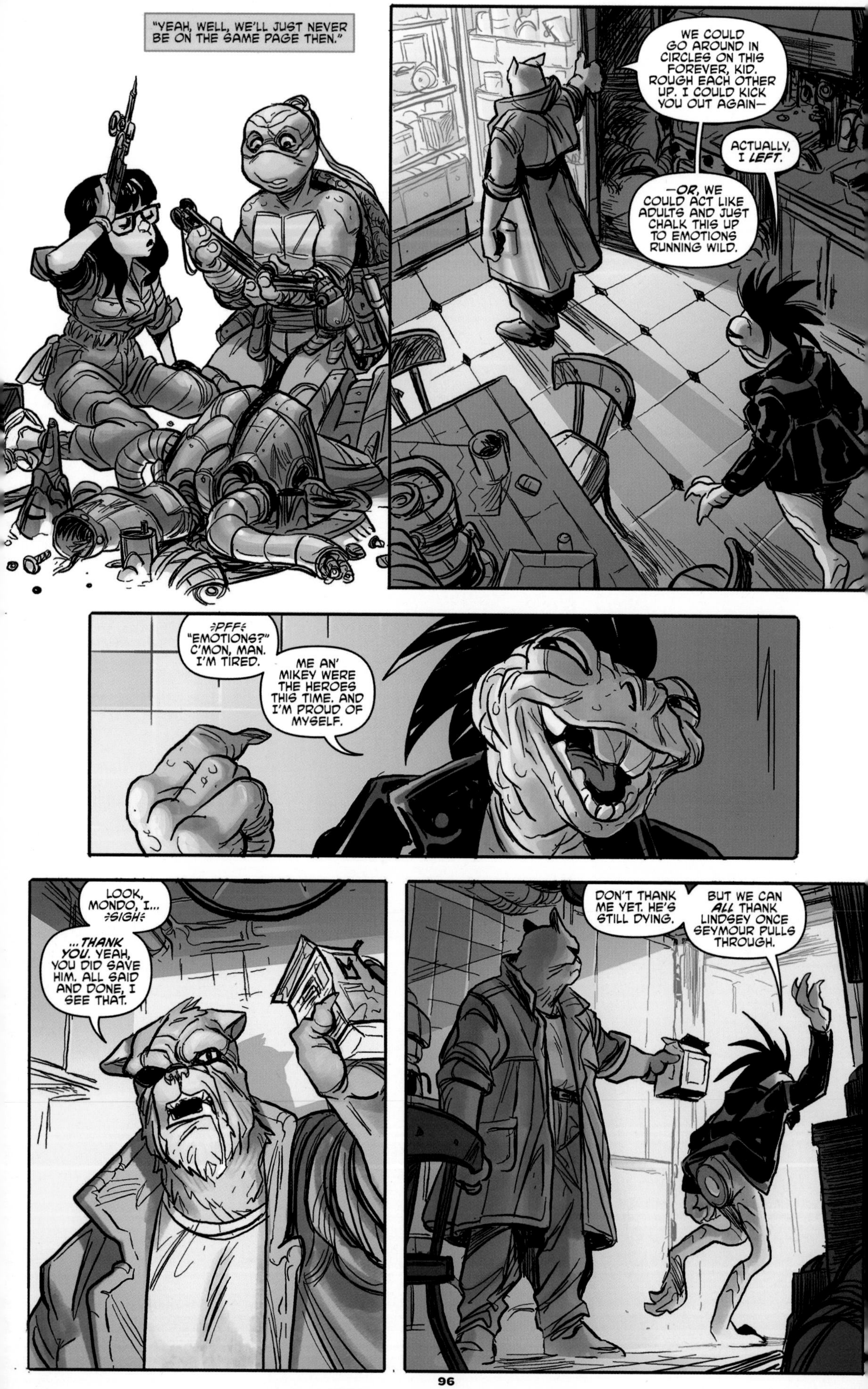

"YEAH, WELL, WE'LL JUST NEVER BE ON THE SAME PAGE THEN."
WE COULD GO AROUND IN CIRCLES ON THIS FOREVER, KID. ROUGH EACH OTHER UP. I COULD KICK YOU OUT AGAIN—
ACTUALLY, I *LEFT*.
—*OR*, WE COULD ACT LIKE ADULTS AND JUST CHALK THIS UP TO EMOTIONS RUNNING WILD.
PFF "EMOTIONS?" C'MON, MAN. I'M TIRED.
ME AN' MIKEY WERE THE HEROES THIS TIME. AND I'M PROUD OF MYSELF.
LOOK, MONDO, I... *SIGH*
...*THANK YOU*. YEAH, YOU DID SAVE HIM. ALL SAID AND DONE, I SEE THAT.
DON'T THANK ME YET. HE'S STILL DYING.
BUT WE CAN *ALL* THANK LINDSEY ONCE SEYMOUR PULLS THROUGH.

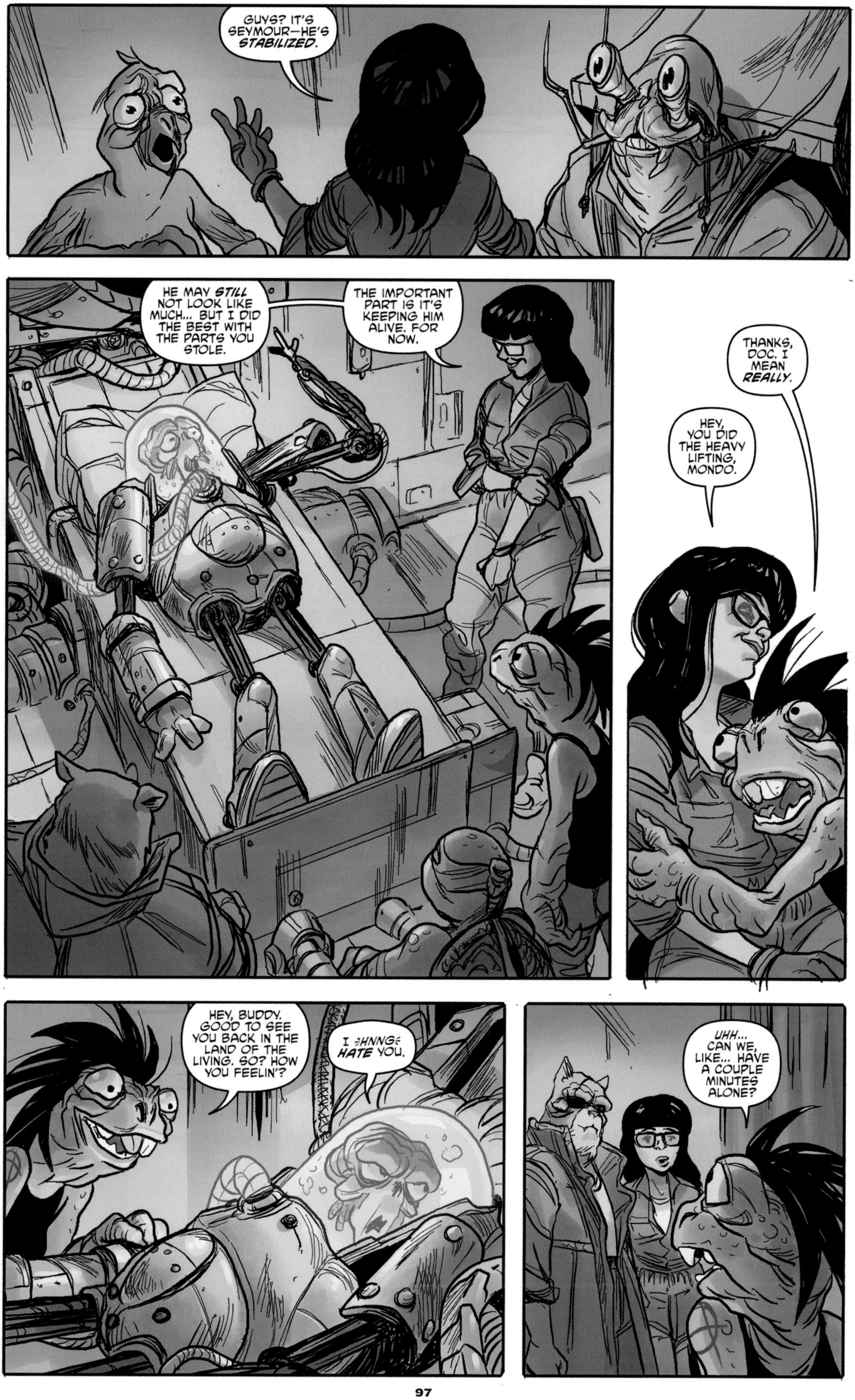
GUYS? IT'S SEYMOUR—HE'S *STABILIZED*.
HE MAY *STILL* NOT LOOK LIKE MUCH... BUT I DID THE BEST WITH THE PARTS YOU STOLE.
THE IMPORTANT PART IS IT'S KEEPING HIM ALIVE. FOR NOW.
THANKS, DOC. I MEAN *REALLY*.
HEY, YOU DID THE HEAVY LIFTING, MONDO.
HEY, BUDDY. GOOD TO SEE YOU BACK IN THE LAND OF THE LIVING. SO? HOW YOU FEELIN'?
I ≶HNNG≶ *HATE* YOU.
UHH... CAN WE, LIKE... HAVE A COUPLE MINUTES ALONE?

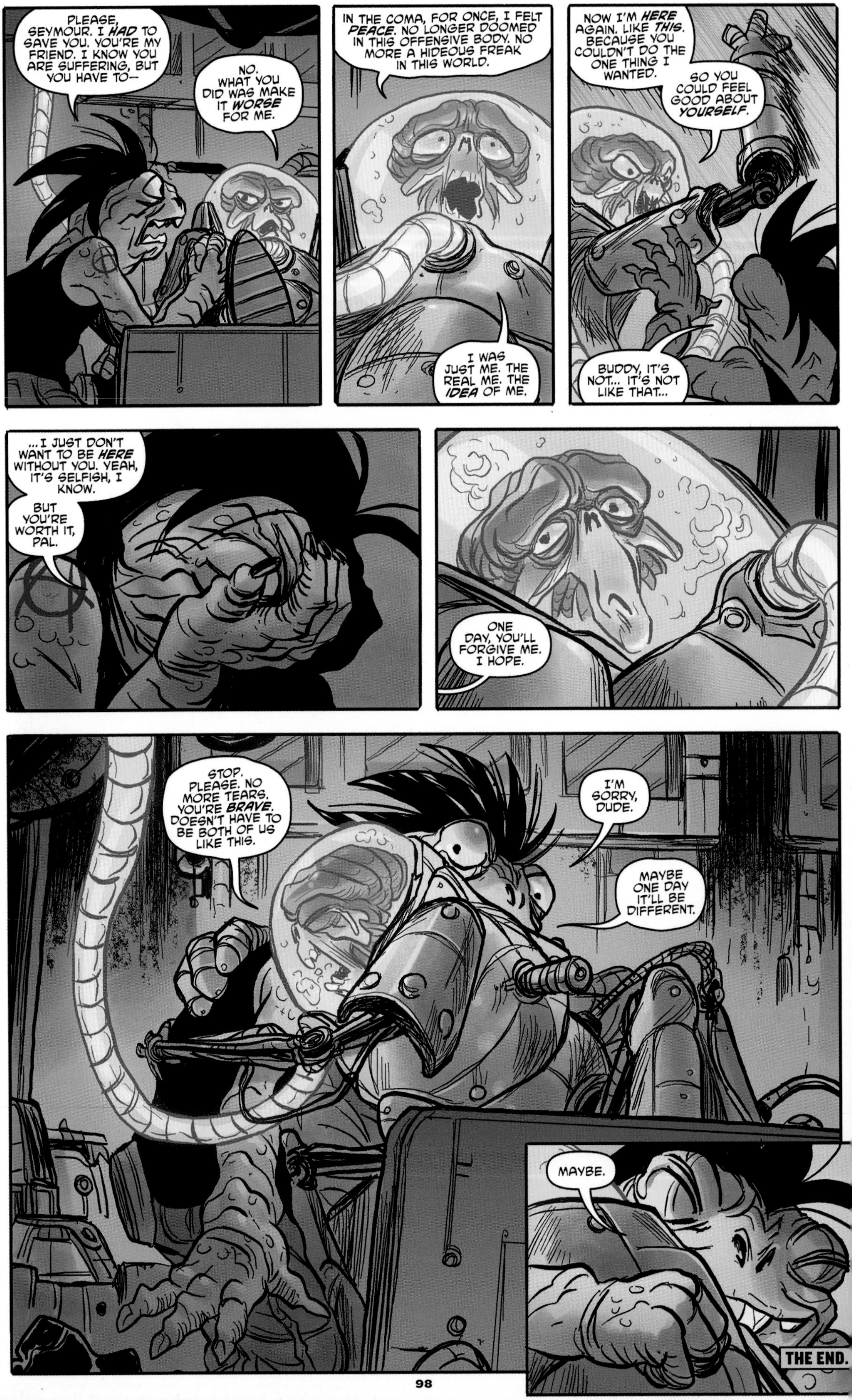
PLEASE, SEYMOUR. I *HAD* TO SAVE YOU. YOU'RE MY FRIEND. I KNOW YOU ARE SUFFERING, BUT YOU HAVE TO—
NO. WHAT YOU DID WAS MAKE IT *WORSE* FOR ME.
IN THE COMA, FOR ONCE, I FELT *PEACE*. NO LONGER DOOMED IN THIS OFFENSIVE BODY. NO MORE A HIDEOUS FREAK IN THIS WORLD.
I WAS JUST ME. THE REAL ME. THE *IDEA* OF ME.
NOW I'M *HERE* AGAIN. LIKE *THIS*. BECAUSE YOU COULDN'T DO THE ONE THING I WANTED.
SO YOU COULD FEEL GOOD ABOUT *YOURSELF*.
BUDDY, IT'S NOT... IT'S NOT LIKE THAT...
...I JUST DON'T WANT TO BE *HERE* WITHOUT YOU. YEAH, IT'S SELFISH, I KNOW.
BUT YOU'RE WORTH IT, PAL.
ONE DAY, YOU'LL FORGIVE ME. I HOPE.
STOP. PLEASE. NO MORE TEARS. YOU'RE *BRAVE*. DOESN'T HAVE TO BE BOTH OF US LIKE THIS.
I'M SORRY, DUDE.
MAYBE ONE DAY IT'LL BE DIFFERENT.
MAYBE.
THE END.

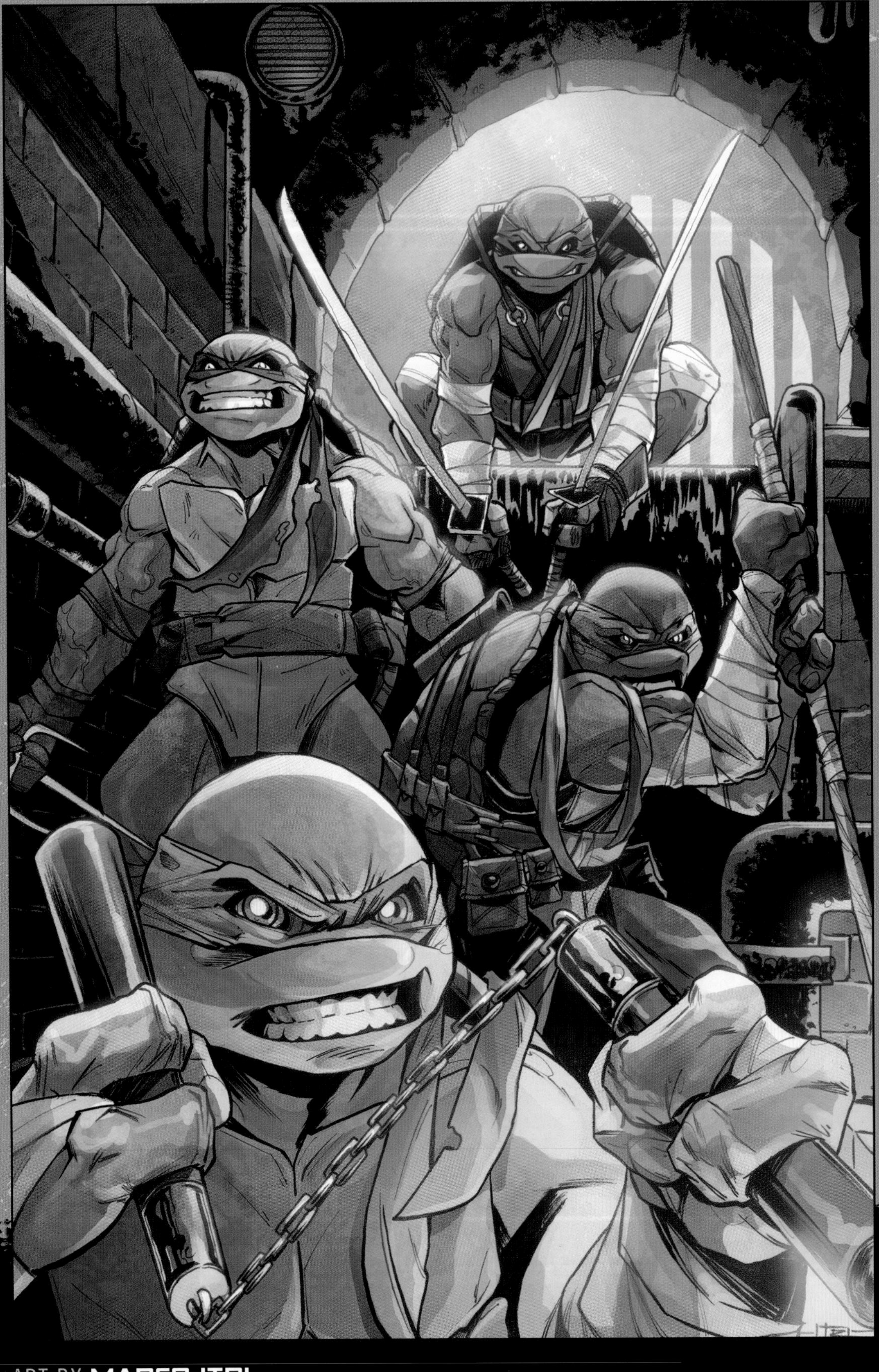

ART BY **MARCO ITRI**
COLORS BY **BRITTANY PEER**

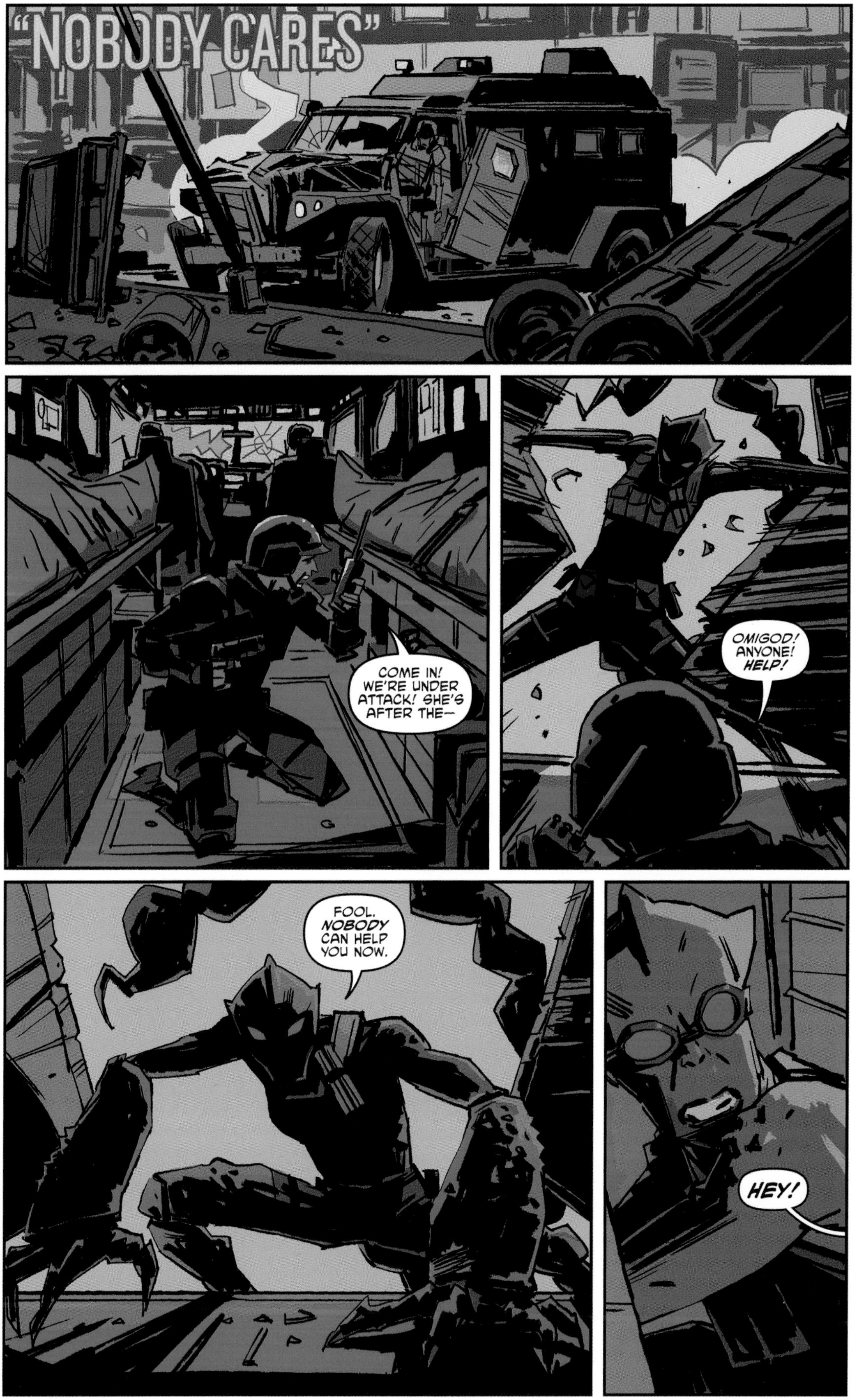
"NOBODY CARES"
COME IN! WE'RE UNDER ATTACK! SHE'S AFTER THE—
OMIGOD! ANYONE! HELP!
FOOL. NOBODY CAN HELP YOU NOW.
HEY!

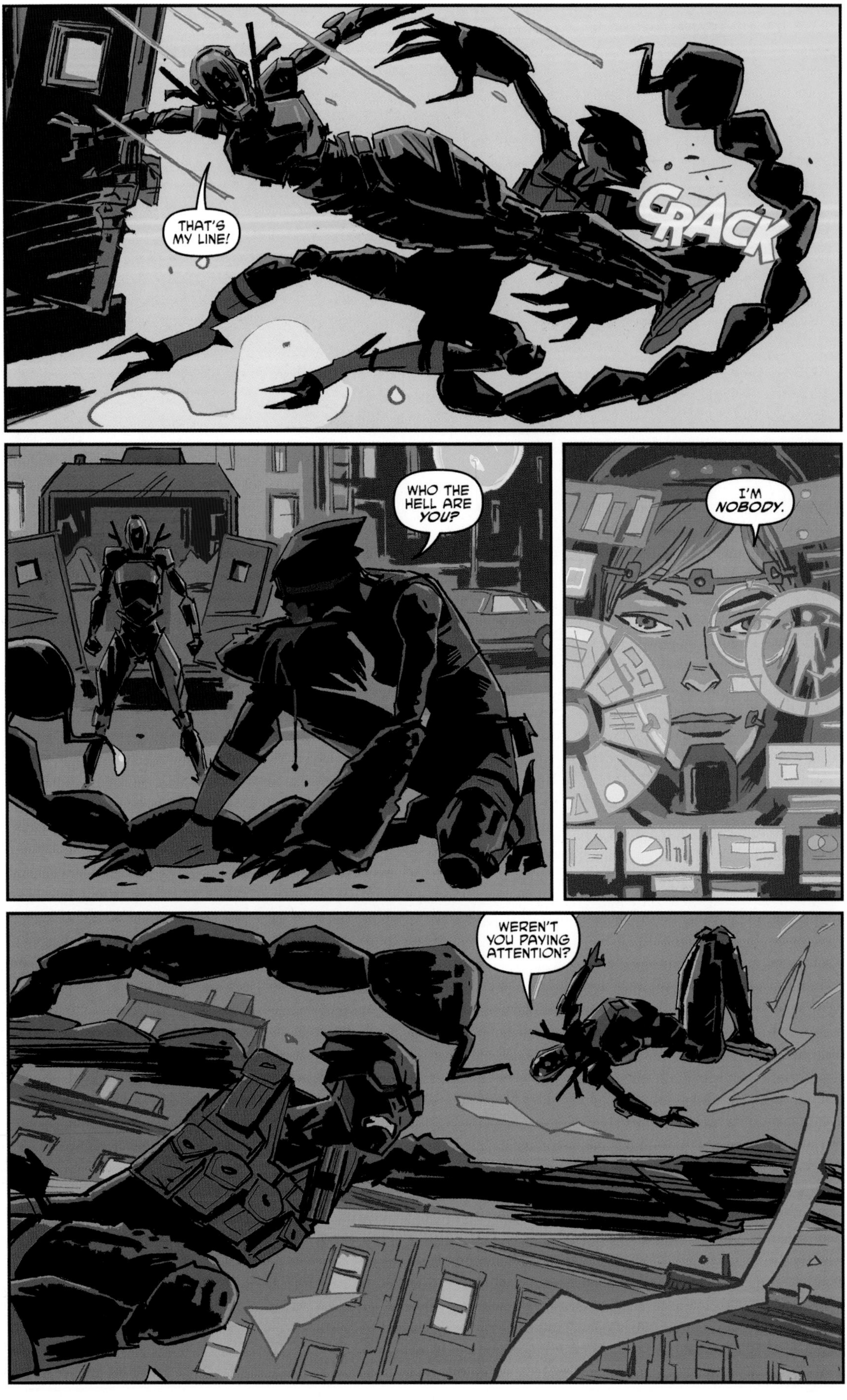
THAT'S MY LINE!
CRACK
WHO THE HELL ARE *YOU?*
I'M *NOBODY.*
WEREN'T YOU PAYING ATTENTION?

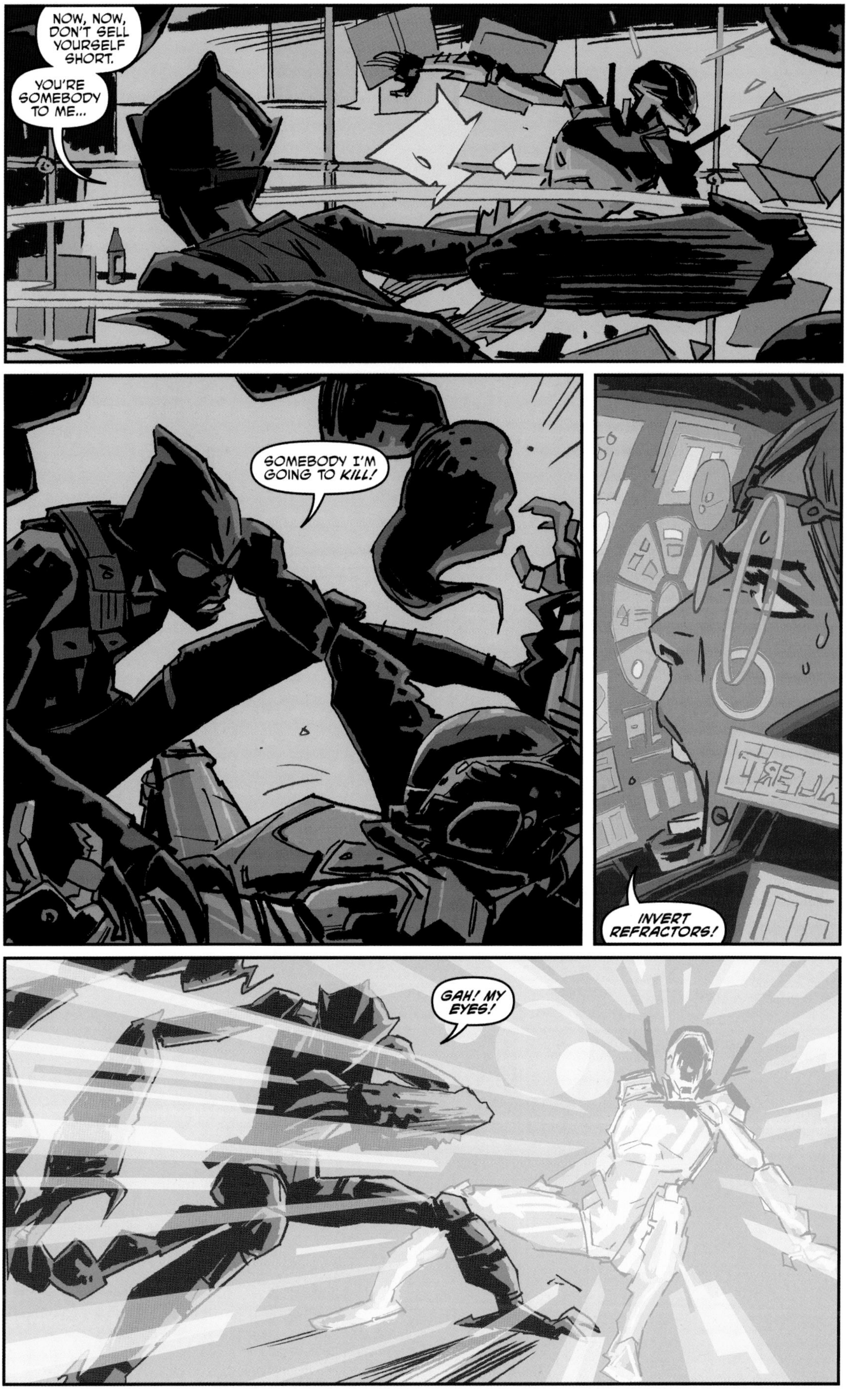
NOW, NOW, DON'T SELL YOURSELF SHORT.
YOU'RE SOMEBODY TO ME...
SOMEBODY I'M GOING TO KILL!
INVERT REFRACTORS!
GAH! MY EYES!

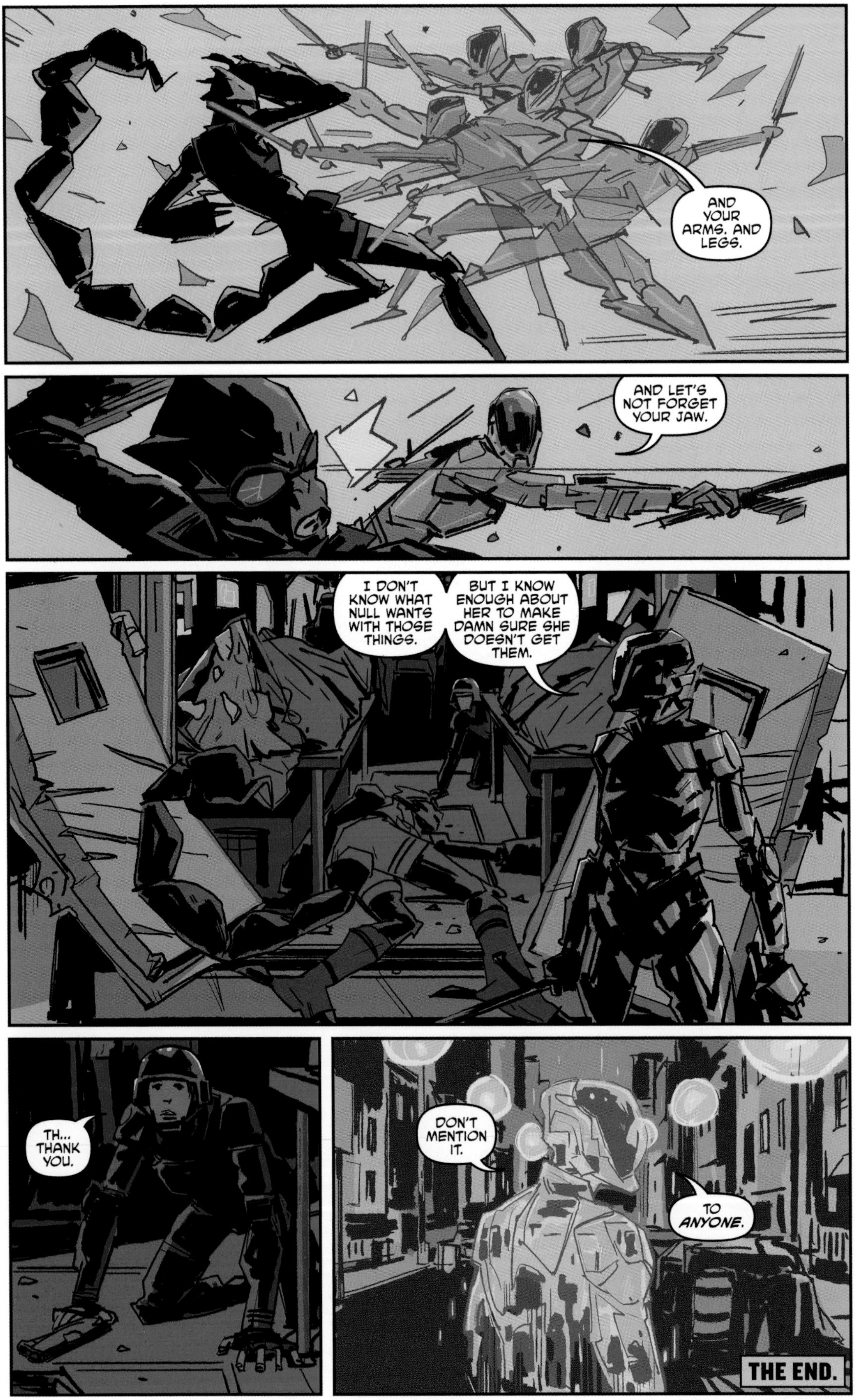
AND YOUR ARMS. AND LEGS.
AND LET'S NOT FORGET YOUR JAW.
I DON'T KNOW WHAT NULL WANTS WITH THOSE THINGS.
BUT I KNOW ENOUGH ABOUT HER TO MAKE DAMN SURE SHE DOESN'T GET THEM.
TH... THANK YOU.
DON'T MENTION IT.
TO *ANYONE*.
THE END.

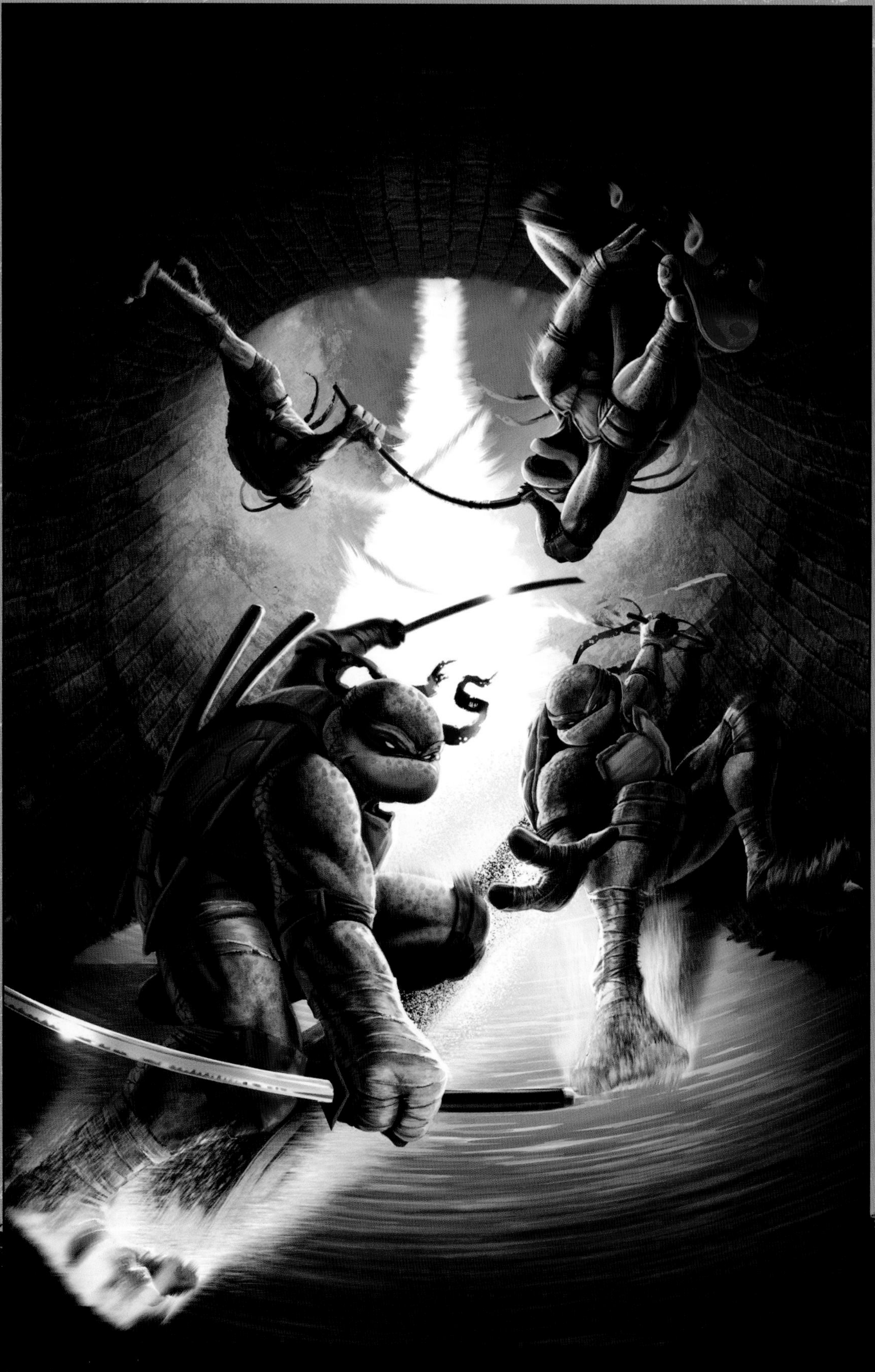

ART BY **TOM VELEZ**

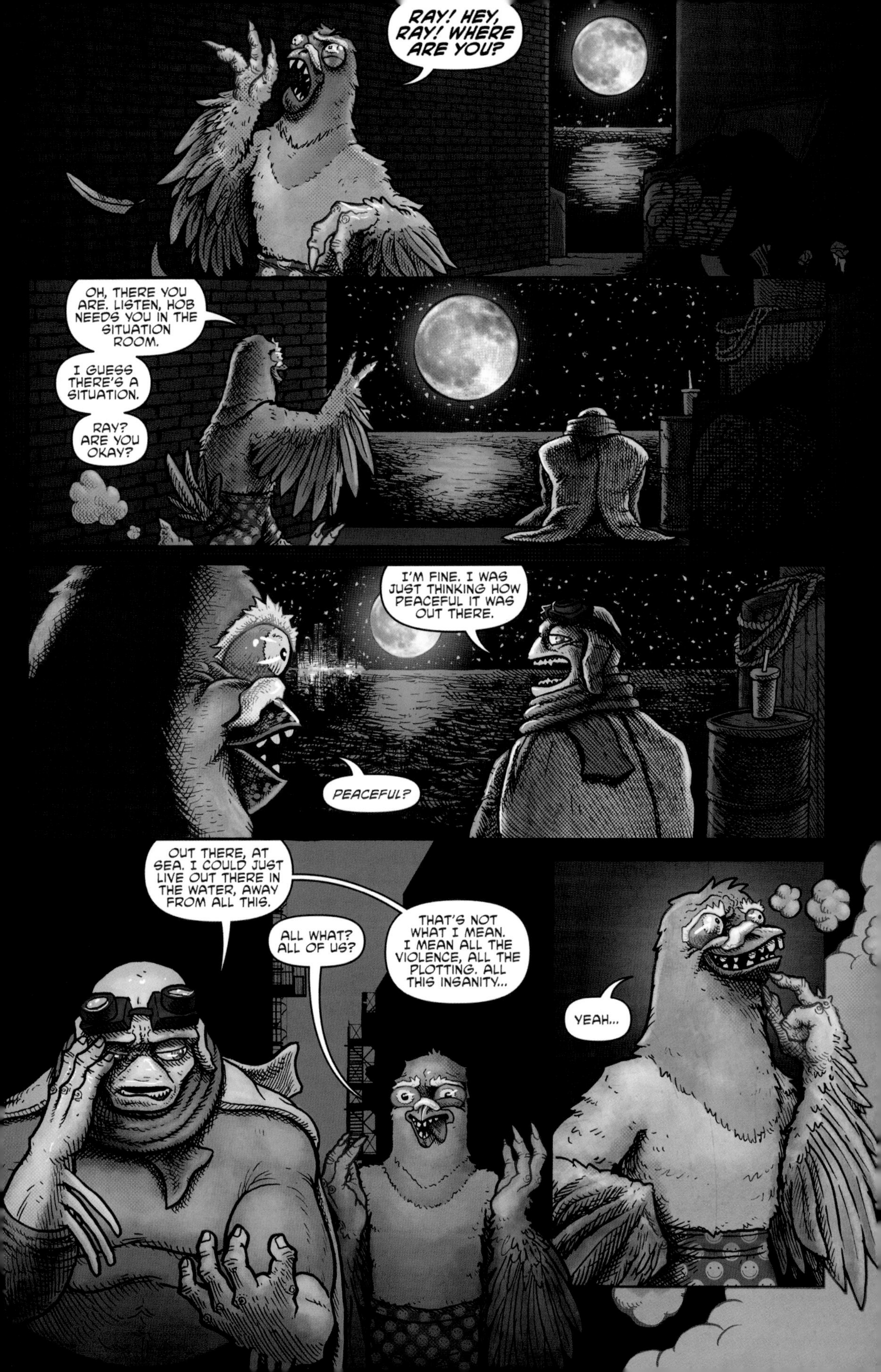
RAY! HEY, RAY! WHERE ARE YOU?
OH, THERE YOU ARE. LISTEN, HOB NEEDS YOU IN THE SITUATION ROOM.
I GUESS THERE'S A SITUATION.
RAY? ARE YOU OKAY?
I'M FINE. I WAS JUST THINKING HOW PEACEFUL IT WAS OUT THERE.
PEACEFUL?
OUT THERE, AT SEA. I COULD JUST LIVE OUT THERE IN THE WATER, AWAY FROM ALL THIS.
ALL WHAT? ALL OF US?
THAT'S NOT WHAT I MEAN. I MEAN ALL THE VIOLENCE, ALL THE PLOTTING. ALL THIS INSANITY...
YEAH...

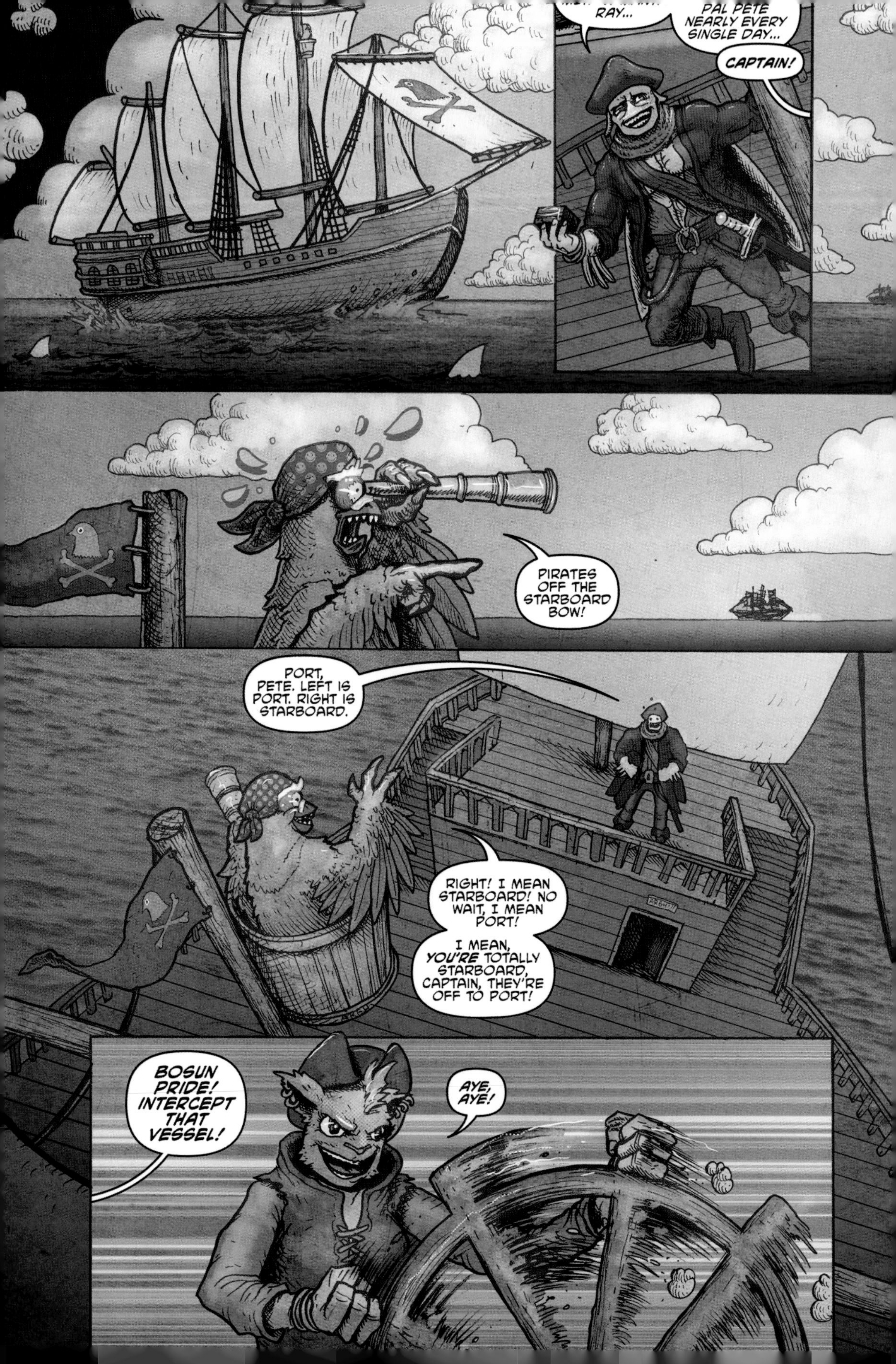
RAY...
PAL PETE NEARLY EVERY SINGLE DAY...
CAPTAIN!
PIRATES OFF THE STARBOARD BOW!
PORT, PETE. LEFT IS PORT. RIGHT IS STARBOARD.
RIGHT! I MEAN STARBOARD! NO WAIT, I MEAN PORT!
I MEAN, *YOU'RE* TOTALLY STARBOARD, CAPTAIN, THEY'RE OFF TO PORT!
BOSUN PRIDE! INTERCEPT THAT VESSEL!
AYE, AYE!

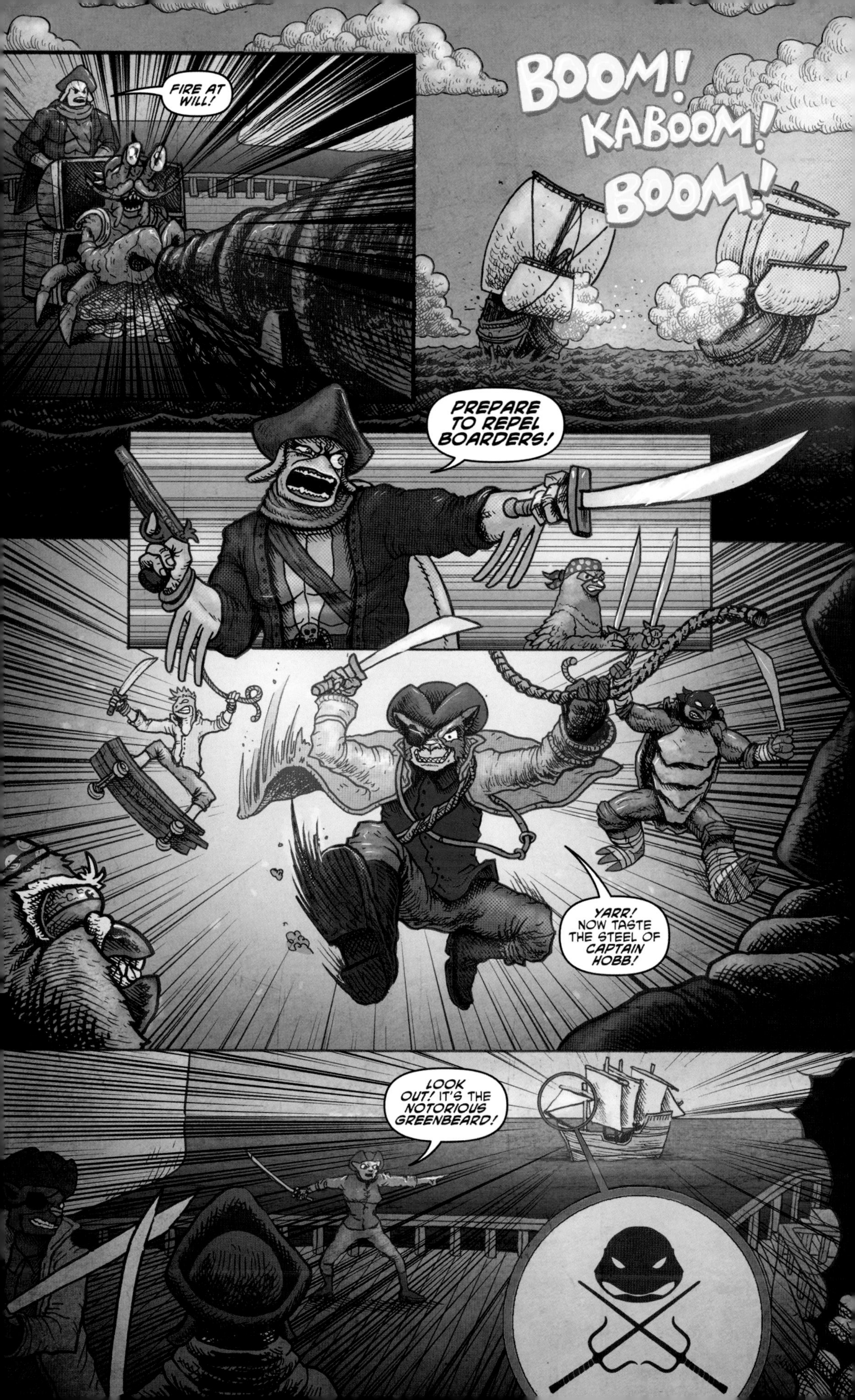
FIRE AT WILL!
BOOM! KABOOM! BOOM!
PREPARE TO REPEL BOARDERS!
YARR! NOW TASTE THE STEEL OF CAPTAIN HOBB!
LOOK OUT! IT'S THE NOTORIOUS GREENBEARD!

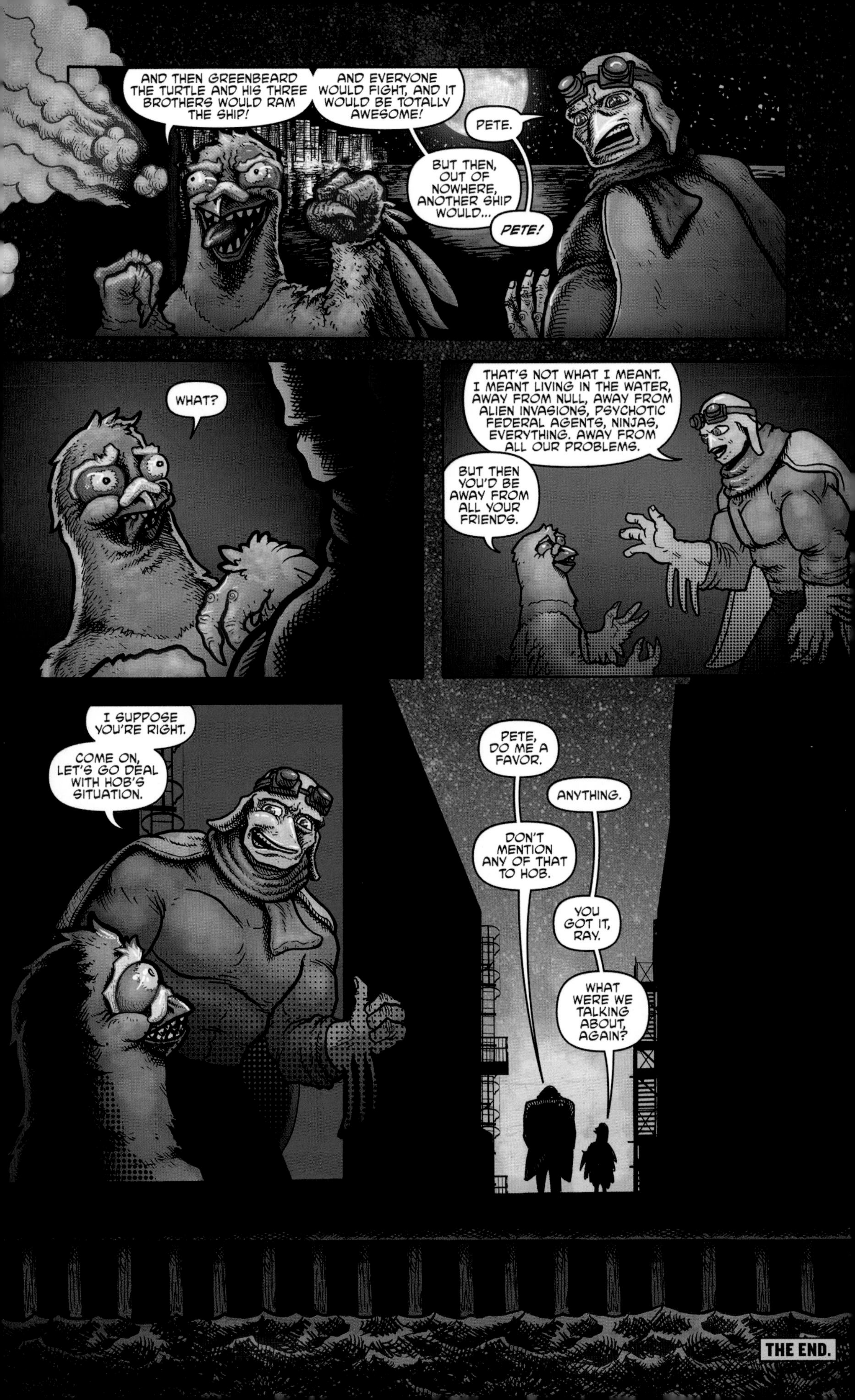
AND THEN GREENBEARD THE TURTLE AND HIS THREE BROTHERS WOULD RAM THE SHIP!
AND EVERYONE WOULD FIGHT, AND IT WOULD BE TOTALLY AWESOME!
PETE.
BUT THEN, OUT OF NOWHERE, ANOTHER SHIP WOULD...
PETE!
WHAT?
THAT'S NOT WHAT I MEANT. I MEANT LIVING IN THE WATER, AWAY FROM NULL, AWAY FROM ALIEN INVASIONS, PSYCHOTIC FEDERAL AGENTS, NINJAS, EVERYTHING. AWAY FROM ALL OUR PROBLEMS.
BUT THEN YOU'D BE AWAY FROM ALL YOUR FRIENDS.
I SUPPOSE YOU'RE RIGHT.
COME ON, LET'S GO DEAL WITH HOB'S SITUATION.
PETE, DO ME A FAVOR.
ANYTHING.
DON'T MENTION ANY OF THAT TO HOB.
YOU GOT IT, RAY.
WHAT WERE WE TALKING ABOUT, AGAIN?
THE END.

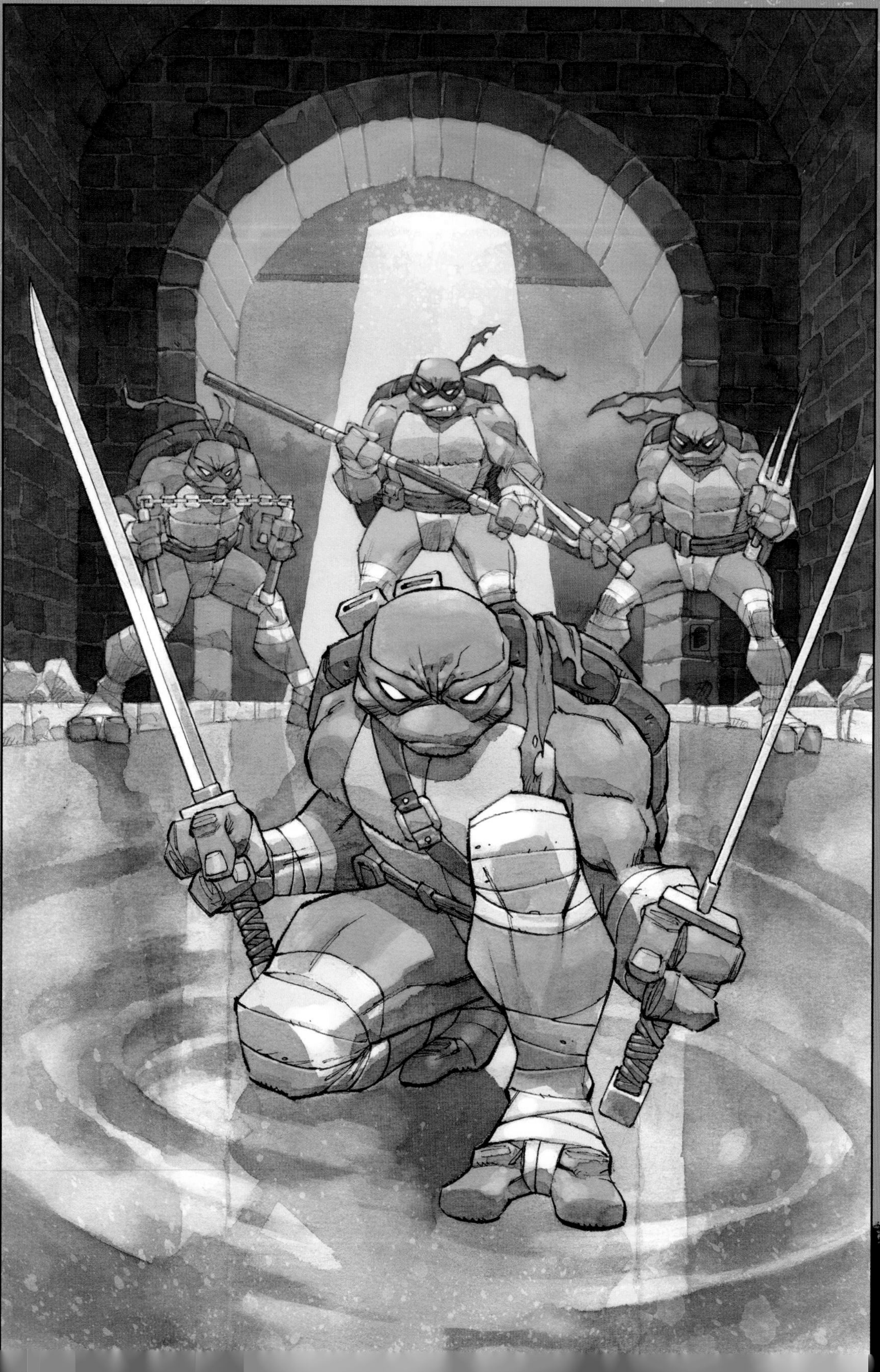

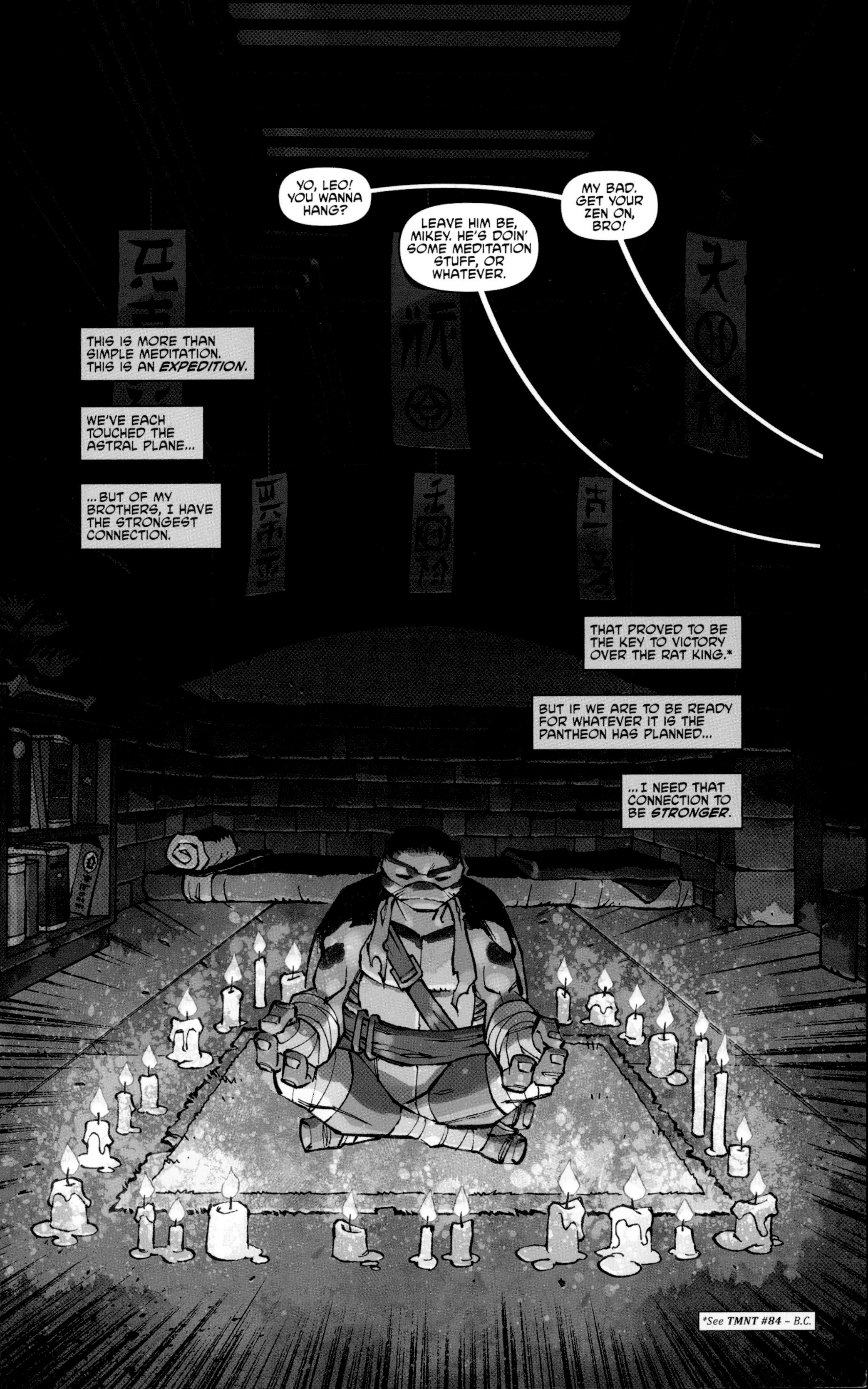
YO, LEO! YOU WANNA HANG?
LEAVE HIM BE, MIKEY. HE'S DOIN' SOME MEDITATION STUFF, OR WHATEVER.
MY BAD. GET YOUR ZEN ON, BRO!
THIS IS MORE THAN SIMPLE MEDITATION. THIS IS AN *EXPEDITION*.
WE'VE EACH TOUCHED THE ASTRAL PLANE...
...BUT OF MY BROTHERS, I HAVE THE STRONGEST CONNECTION.
THAT PROVED TO BE THE KEY TO VICTORY OVER THE RAT KING.*
BUT IF WE ARE TO BE READY FOR WHATEVER IT IS THE PANTHEON HAS PLANNED...
...I NEED THAT CONNECTION TO BE ***STRONGER***.
*See **TMNT #84** – B.C.

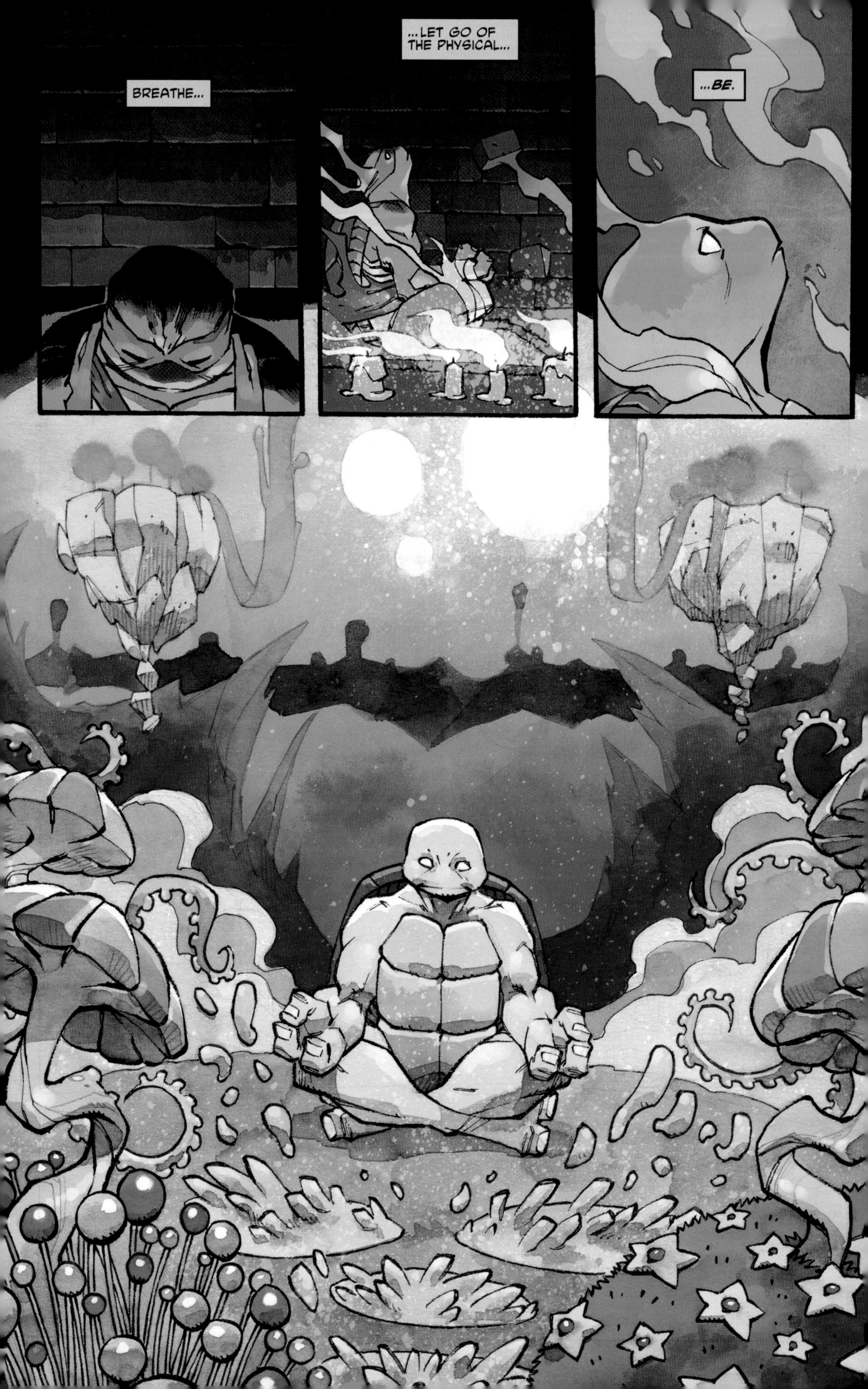
BREATHE...
...LET GO OF THE PHYSICAL...
...BE.

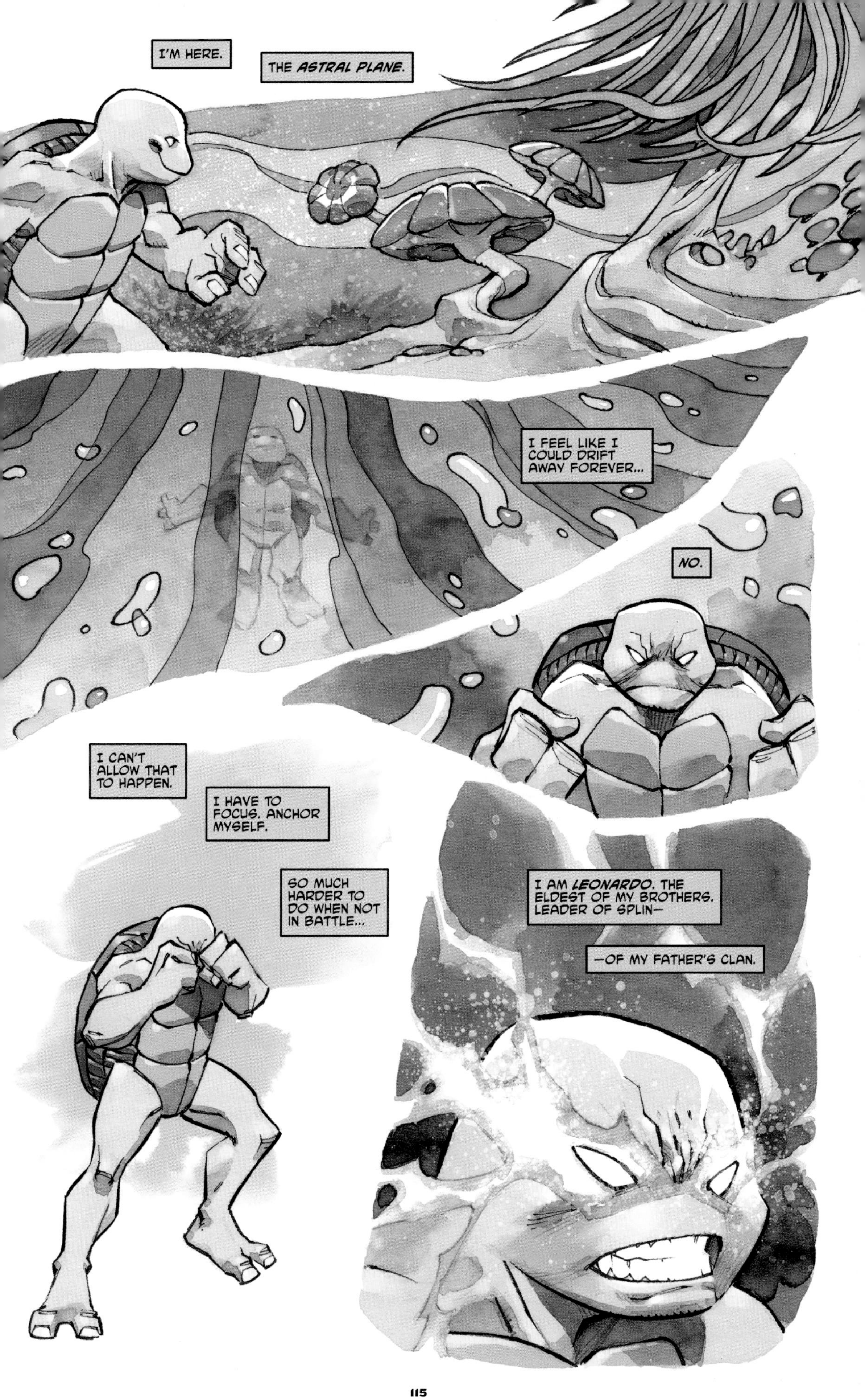
I'M HERE.
THE *ASTRAL PLANE*.
I FEEL LIKE I COULD DRIFT AWAY FOREVER...
NO.
I CAN'T ALLOW THAT TO HAPPEN.
I HAVE TO FOCUS. ANCHOR MYSELF.
SO MUCH HARDER TO DO WHEN NOT IN BATTLE...
I AM *LEONARDO*. THE ELDEST OF MY BROTHERS. LEADER OF SPLIN—
—OF MY FATHER'S CLAN.

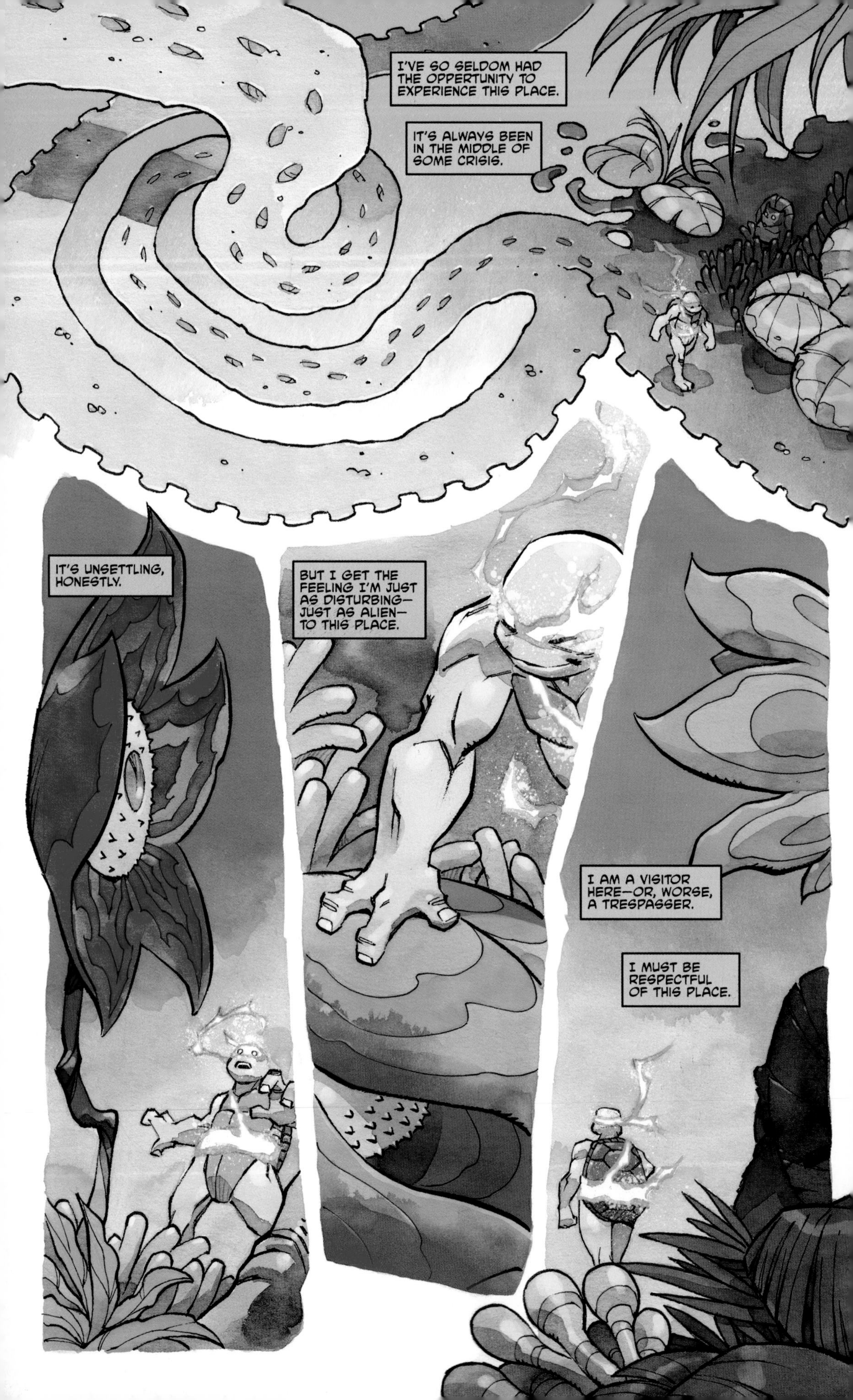
I'VE SO SELDOM HAD THE OPPERTUNITY TO EXPERIENCE THIS PLACE.
IT'S ALWAYS BEEN IN THE MIDDLE OF SOME CRISIS.
IT'S UNSETTLING, HONESTLY.
BUT I GET THE FEELING I'M JUST AS DISTURBING— JUST AS ALIEN— TO THIS PLACE.
I AM A VISITOR HERE—OR, WORSE, A TRESPASSER.
I MUST BE RESPECTFUL OF THIS PLACE.

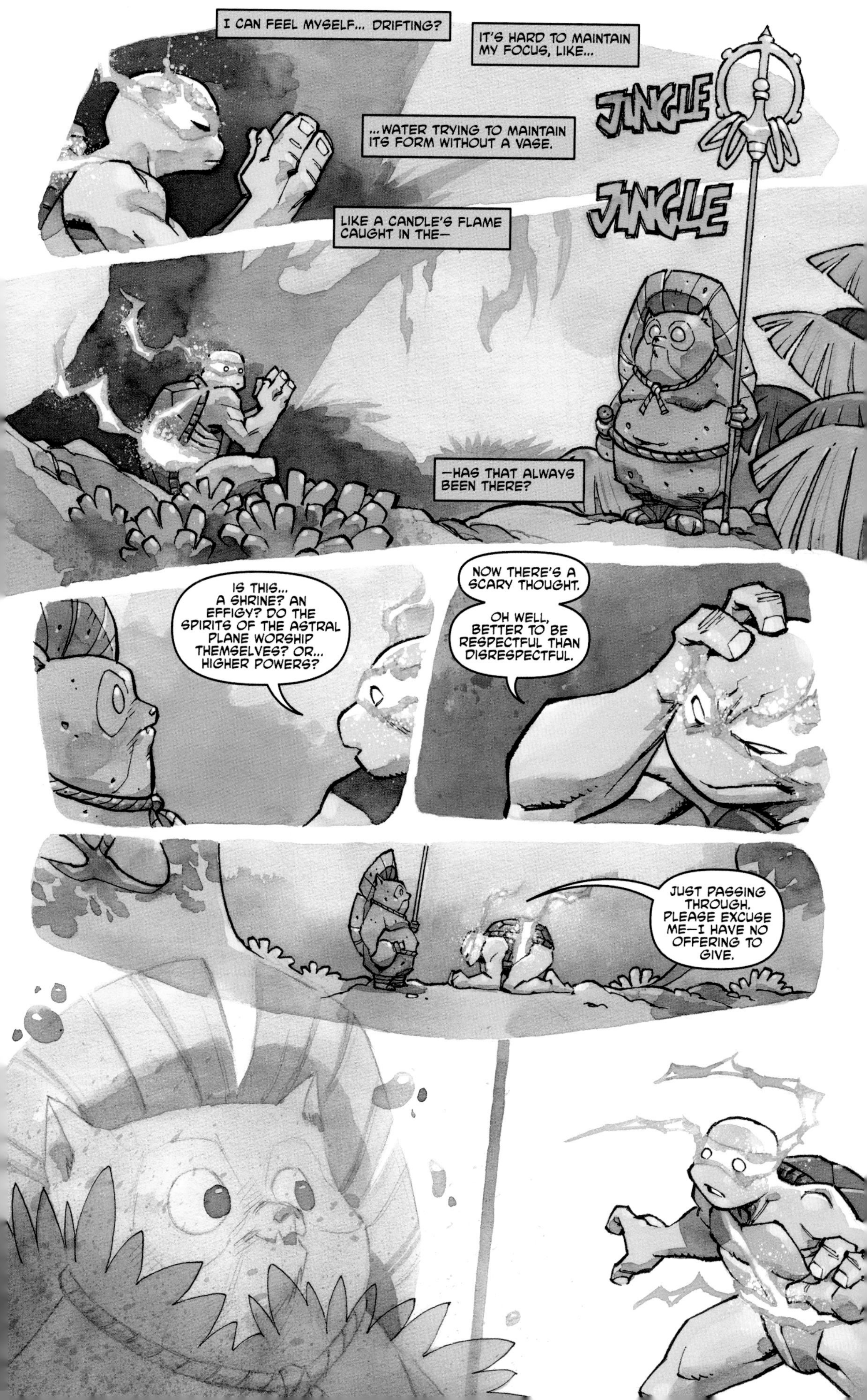
I CAN FEEL MYSELF... DRIFTING?
IT'S HARD TO MAINTAIN MY FOCUS, LIKE...
...WATER TRYING TO MAINTAIN ITS FORM WITHOUT A VASE.
JINGLE
JINGLE
LIKE A CANDLE'S FLAME CAUGHT IN THE—
—HAS THAT ALWAYS BEEN THERE?
IS THIS... A SHRINE? AN EFFIGY? DO THE SPIRITS OF THE ASTRAL PLANE WORSHIP THEMSELVES? OR... HIGHER POWERS?
NOW THERE'S A SCARY THOUGHT.
OH WELL, BETTER TO BE RESPECTFUL THAN DISRESPECTFUL.
JUST PASSING THROUGH. PLEASE EXCUSE ME—I HAVE NO OFFERING TO GIVE.

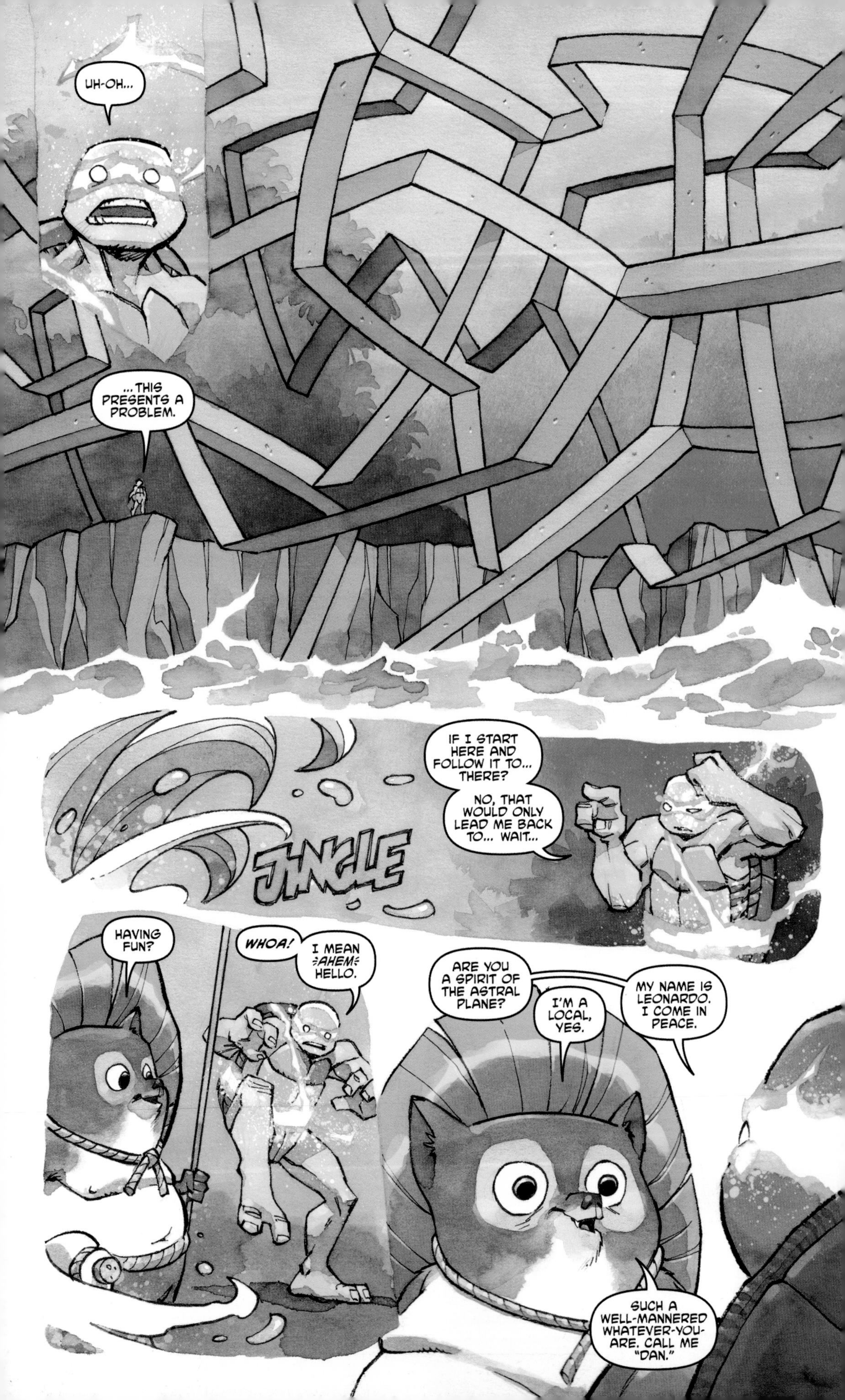
UH-OH...
...THIS PRESENTS A PROBLEM.
IF I START HERE AND FOLLOW IT TO... THERE?
NO, THAT WOULD ONLY LEAD ME BACK TO... WAIT...
JINGLE
HAVING FUN?
WHOA!
I MEAN *AHEM* HELLO.
ARE YOU A SPIRIT OF THE ASTRAL PLANE?
I'M A LOCAL, YES.
MY NAME IS LEONARDO. I COME IN PEACE.
SUCH A WELL-MANNERED WHATEVER-YOU-ARE. CALL ME "DAN."

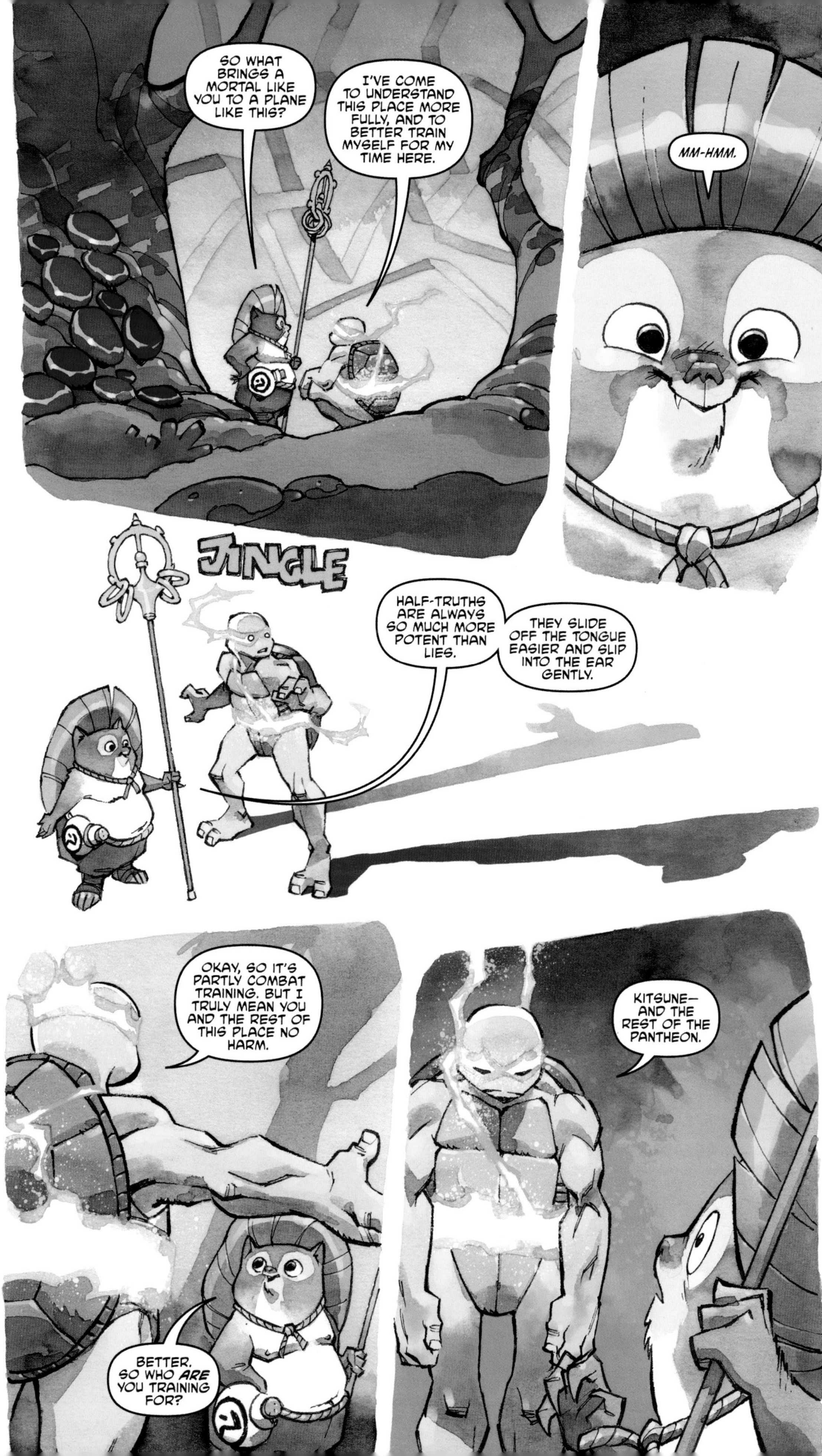
SO WHAT BRINGS A MORTAL LIKE YOU TO A PLANE LIKE THIS?
I'VE COME TO UNDERSTAND THIS PLACE MORE FULLY, AND TO BETTER TRAIN MYSELF FOR MY TIME HERE.
MM-HMM.
JINGLE
HALF-TRUTHS ARE ALWAYS SO MUCH MORE POTENT THAN LIES.
THEY SLIDE OFF THE TONGUE EASIER AND SLIP INTO THE EAR GENTLY.
OKAY, SO IT'S PARTLY COMBAT TRAINING. BUT I TRULY MEAN YOU AND THE REST OF THIS PLACE NO HARM.
BETTER. SO WHO *ARE* YOU TRAINING FOR?
KITSUNE— AND THE REST OF THE PANTHEON.

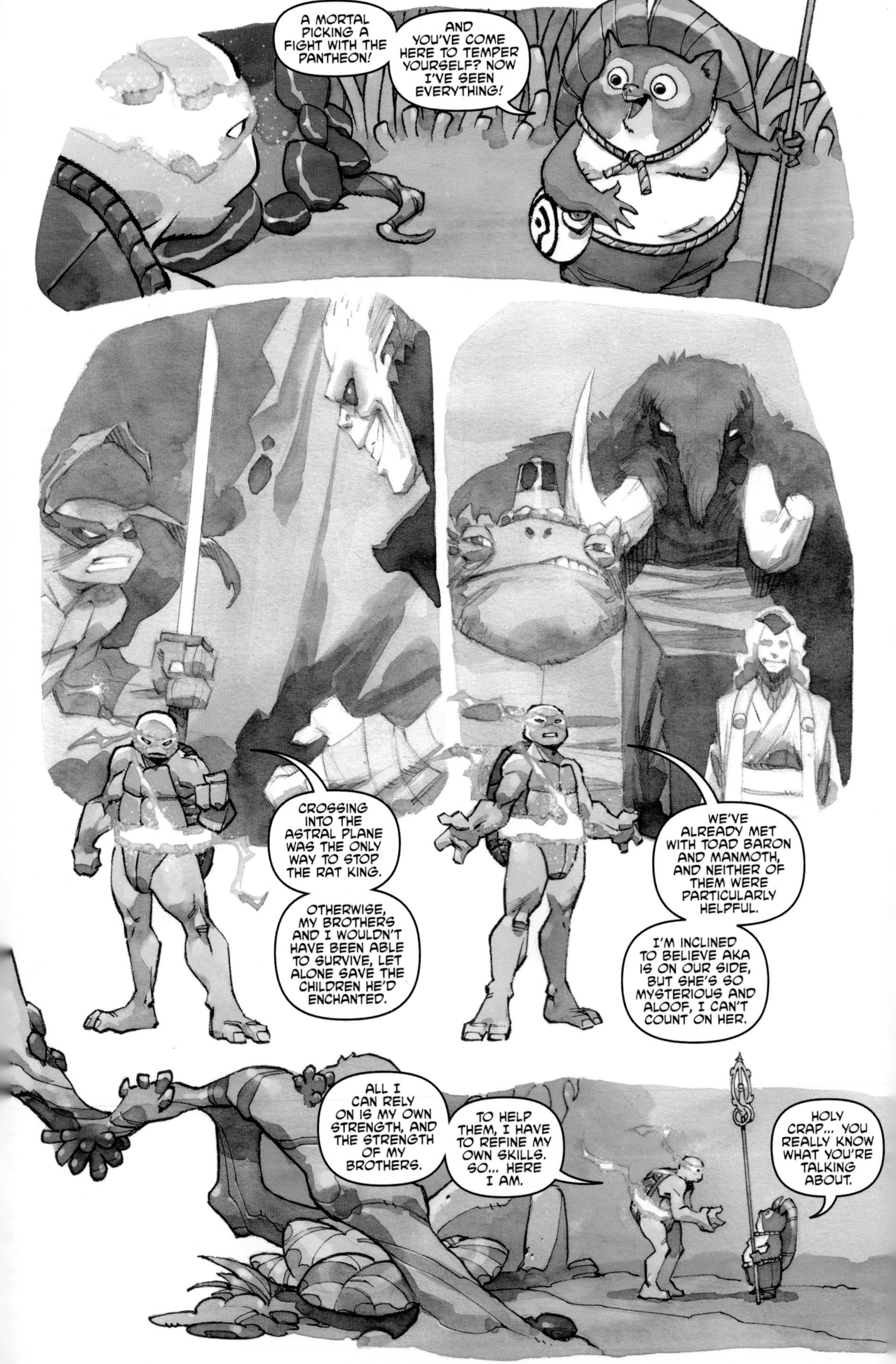
A MORTAL PICKING A FIGHT WITH THE PANTHEON!
AND YOU'VE COME HERE TO TEMPER YOURSELF? NOW I'VE SEEN EVERYTHING!
CROSSING INTO THE ASTRAL PLANE WAS THE ONLY WAY TO STOP THE RAT KING.
OTHERWISE, MY BROTHERS AND I WOULDN'T HAVE BEEN ABLE TO SURVIVE, LET ALONE SAVE THE CHILDREN HE'D ENCHANTED.
WE'VE ALREADY MET WITH TOAD BARON AND MANMOTH, AND NEITHER OF THEM WERE PARTICULARLY HELPFUL.
I'M INCLINED TO BELIEVE AKA IS ON OUR SIDE, BUT SHE'S SO MYSTERIOUS AND ALOOF, I CAN'T COUNT ON HER.
ALL I CAN RELY ON IS MY OWN STRENGTH, AND THE STRENGTH OF MY BROTHERS.
TO HELP THEM, I HAVE TO REFINE MY OWN SKILLS. SO... HERE I AM.
HOLY CRAP... YOU REALLY KNOW WHAT YOU'RE TALKING ABOUT.

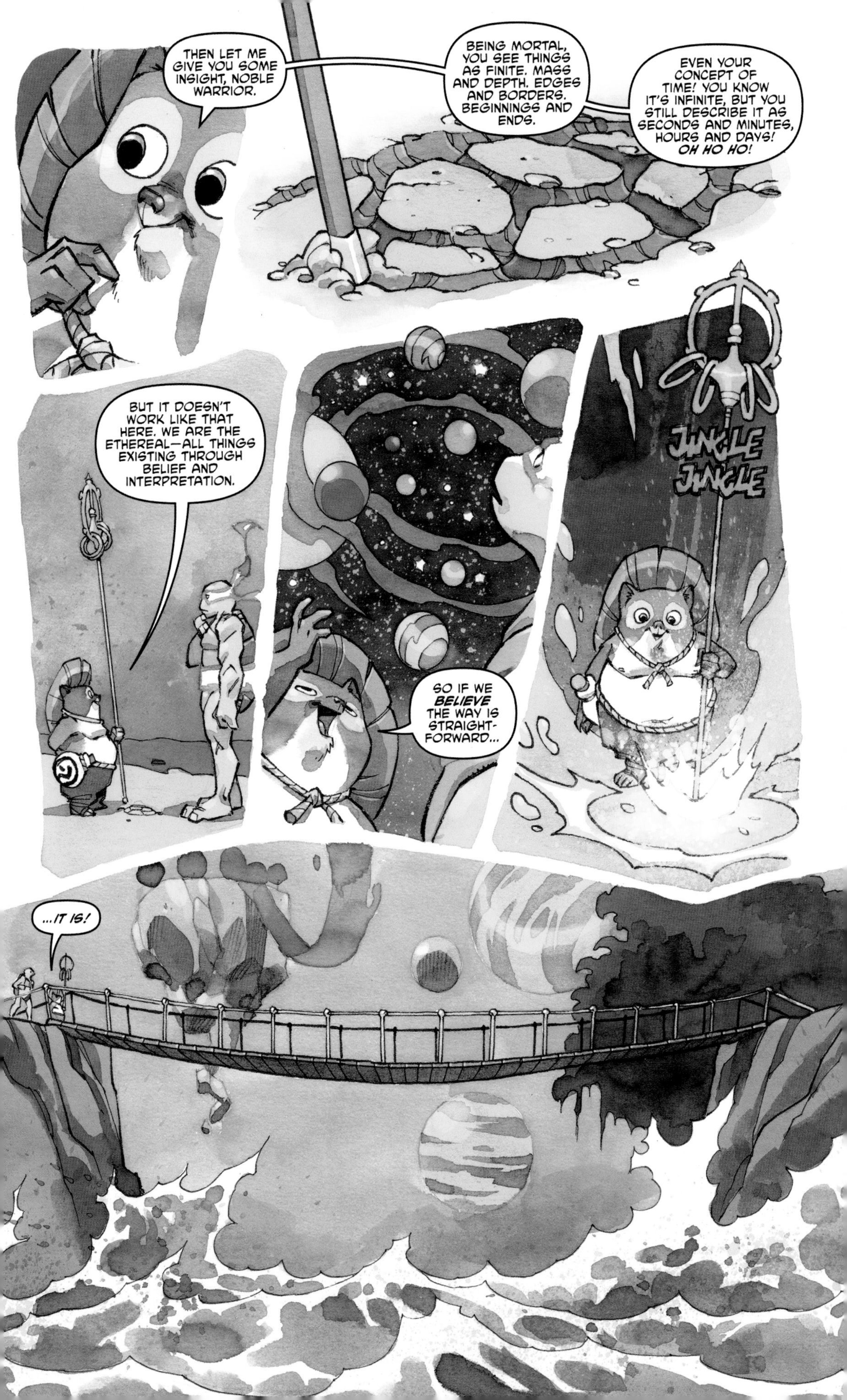

THEN LET ME GIVE YOU SOME INSIGHT, NOBLE WARRIOR.
BEING MORTAL, YOU SEE THINGS AS FINITE. MASS AND DEPTH. EDGES AND BORDERS. BEGINNINGS AND ENDS.
EVEN YOUR CONCEPT OF TIME! YOU KNOW IT'S INFINITE, BUT YOU STILL DESCRIBE IT AS SECONDS AND MINUTES, HOURS AND DAYS! *OH HO HO!*
BUT IT DOESN'T WORK LIKE THAT HERE. WE ARE THE ETHEREAL—ALL THINGS EXISTING THROUGH BELIEF AND INTERPRETATION.
SO IF WE *BELIEVE* THE WAY IS STRAIGHT-FORWARD...
JINGLE JINGLE
...IT IS!

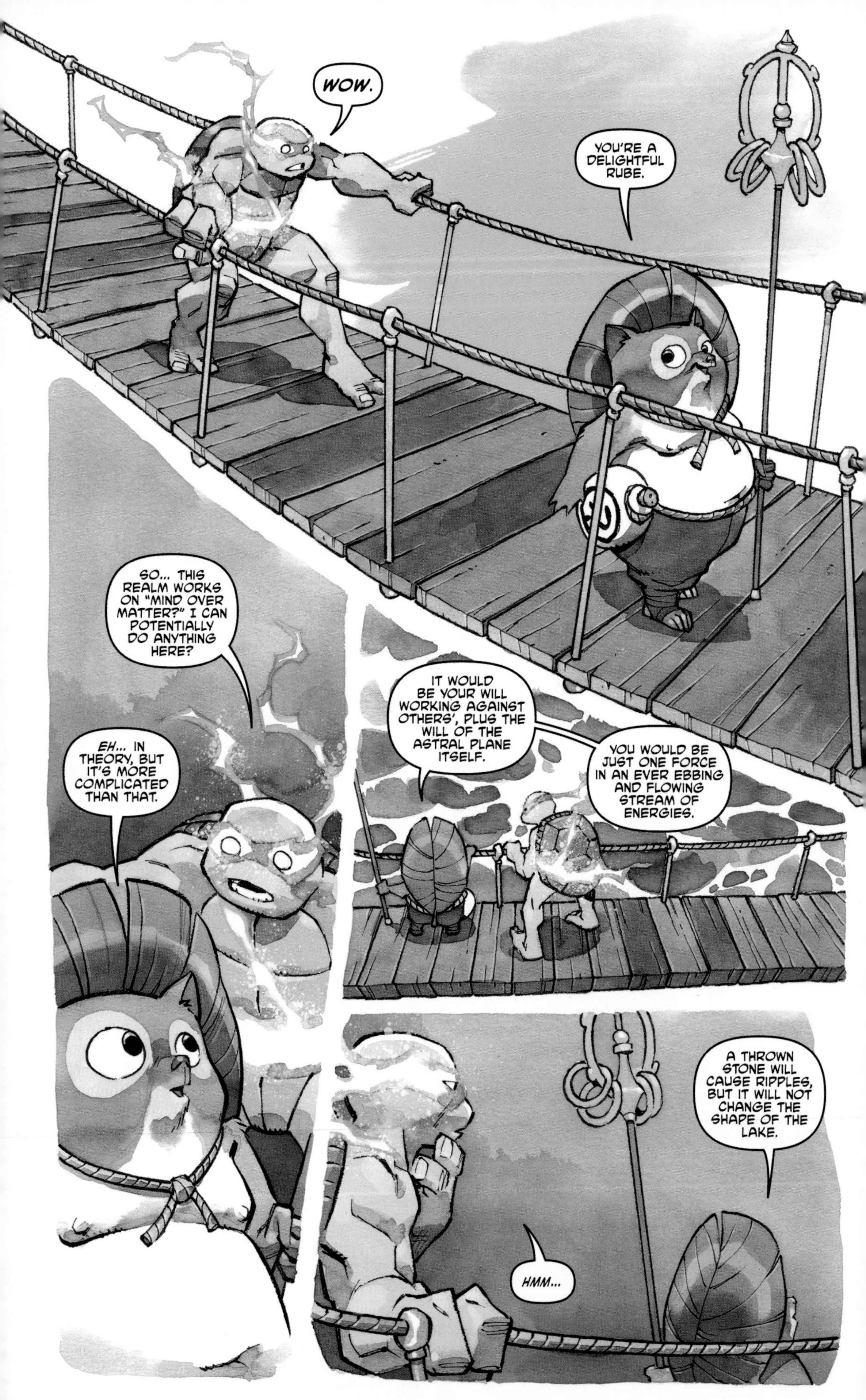
WOW.
YOU'RE A DELIGHTFUL RUBE.
SO... THIS REALM WORKS ON "MIND OVER MATTER?" I CAN POTENTIALLY DO ANYTHING HERE?
EH... IN THEORY, BUT IT'S MORE COMPLICATED THAN THAT.
IT WOULD BE YOUR WILL WORKING AGAINST OTHERS', PLUS THE WILL OF THE ASTRAL PLANE ITSELF.
YOU WOULD BE JUST ONE FORCE IN AN EVER EBBING AND FLOWING STREAM OF ENERGIES.
A THROWN STONE WILL CAUSE RIPPLES, BUT IT WILL NOT CHANGE THE SHAPE OF THE LAKE.
HMM...

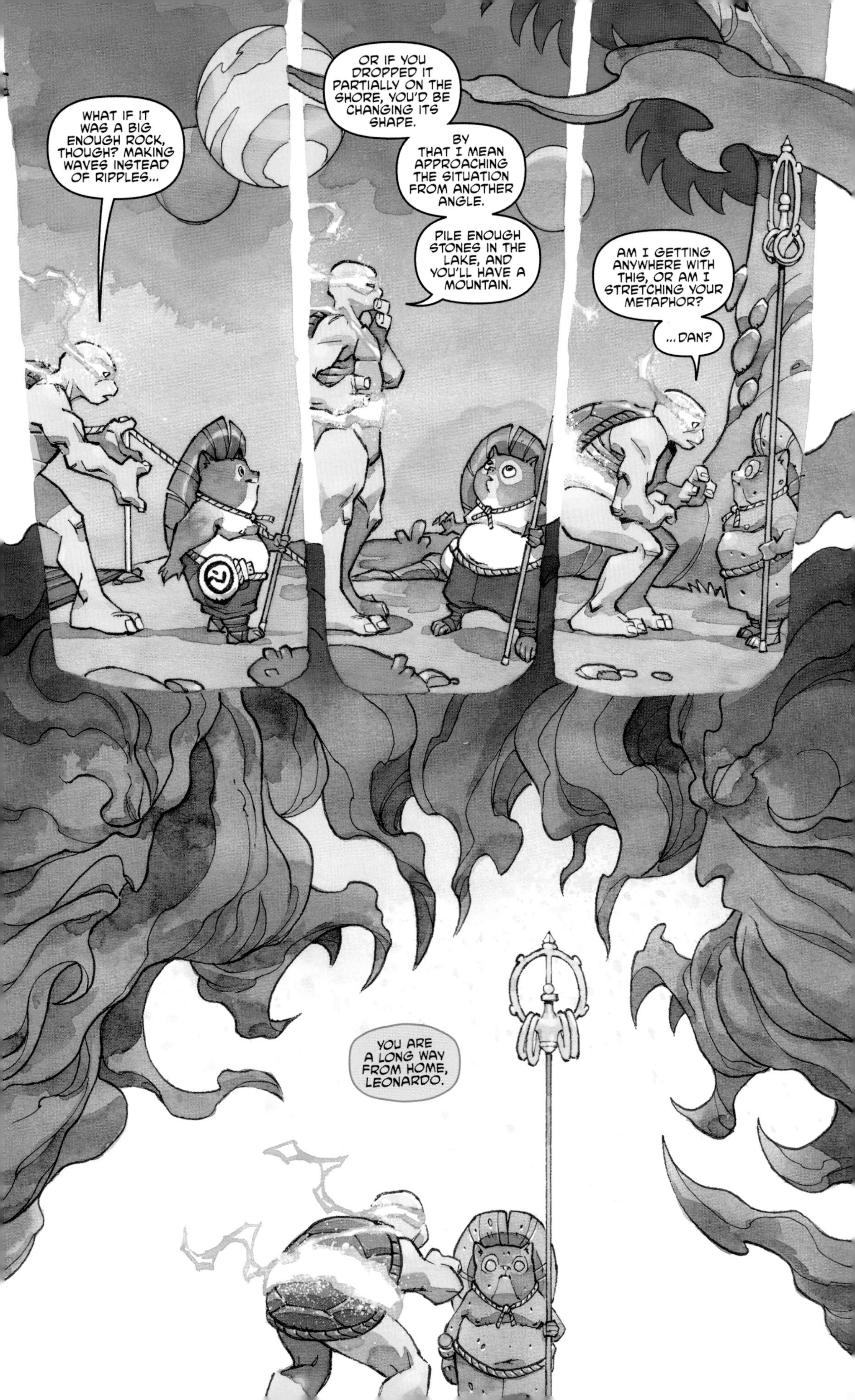
WHAT IF IT WAS A BIG ENOUGH ROCK, THOUGH? MAKING WAVES INSTEAD OF RIPPLES...
OR IF YOU DROPPED IT PARTIALLY ON THE SHORE, YOU'D BE CHANGING ITS SHAPE.
BY THAT I MEAN APPROACHING THE SITUATION FROM ANOTHER ANGLE.
PILE ENOUGH STONES IN THE LAKE, AND YOU'LL HAVE A MOUNTAIN.
AM I GETTING ANYWHERE WITH THIS, OR AM I STRETCHING YOUR METAPHOR?
...DAN?
YOU ARE A LONG WAY FROM HOME, LEONARDO.

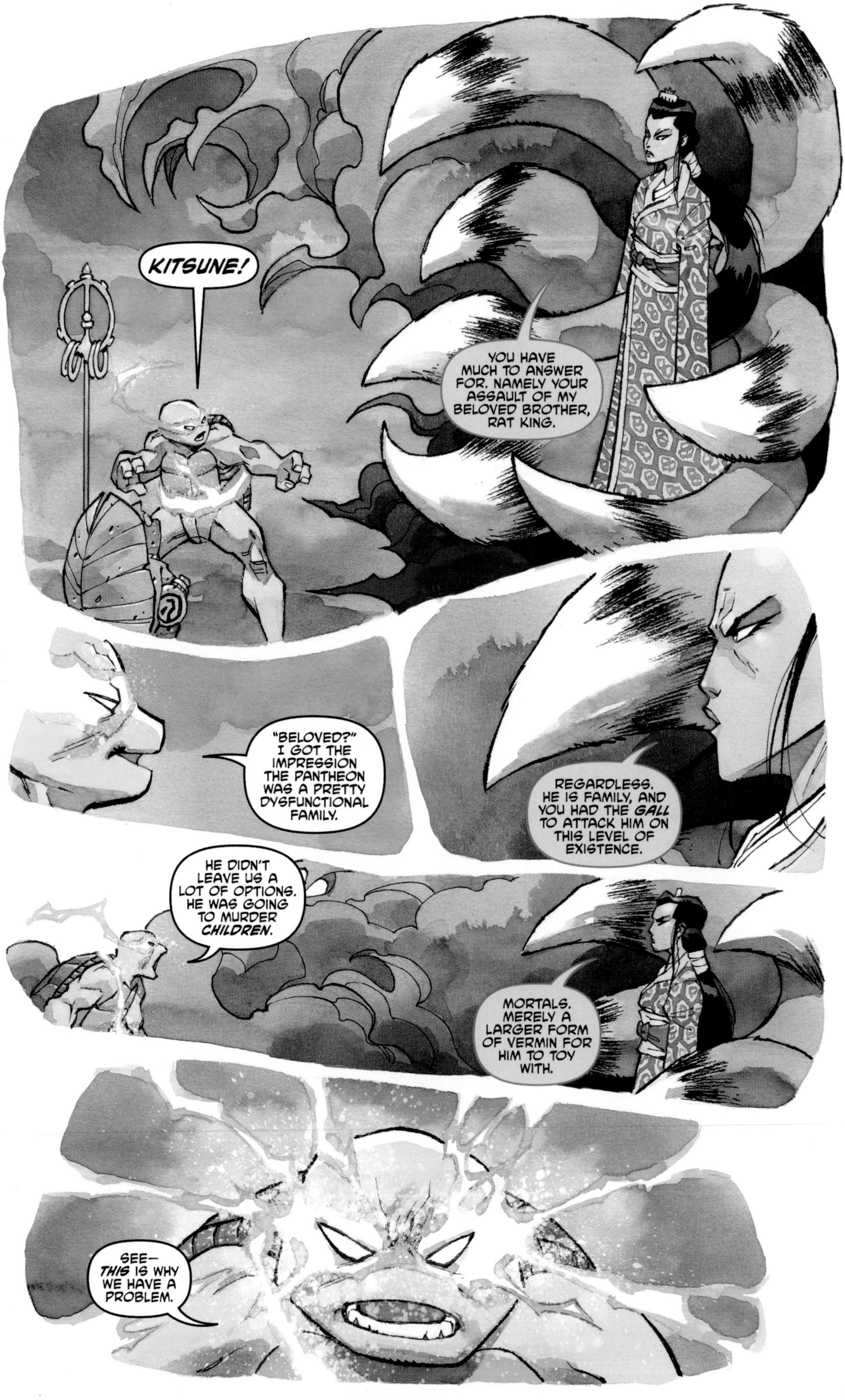
KITSUNE!
YOU HAVE MUCH TO ANSWER FOR. NAMELY YOUR ASSAULT OF MY BELOVED BROTHER, RAT KING.
"BELOVED?" I GOT THE IMPRESSION THE PANTHEON WAS A PRETTY DYSFUNCTIONAL FAMILY.
REGARDLESS. HE IS FAMILY, AND YOU HAD THE GALL TO ATTACK HIM ON THIS LEVEL OF EXISTENCE.
HE DIDN'T LEAVE US A LOT OF OPTIONS. HE WAS GOING TO MURDER CHILDREN.
MORTALS. MERELY A LARGER FORM OF VERMIN FOR HIM TO TOY WITH.
SEE— THIS IS WHY WE HAVE A PROBLEM.

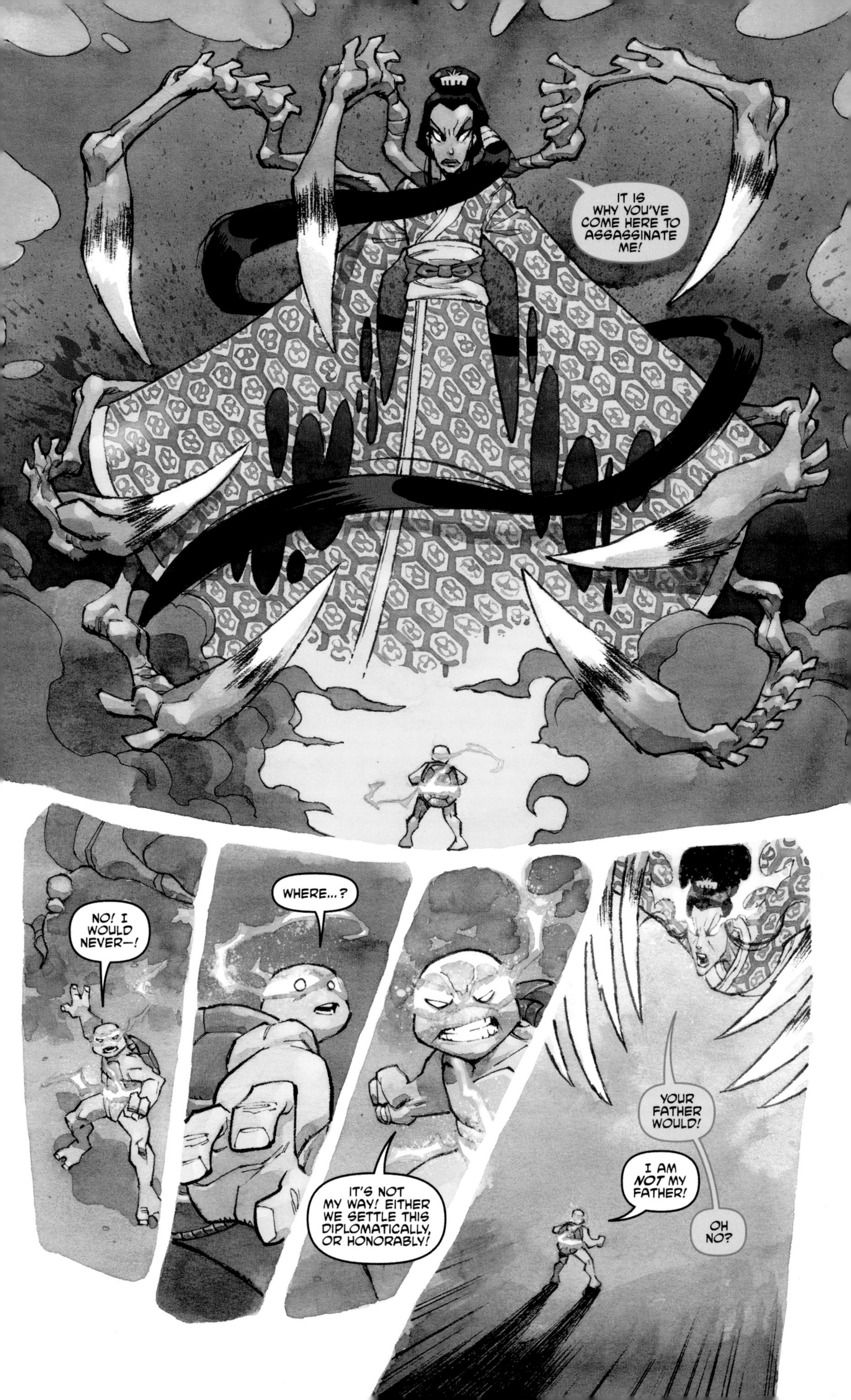
IT IS WHY YOU'VE COME HERE TO ASSASSINATE ME!
NO! I WOULD NEVER—!
WHERE...?
IT'S NOT MY WAY! EITHER WE SETTLE THIS DIPLOMATICALLY, OR HONORABLY!
YOUR FATHER WOULD!
I AM NOT MY FATHER!
OH NO?

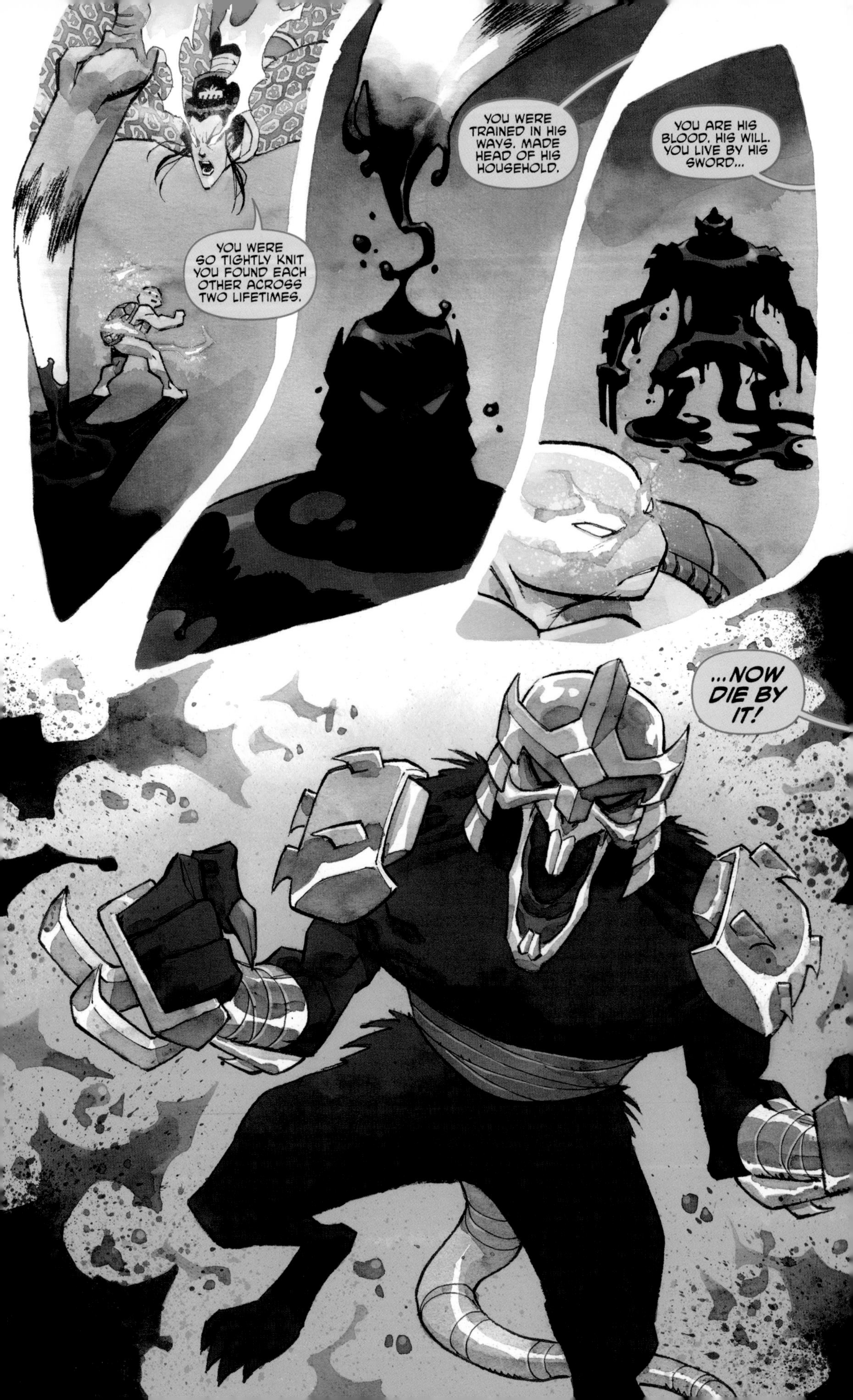
YOU WERE SO TIGHTLY KNIT YOU FOUND EACH OTHER ACROSS TWO LIFETIMES.
YOU WERE TRAINED IN HIS WAYS. MADE HEAD OF HIS HOUSEHOLD.
YOU ARE HIS BLOOD. HIS WILL. YOU LIVE BY HIS SWORD...
...NOW DIE BY IT!

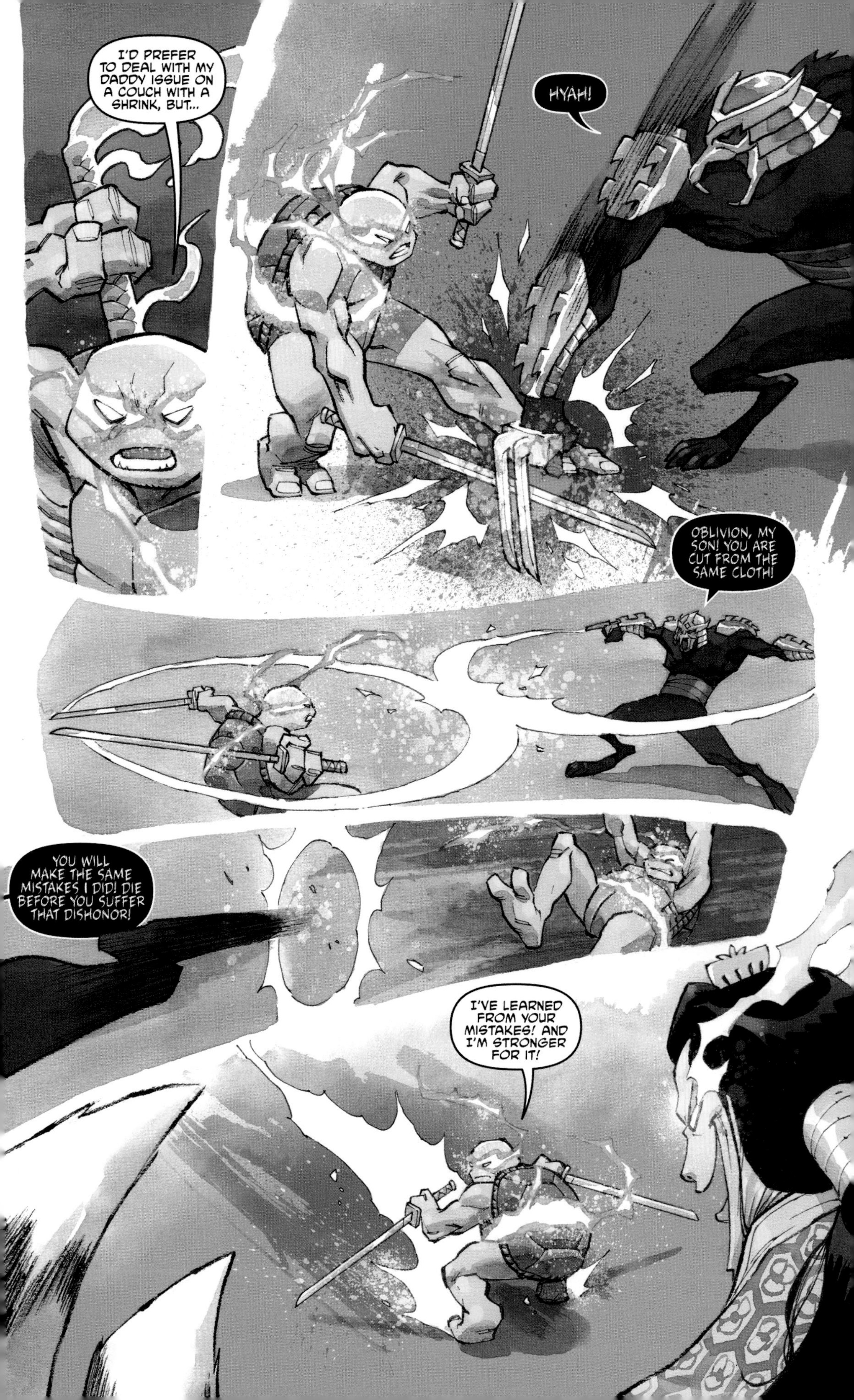
I'D PREFER TO DEAL WITH MY DADDY ISSUE ON A COUCH WITH A SHRINK, BUT...
HYAH!
OBLIVION, MY SON! YOU ARE CUT FROM THE SAME CLOTH!
YOU WILL MAKE THE SAME MISTAKES I DID! DIE BEFORE YOU SUFFER THAT DISHONOR!
I'VE LEARNED FROM YOUR MISTAKES! AND I'M STRONGER FOR IT!

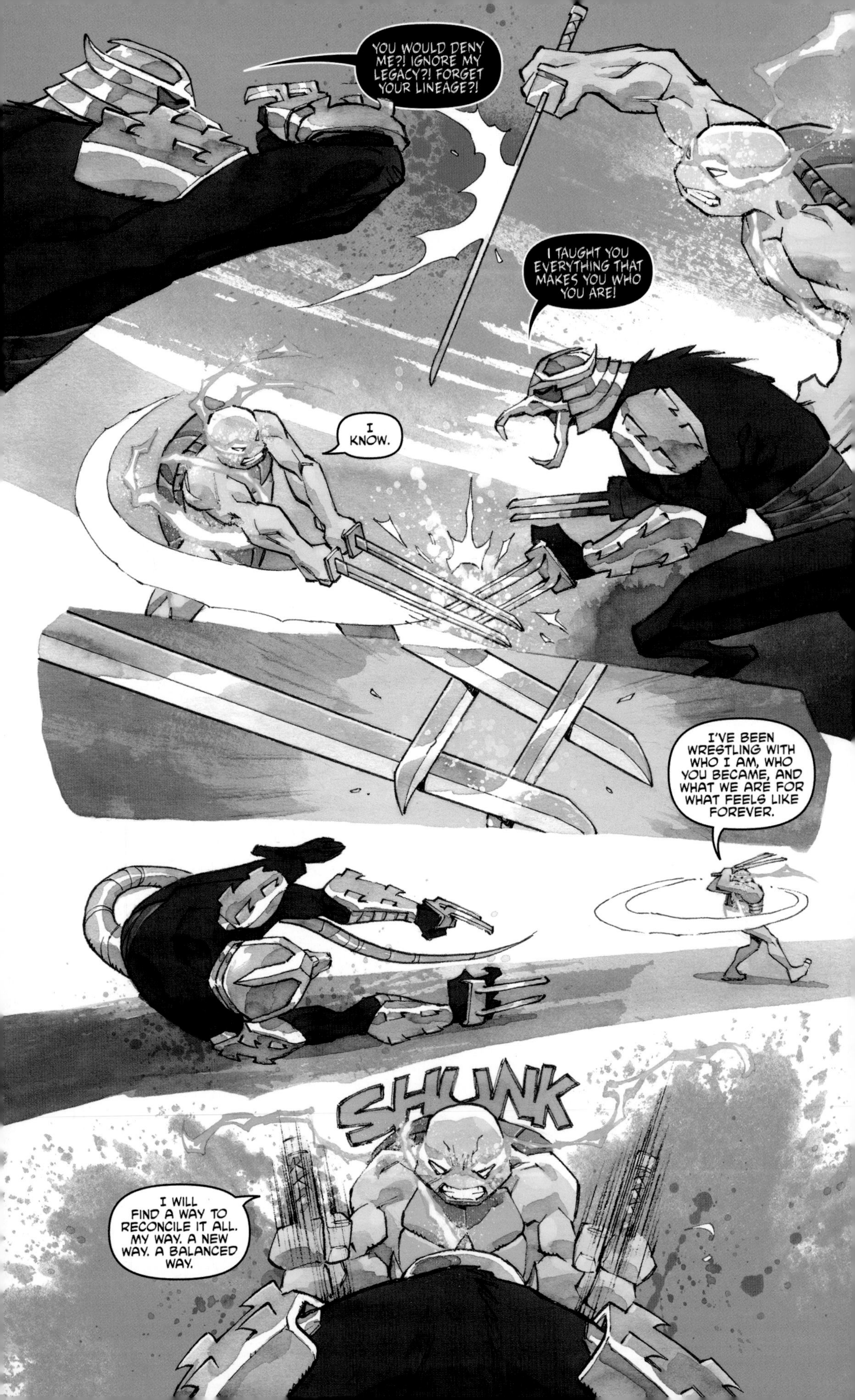
YOU WOULD DENY ME?! IGNORE MY LEGACY?! FORGET YOUR LINEAGE?!
I TAUGHT YOU EVERYTHING THAT MAKES YOU WHO YOU ARE!
I KNOW.
I'VE BEEN WRESTLING WITH WHO I AM, WHO YOU BECAME, AND WHAT WE ARE FOR WHAT FEELS LIKE FOREVER.
SHUNK
I WILL FIND A WAY TO RECONCILE IT ALL. MY WAY. A NEW WAY. A BALANCED WAY.

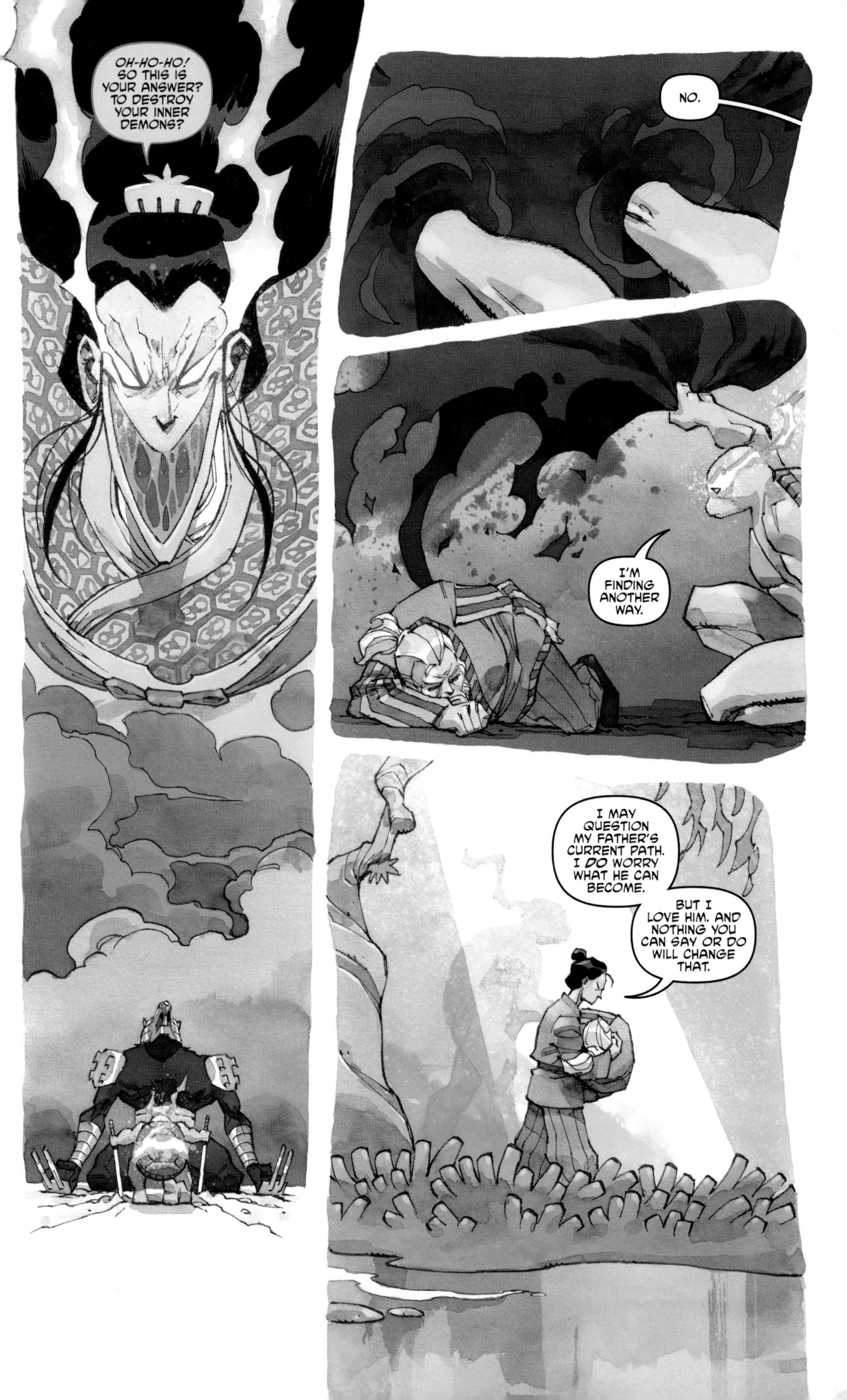
OH-HO-HO! SO THIS IS YOUR ANSWER? TO DESTROY YOUR INNER DEMONS?
NO.
I'M FINDING ANOTHER WAY.
I MAY QUESTION MY FATHER'S CURRENT PATH. I DO WORRY WHAT HE CAN BECOME.
BUT I LOVE HIM. AND NOTHING YOU CAN SAY OR DO WILL CHANGE THAT.

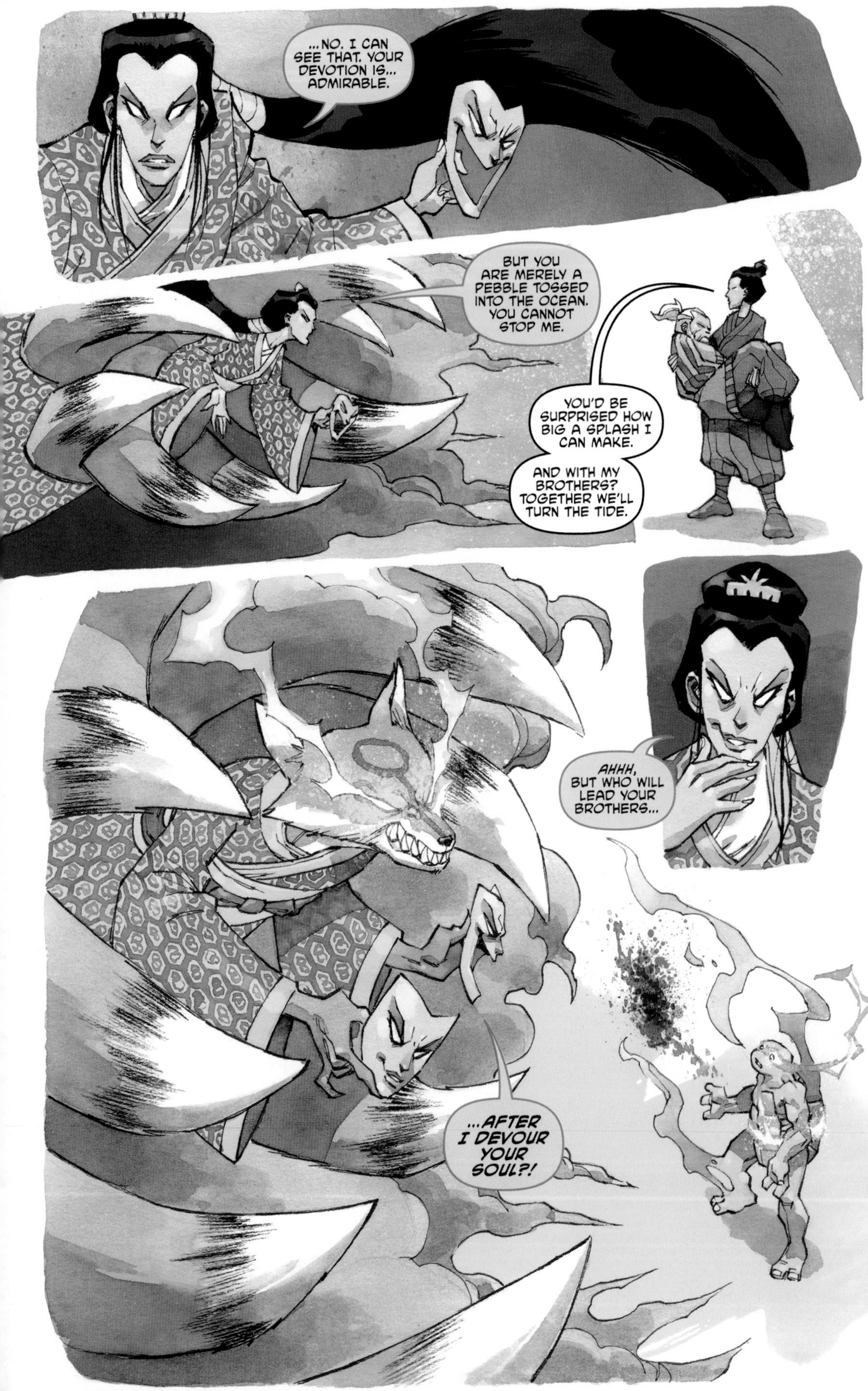
...NO. I CAN SEE THAT. YOUR DEVOTION IS... ADMIRABLE.
BUT YOU ARE MERELY A PEBBLE TOSSED INTO THE OCEAN. YOU CANNOT STOP ME.
YOU'D BE SURPRISED HOW BIG A SPLASH I CAN MAKE.
AND WITH MY BROTHERS? TOGETHER WE'LL TURN THE TIDE.
AHHH, BUT WHO WILL LEAD YOUR BROTHERS...
...AFTER I DEVOUR YOUR SOUL?!

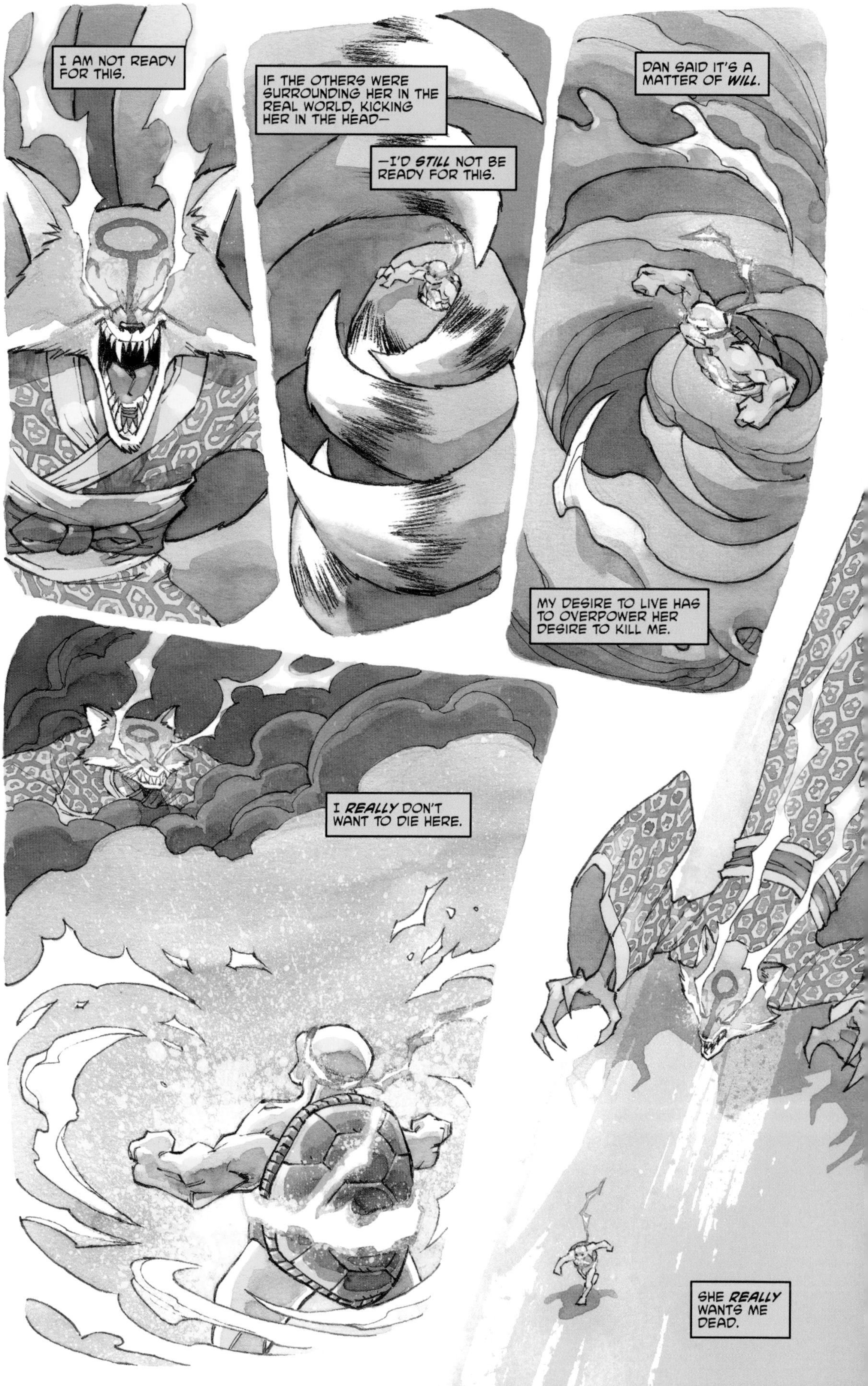
I AM NOT READY FOR THIS.
IF THE OTHERS WERE SURROUNDING HER IN THE REAL WORLD, KICKING HER IN THE HEAD—
—I'D *STILL* NOT BE READY FOR THIS.
DAN SAID IT'S A MATTER OF *WILL*.
MY DESIRE TO LIVE HAS TO OVERPOWER HER DESIRE TO KILL ME.
I *REALLY* DON'T WANT TO DIE HERE.
SHE *REALLY* WANTS ME DEAD.

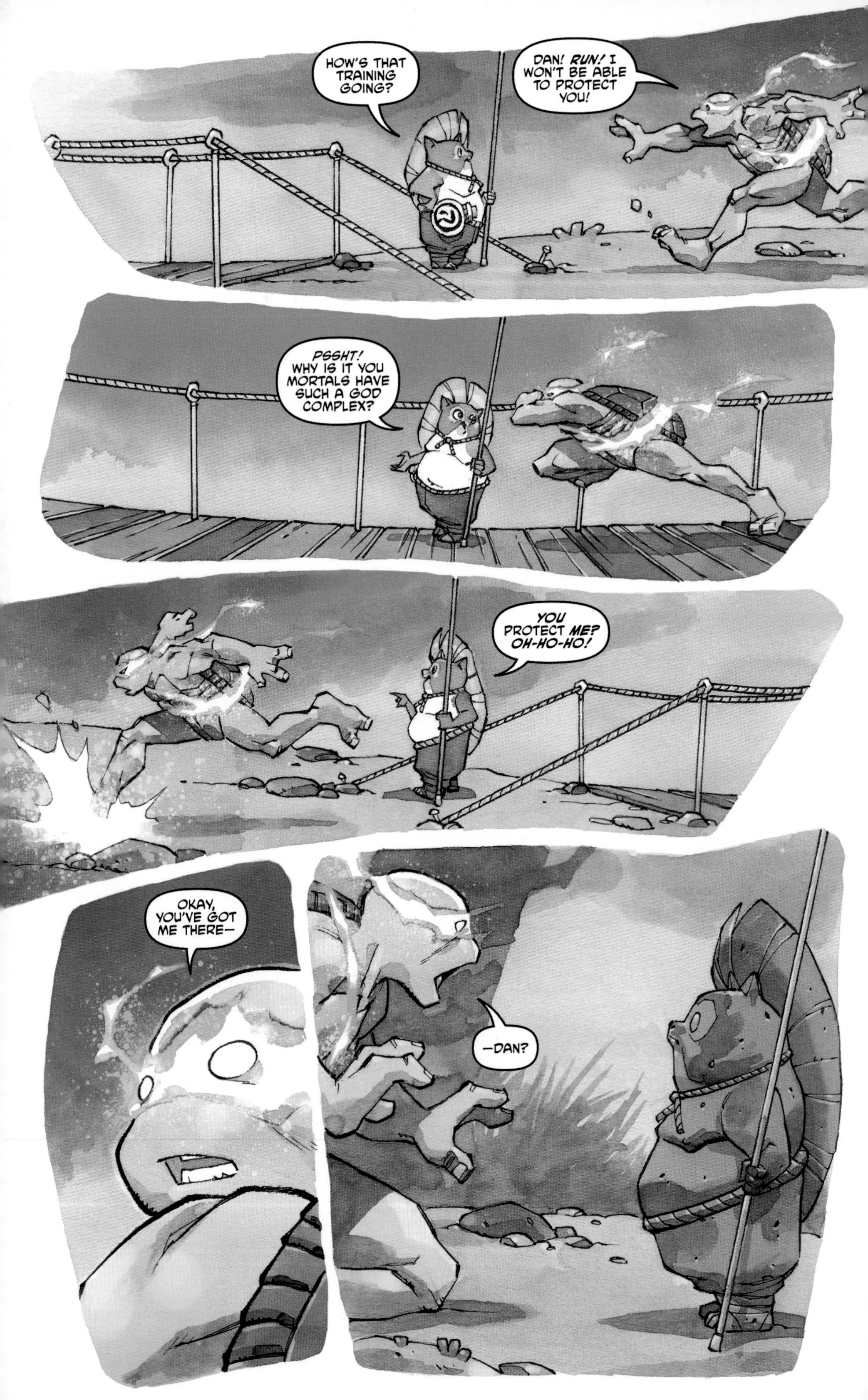
HOW'S THAT TRAINING GOING?
DAN! RUN! I WON'T BE ABLE TO PROTECT YOU!
PSSHT! WHY IS IT YOU MORTALS HAVE SUCH A GOD COMPLEX?
YOU PROTECT ME? OH-HO-HO!
OKAY, YOU'VE GOT ME THERE—
—DAN?

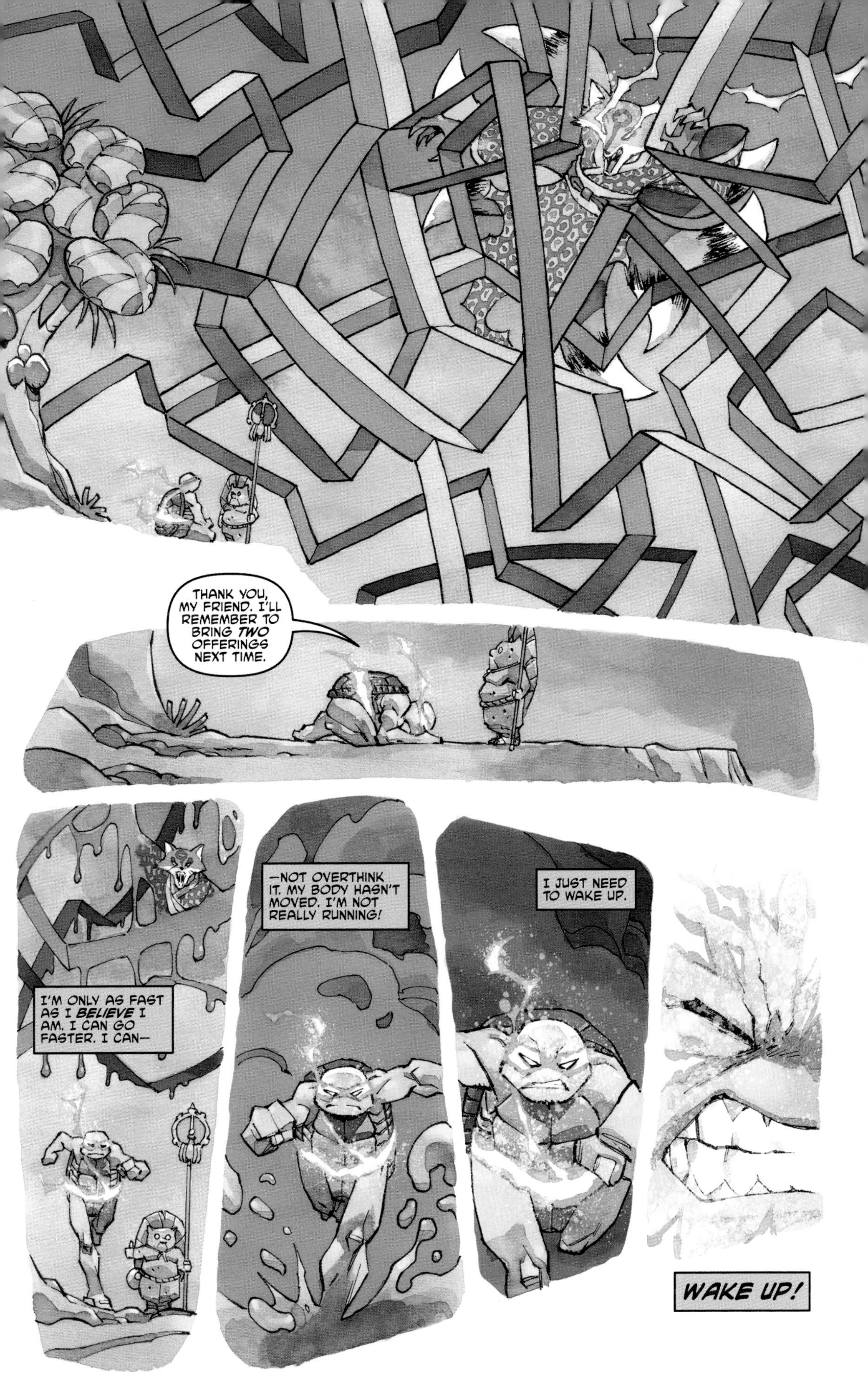
THANK YOU, MY FRIEND. I'LL REMEMBER TO BRING *TWO* OFFERINGS NEXT TIME.
I'M ONLY AS FAST AS I *BELIEVE* I AM. I CAN GO FASTER. I CAN—
—NOT OVERTHINK IT. MY BODY HASN'T MOVED. I'M NOT REALLY RUNNING!
I JUST NEED TO WAKE UP.
WAKE UP!

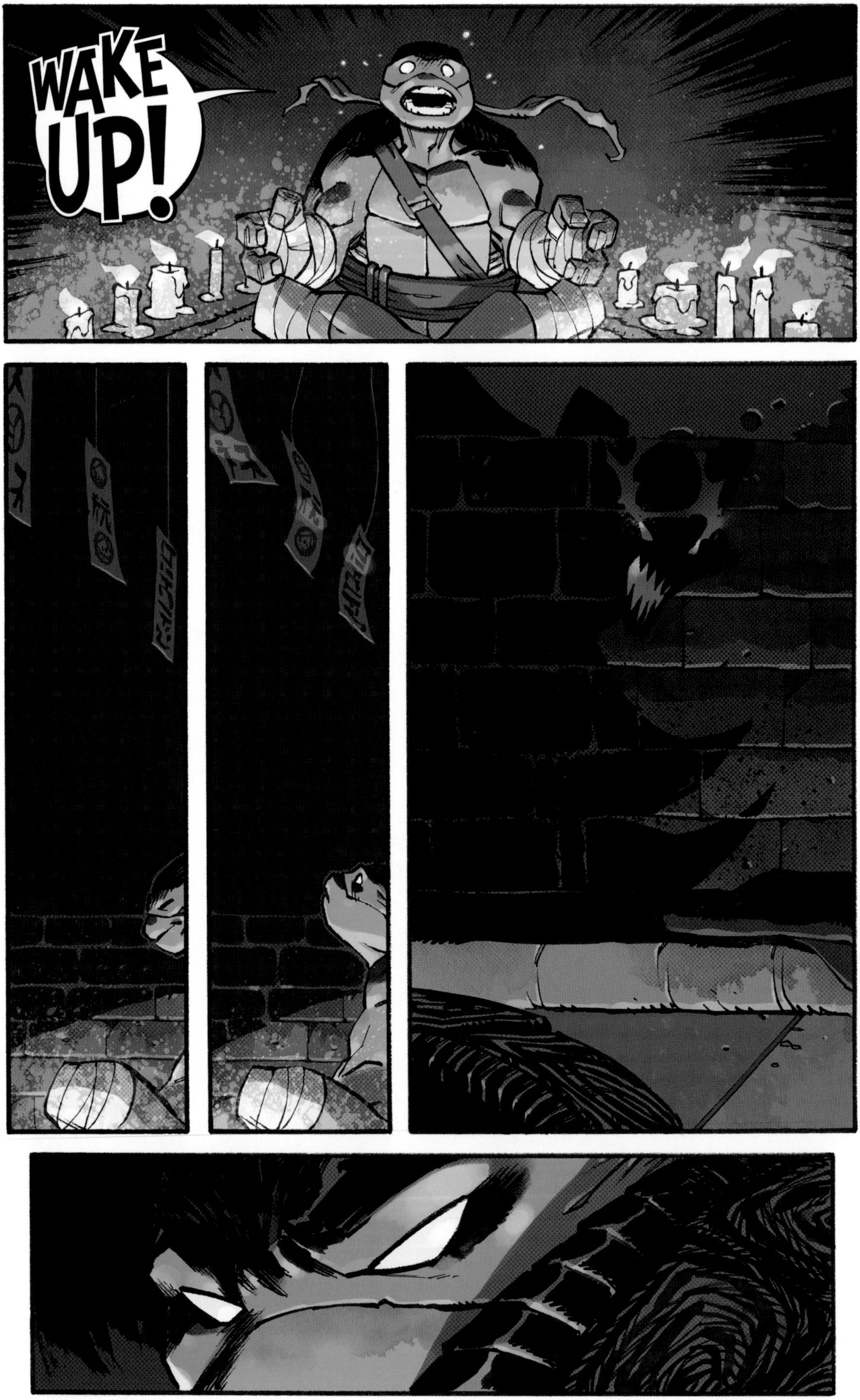
WAKE UP!

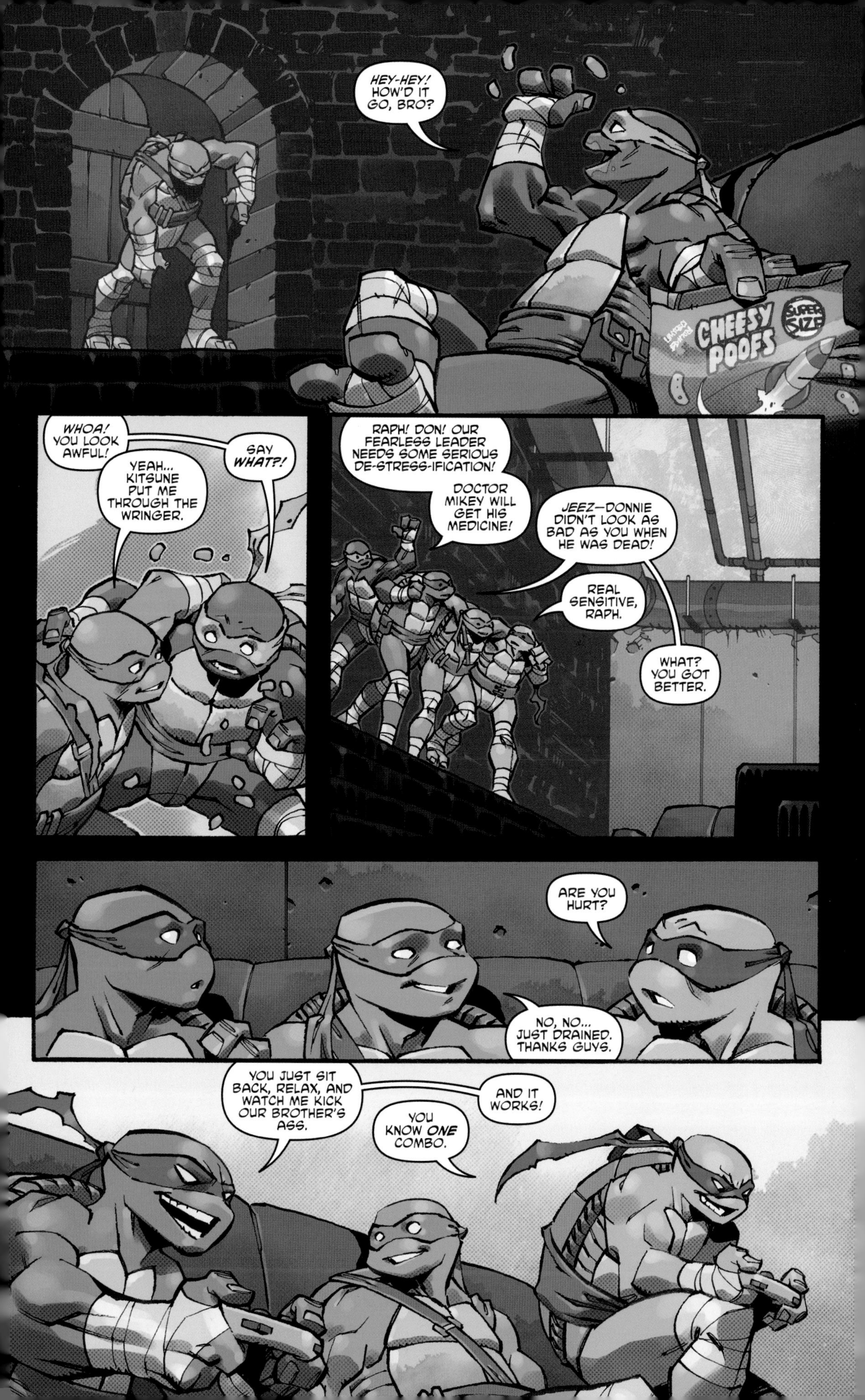
HEY-HEY! HOW'D IT GO, BRO?
CHEESY POOFS
SUPER SIZE
WHOA! YOU LOOK AWFUL!
SAY WHAT?!
YEAH... KITSUNE PUT ME THROUGH THE WRINGER.
RAPH! DON! OUR FEARLESS LEADER NEEDS SOME SERIOUS DE-STRESS-IFICATION!
DOCTOR MIKEY WILL GET HIS MEDICINE!
JEEZ—DONNIE DIDN'T LOOK AS BAD AS YOU WHEN HE WAS DEAD!
REAL SENSITIVE, RAPH.
WHAT? YOU GOT BETTER.
ARE YOU HURT?
NO, NO... JUST DRAINED. THANKS GUYS.
YOU JUST SIT BACK, RELAX, AND WATCH ME KICK OUR BROTHER'S ASS.
YOU KNOW ONE COMBO.
AND IT WORKS!

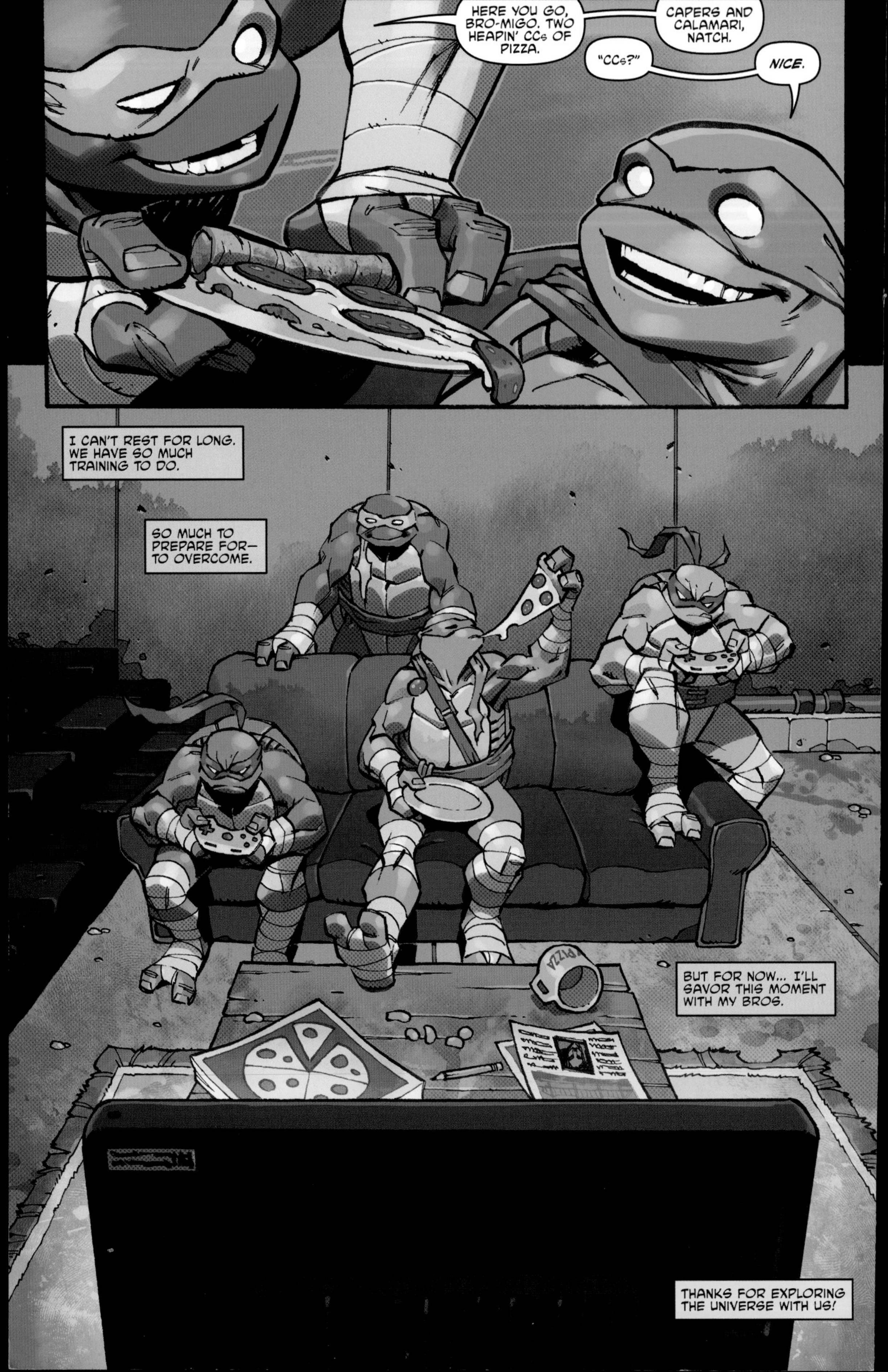
HERE YOU GO, BRO-MIGO. TWO HEAPIN' CCs OF PIZZA.
CAPERS AND CALAMARI, NATCH.
"CCs?"
NICE.
I CAN'T REST FOR LONG. WE HAVE SO MUCH TRAINING TO DO.
SO MUCH TO PREPARE FOR— TO OVERCOME.
PIZZA
BUT FOR NOW... I'LL SAVOR THIS MOMENT WITH MY BROS.
THANKS FOR EXPLORING THE UNIVERSE WITH US!

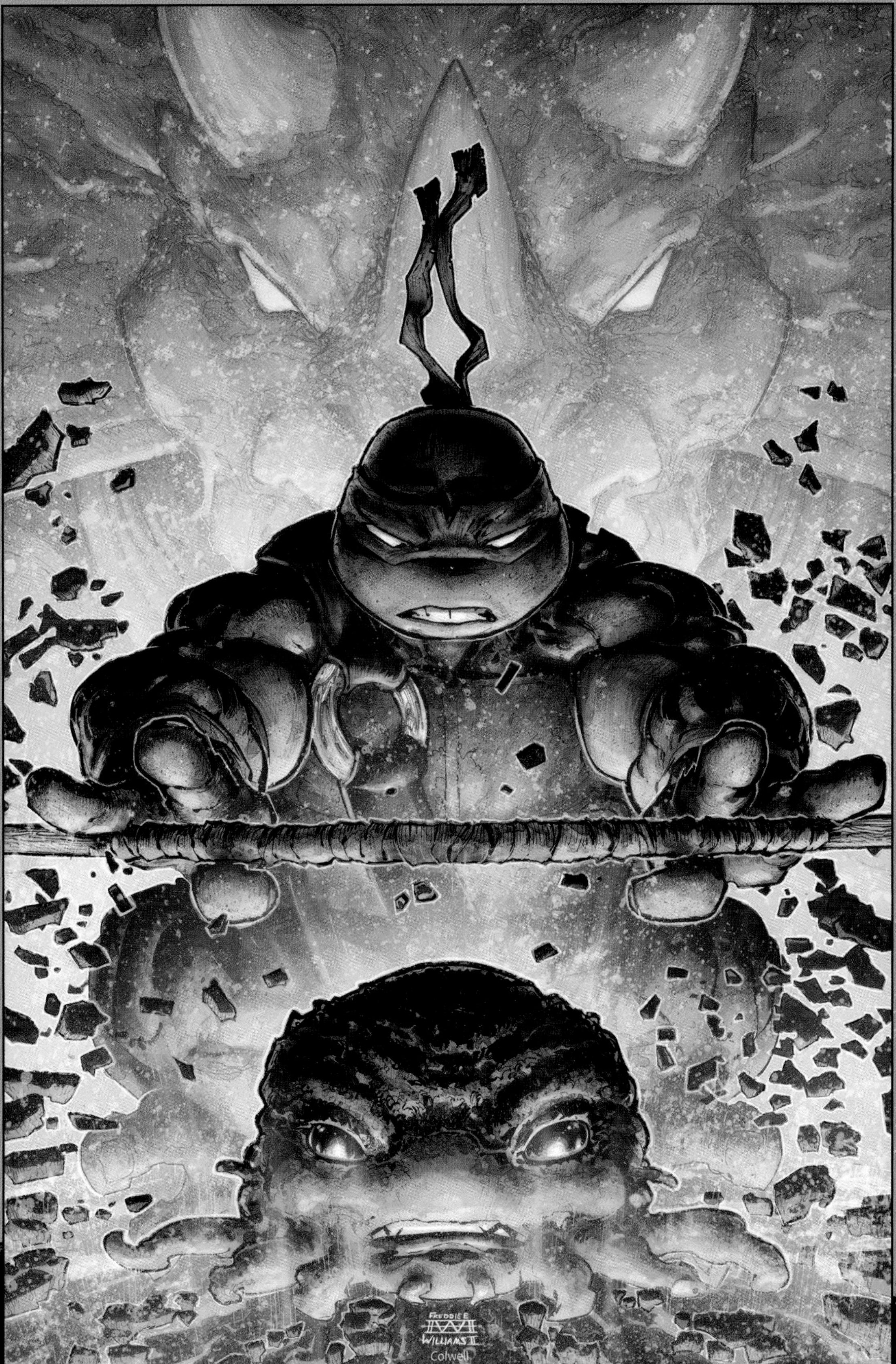
FREDDIE E. WILLIAMS II
Colwell

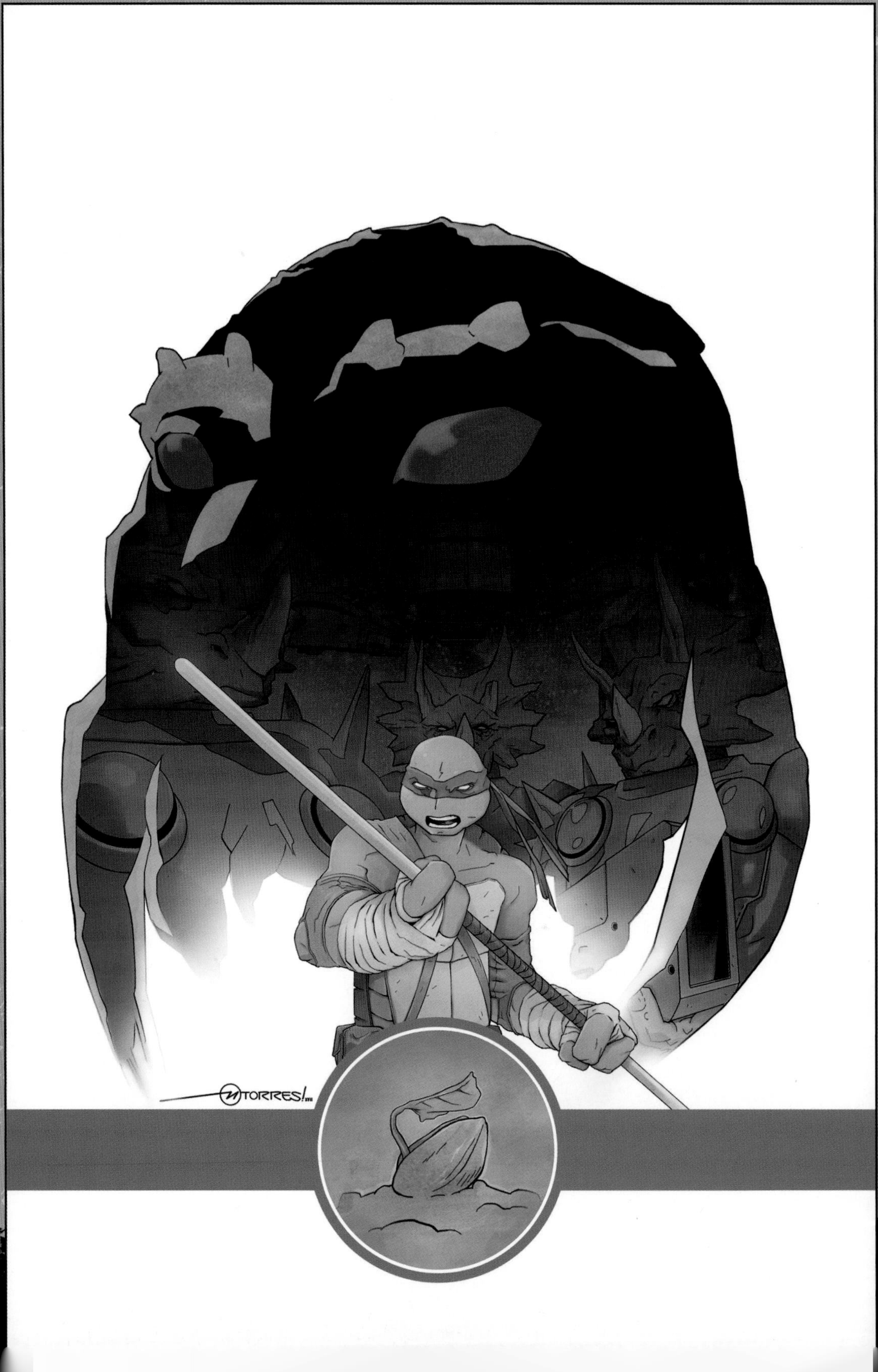
TORRES!

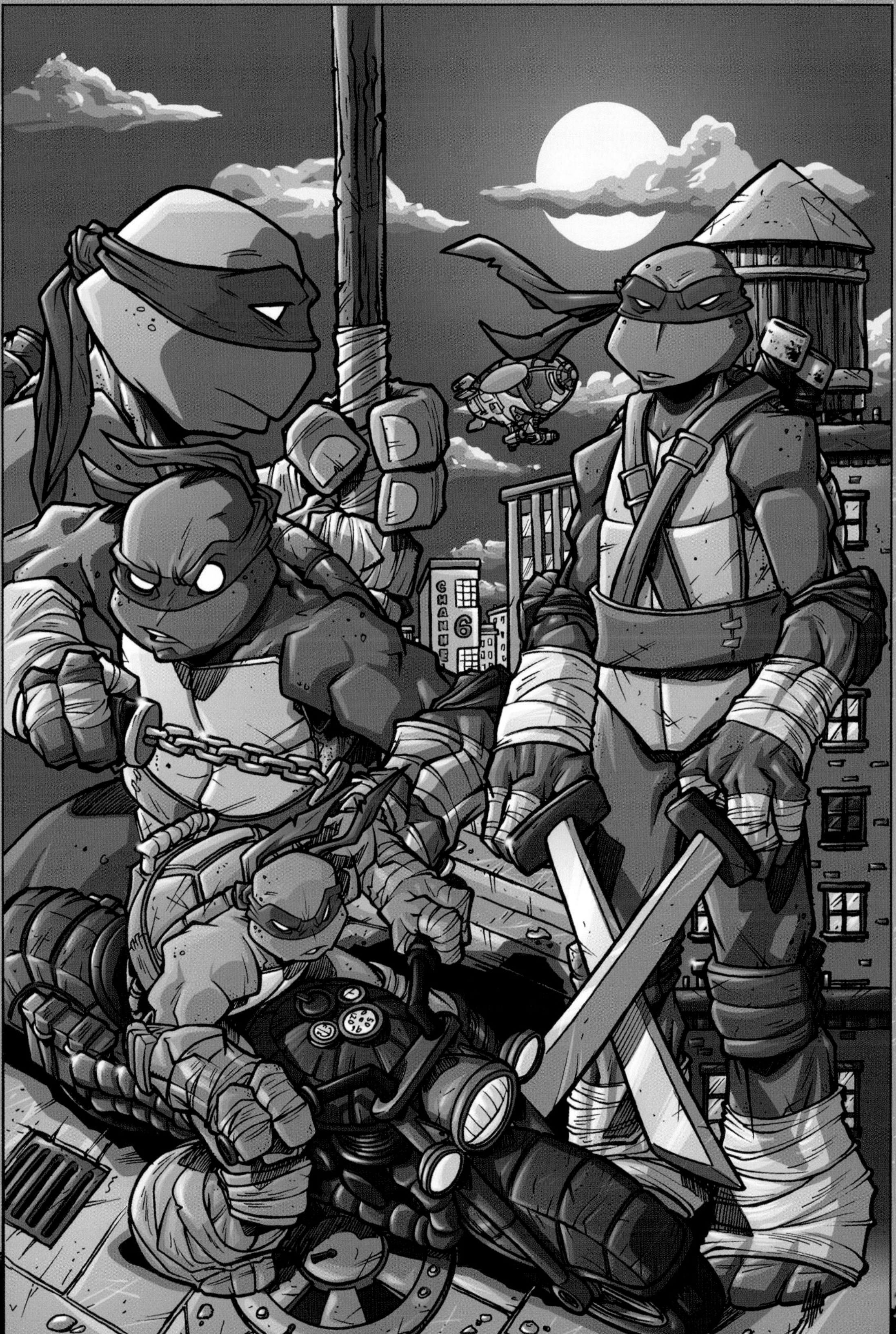

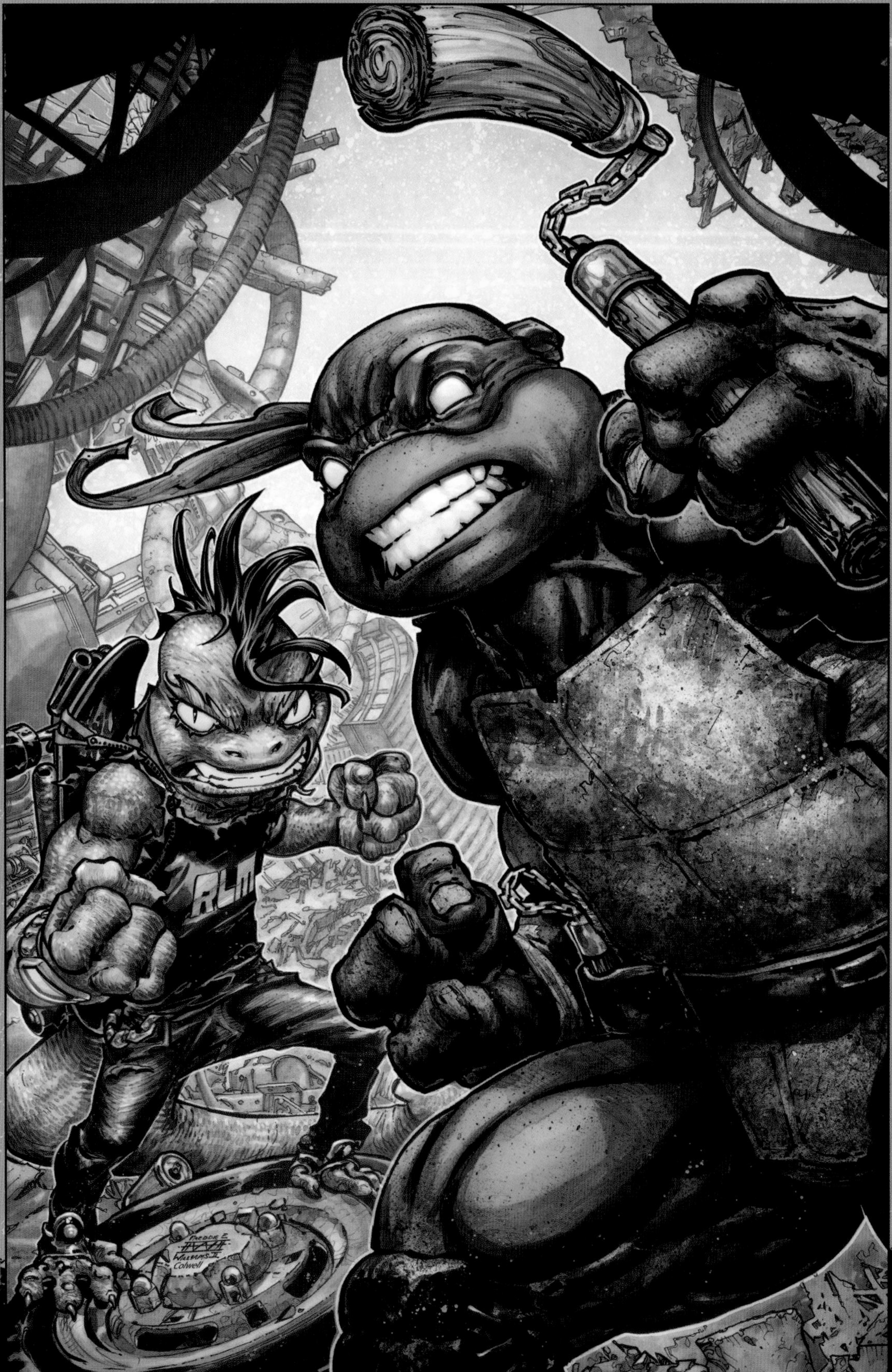
RLM

ART BY FREDDIE E. WILLIAMS II

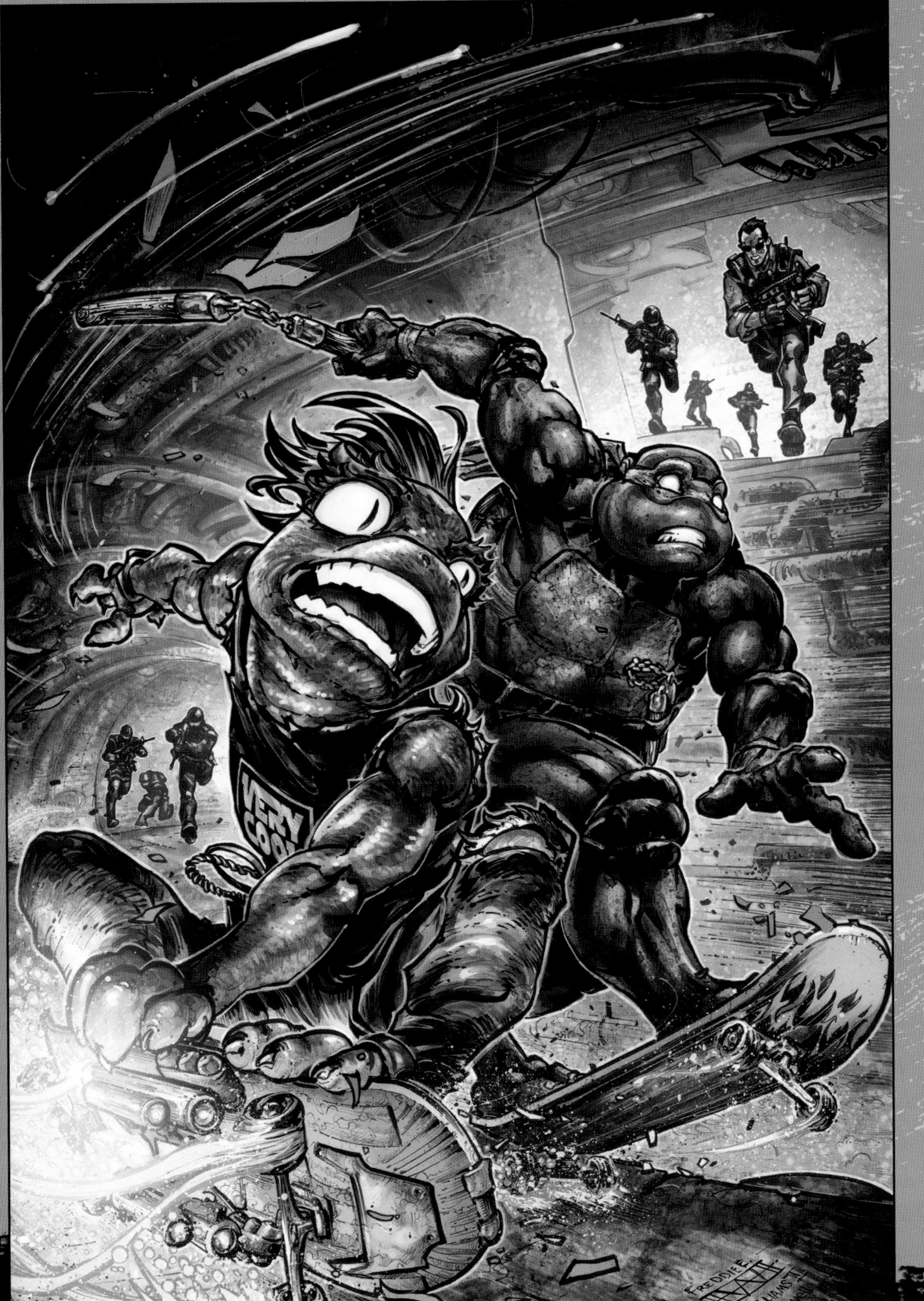
VERY

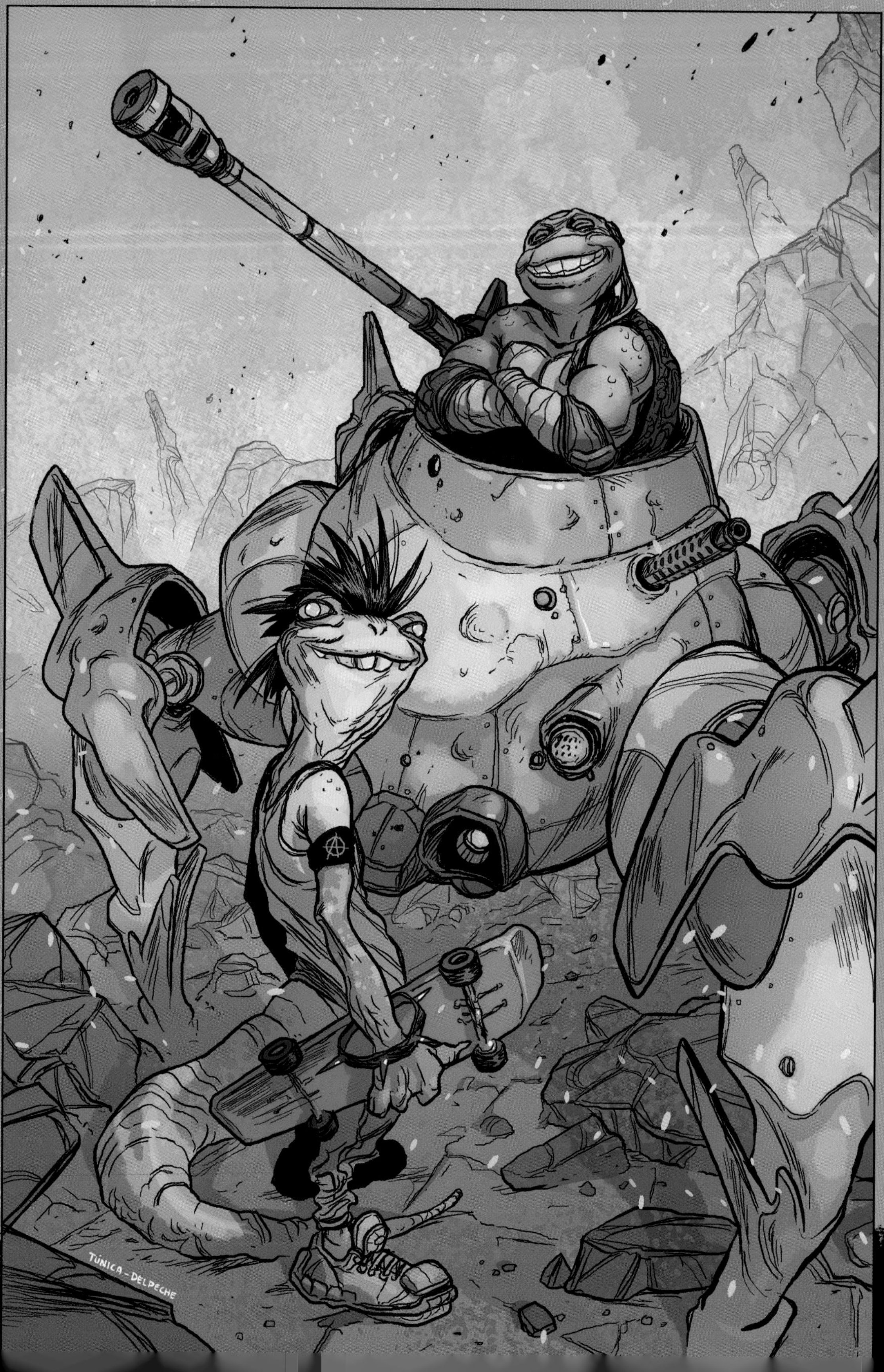
TÚNICA - DELPECHE

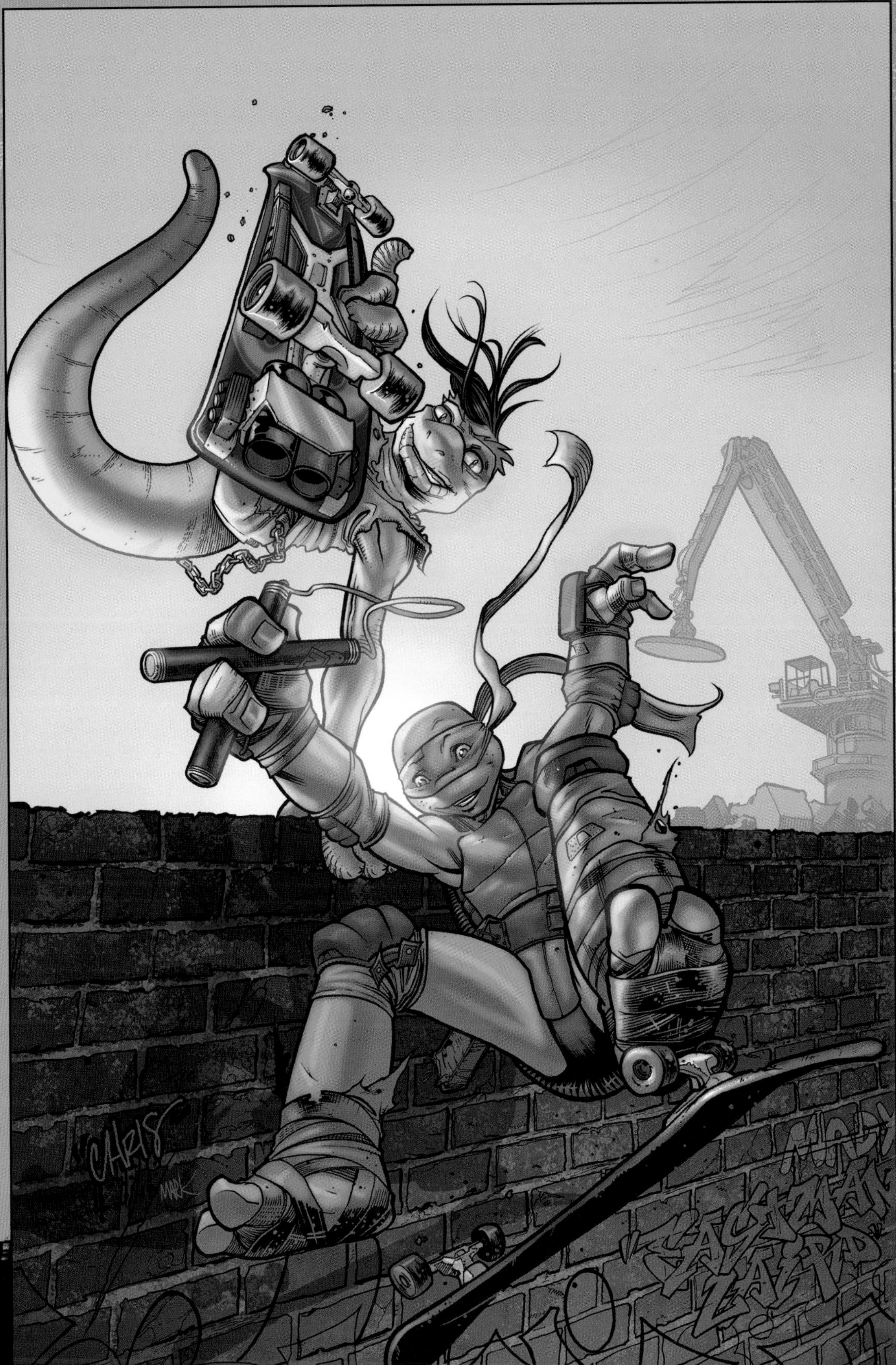
CHRIS
MARK

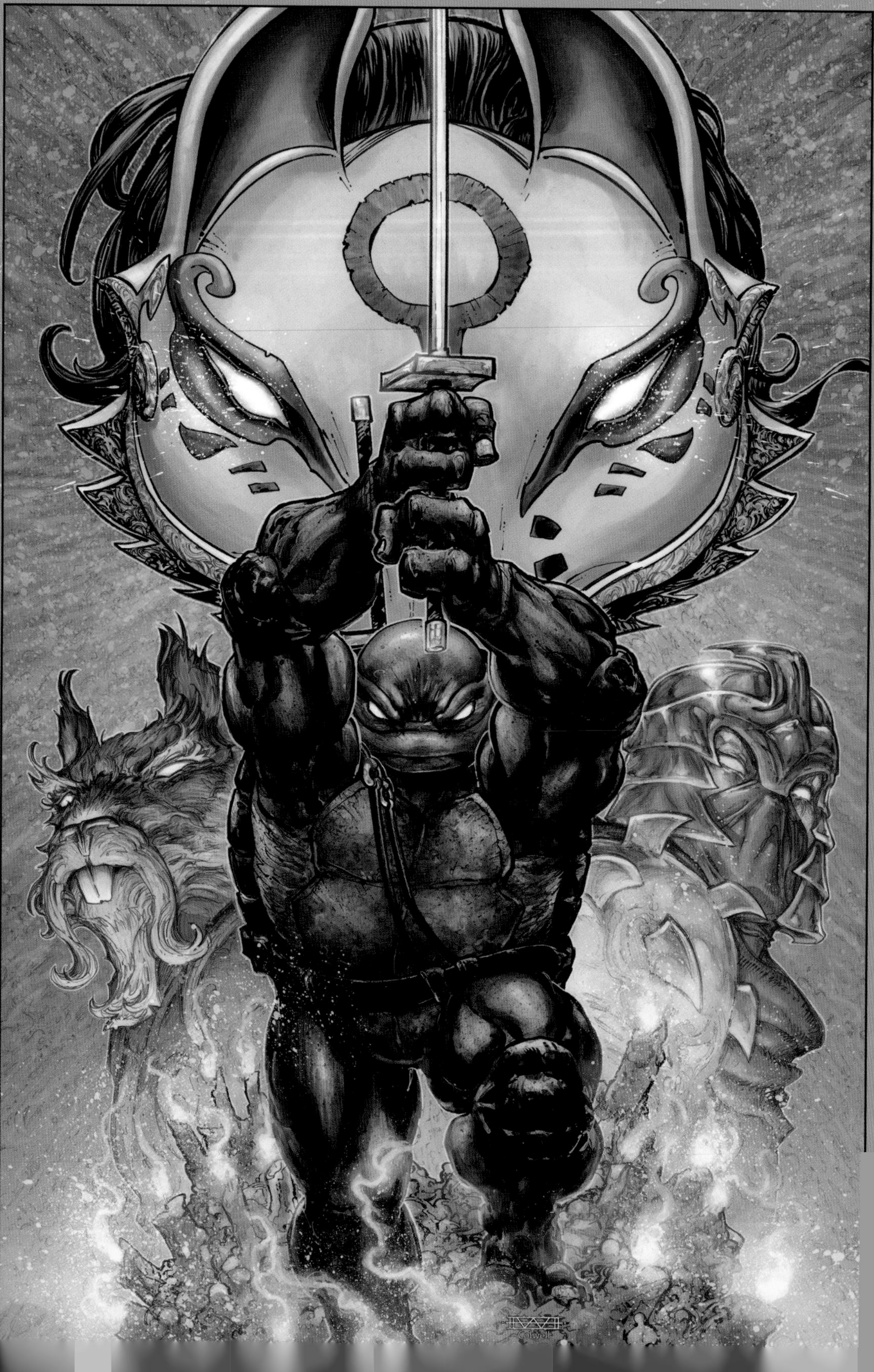